# The Garden of the Finzi-Continis

## A Novel by
## Giorgio Bassani

Translated from the Italian by William Weaver

**MJF BOOKS**
NEW YORK

Published by MJF Books
Fine Communications
Two Lincoln Square
60 West 66th Street
New York, NY 10023

Library of Congress Catalog Card Number 96-76468
ISBN 1-56731-099-0

Copyright © 1962 by Giulio Einaudi editore s.p.a.
English translation copyright © 1977 by Harcourt Brace & Company

This edition published by arrangement with Harcourt Brace & Company, Inc.

Manufactured in the United States of America on acid-free paper    ∞

MJF Books and the MJF colophon are trademarks of Fine Creative Media, Inc.

10   9   8   7   6   5   4   3   2   1

The heart, to be sure, always has something to say about what is to come, to him who heeds it. But what does the heart know? Only a little of what has already happened.

—*I promessi sposi*, chapter viii

# Prologue

For many years I wanted to write about the Finzi-Continis—about Micòl and Alberto, about Professor Ermanno and Signora Olga—and about all the others who inhabited or, like me, frequented the house in Corso Ercole I d'Este, in Ferrara, just before the outbreak of the last war. But the stimulus, the impulse to do it really came to me only a year ago, on a Sunday in April 1957.

It was during one of those usual weekend excursions. I was with a group of friends, divided between two automobiles, and we had set off along the Via Aurelia immediately after midday dinner, without a specific destination. A few miles from Santa Marinella, attracted by the towers of a medieval castle that had suddenly loomed up on the left, we turned off onto a narrow dirt road, then ended up strolling, scattered along the desolate beach that extended at the foot of the castle: the building, on closer inspection, much less medieval than it had promised from afar, when, from the highway, we had seen it outlined against the light over the blue and dazzling desert of the Tyrrhenian. With the wind blowing straight at us, sand in our eyes, deafened by the din of the backwash, unable even to visit the interior of the castle, because we were not provided with written permission from some Roman bank or other; we felt deeply discontent, irritated at having decided to leave Rome on a day like this, which now, at the seaside, was proving as inclement as if it were winter.

We walked up and down for perhaps twenty minutes, following the arc of the beach. The only jolly person of the company was a little girl of nine, daughter of the young couple in whose car I was riding. Thrilled by the same wind, the sea, the mad eddies of sand, Giannina gave her gay, expansive nature free rein. Though her mother tried to forbid it, she had taken off her shoes and stockings. She rushed towards the waves attacking the shore, and allowed her legs to get wet up to the knees. She seemed to be having the time of her life, in other words; and in fact, a little later, when we climbed back into the cars, I saw in her lively black eyes, sparkling above a pair of tender, flushed little cheeks, a passing shadow of frank regret.

After we had reached the Via Aurelia again, in five minutes' time we were in sight of the turnoff for Cerveteri. Since it had been decided that we were going straight back to Rome, I was sure we would go on. But instead, at this point, our car slowed down more than was necessary, and Giannina's father thrust his arm out of the window. He was signaling to the second car, about thirty yards behind us, his intention to turn left. He had changed his mind.

Thus we found ourselves driving along the smooth little paved road that quickly takes you to a small cluster of houses, mostly recent, and from there, proceeding tortuously towards the inland hills, to the famous Etruscan necropolis. Nobody asked for explanations, and I also remained silent.

After the village, the road began to climb slightly, forcing the car to slow down. We were now passing, at a few yards' distance, the so-called *montarozzi*, or mounds, which as far as Tarquinia, and even beyond, are scattered throughout that stretch of Latium north of Rome, more towards the hills than towards the sea. The area, really, is nothing but an immense, almost uninterrupted cemetery. Here the grass is greener, thicker, darker than that of the plain below, between the Aurelia and the Tyrrhenian: a sign that the eternal sirocco, blowing obliquely from the sea, when it arrives up here, has lost much of its brine along the way, and the moisture of the nearby mountains begins to exercise its beneficial influence on the vegetation.

"Where are we going?" Giannina asked.

Husband and wife were both sitting on the front seat, the child between them. The father took his hand off the wheel and placed it on his daughter's dark curls.

"We're going to take a look at some tombs that date back four or five thousand years," he answered, in the tone of somebody beginning to tell a fairy tale, who therefore has no hesitation about exaggerating numbers. "Etruscan tombs."

"How sad!" Giannina sighed, pressing her neck against the back of the seat.

"Sad? Why? In school haven't they told you about the Etruscans?"

"In our history book the Etruscans are at the beginning, next to the

Egyptians and the Jews. Tell me, Papà: who do you think were more ancient, the Etruscans or the Jews?''

Her father burst out laughing.

"Ask that gentleman back there," he said, jerking his thumb towards me.

Giannina turned. Her mouth hidden by the top of the seat, she gave me a rapid glance, severe, filled with mistrust. I waited for her to repeat the question. But she didn't: she promptly turned around and looked straight ahead.

Coming down the road, which continued to rise slightly, flanked by a double row of cypresses, groups of villagers were approaching us, girls and young men. It was the Sunday stroll. Arm in arm, the girls at times formed chains that stretched to the center of the road. At the moment we passed them, we felt ourselves inspected through the windows by their laughing eyes, in which curiosity was mixed with a kind of strange pride, barely dissimulated contempt.

"Papà," Giannina asked again, "why is it that ancient tombs are not as sad as new ones?"

A group more numerous than the others, occupying a good part of the road, and singing in chorus with no thought of making way for us, had forced the car almost to a stop. Her father shifted into second.

"That's obvious," he answered. "People who have just died are closer to us, and so we are fonder of them. The Etruscans, after all, have been dead for a long time"—again he was telling a fairy tale—"so long it's as if they had never lived, as if they had *always* been dead."

Another, longer pause. At the end of it (we were already near the open space in front of the entrance to the necropolis, full of automobiles and buses), it was Giannina's turn to impart the lesson.

"But now, if you say that," she ventured softly, "you remind me that the Etruscans were also alive once, and so I'm fond of them, like everyone else."

Our visit then to the necropolis, I recall, was completely affected by the extraordinary tenderness of this sentence. Giannina had prepared us to understand. It was she, the youngest, who somehow guided us.

We entered the most important tomb, the one that had belonged to the noble Matuta family: a low underground room that contains about twenty funeral beds set inside as many niches in the tufa walls, and heavily decorated with polychrome stucco figures of the dead, trusted objects of everyday life: hoes, ropes, hatchets, scissors, spades, knives, bows, arrows, even hunting dogs and marsh fowl. And meanwhile, gladly dismissing any lingering notions of scrupulous philology, I tried to imagine what tangible significance, for the later Etruscans of Cerveteri, the Etruscans after the Roman conquest, there could be in the constant visiting of the cemetery at the edge of their city.

They came from the nearby village probably on foot—I let my imagination range—in family groups, packs of young people similar to those we had just encountered on the road, pairs of lovers or friends, or else alone; just as today, in provincial Italian villages, the cemetery gate is still the inevitable terminal point of every evening stroll. They moved among the cone-shaped tombs, solid and massive as the bunkers that the German soldiers scattered over Europe in vain during the last war (gradually, through the centuries, the hearses' iron wheels had hollowed two deep parallel furrows in the paved street that ran from one end of the cemetery to the other): tombs that certainly resembled, also in their interior form, the fortified dwellings of the living. The world changed, of course—they must have said to themselves—it was no longer what it had once been, when Etruria, with its confederation of free, aristocratic city-states, had dominated almost the whole Italian peninsula. New civilizations, more crude and popular, but also stronger and more inured, now reigned. But what did it matter?

Having entered the cemetery, where each of them possessed a second home, and within its resting place, all prepared, where soon he would lie beside his fathers, he must have considered eternity no longer an illusion, a fable, a promise of the priests. The future might cause all the upheavals it liked in the world. But still, there, in the brief enclosure sacred to the familiar dead, in the heart of those tombs where, along with the dead, they arranged to carry down everything that made life beautiful and desirable, in that defended, sheltered corner of the world: there at least (and their thought, their madness still hovered, after twenty-five centuries, around the conical mounds, covered with wild grasses), there at least nothing would ever change.

When we left, it was dark.

From Cerveteri to Rome the distance is not great, barely twenty-five miles. And yet it was not a brief journey. When we had gone halfway, the

Aurelia began to grow jammed with cars coming from Ladispoli and Fregene. We had to proceed almost at walking pace.

But already, once again, in the calm and the somnolence (Giannina had also fallen asleep), I was returning in my memory to the years of my early youth, and to Ferrara, and to the Jewish cemetery at the end of Via Montebello. I saw again the great lawns dotted with trees, the tombstones and the pillars, more dense along the outside walls and the dividing walls inside, and, as if I actually had it before my eyes, the monumental tomb of the Finzi-Continis: an ugly tomb, of course—at home I had always heard them say so, since my childhood—but still imposing, signifying, if only for this reason, the family's importance.

And my heart ached as never before at the thought that in that tomb, erected, it seemed, to guarantee the perpetual repose of the man who commissioned it—his and his descendants'—only one, among all the Finzi-Continis I had known and loved, had managed to gain that repose. In fact the only one buried there is Alberto, the older son, who died in 1942 of a lymphogranuloma. Whereas for Micòl, the second child, the daughter, and for her father, Professor Ermanno, and her mother, Signora Olga, and Signora Regina, Signora Olga's ancient, paralytic mother, all deported to Germany in the autumn of '43, who could say if they found any sort of burial at all?

# Part
# One

The tomb was big, massive, really imposing: a kind of half-ancient, half-Oriental temple of the sort seen in the sets of *Aïda* and *Nabucco* in vogue in our opera houses until a few years ago. In any other cemetery, the neighboring Municipal Cemetery included, a tomb of such pretensions would not have been the least amazing; indeed, confused in the general array, it would have gone unremarked. But in ours, it was unique; and so, though it rose quite far from the entrance gate, at the end of an abandoned field where no one had been buried for more than half a century, it stood out, it was immediately noticeable.

It seemed that the construction had been entrusted to a distinguished professor of architecture, responsible for many other contemporary outrages in the city, by Moisè Finzi-Contini, the paternal great-grandfather of Alberto and Micòl, who had died in 1863, shortly after the territories of the Papal States had been annexed to the Kingdom of Italy, with the consequent, definitive abolition, also in Ferrara, of the ghetto for the Jews. A great landowner, "reformer of Ferrarese agriculture"—as we could read on the plaque the community had placed along the stairs in the temple on Via Mazzini, at the top of the third landing, to immortalize his merits as "Italian and Jew"—but a man, obviously, of rather uncultivated artistic taste, once he had made the decision to set up a tomb *sibi et suis,* he had given the designer a free hand. The times seemed beautiful, flourishing: everything encouraged hope, daring. Overcome by the euphoria of the newly won civil equality, the same that, at the time of the Cisalpine Republic, had allowed him as a young man to make his the first thousand hectares of reclaimed land, the stern patriarch had understandably been led, on that solemn occasion, not to pinch pennies. Very probably the distinguished professor of architecture had been given carte blanche. And with such quantities of fine marble available, snow-white Carrara, flesh-pink Verona, gray speckled with black, yellow marble, blue marble, green marble, he had, in turn, definitely lost all self-control.

The result was an incredible pastiche, in which architectonic echoes of Theodoric's mausoleum in Ravenna mingled with those of the Egyptian temples at Luxor, with Roman baroque, and even, as the squat columns of the peristyle indicated, the archaic Greek of Knossos. But so it went. Little by little, year after year, time, which, in its way, always adjusts everything, had succeeded in harmonizing that unlikely mixture of heterogeneous styles. Moisè Finzi-Contini, here called "austere and tireless worker," had died in 1863; his wife, Allegrina Camaioli, "angel of the household," in '75, in '77, still young, the only son, Menotti, doctor of engineering; followed twenty years later, in '98, by his wife, Josette, daughter of Baron Artom of the Treviso branch of that family. After that, the maintenance of the chapel, which, in 1914, had received only one more member of the family Guido, a boy of six, had passed clearly into hands gradually less prompt in cleaning, tidying, repairing damage when necessary, and above all, fighting off the relentless siege of the surrounding vegetation. The clumps of grass, a dark, almost black grass, metallic in its toughness, and ferns, weeds, thistles, poppies, had been allowed to advance and invade with ever-greater license. So that in '24, or '25, sixty years after its inauguration, when I, as a little boy, was to see it for the first time, the funeral chapel of the Finzi-Continis ("A real horror," my mother, whose hand I was holding, never failed to call it) already looked more or less as it does now, when for a long time there has been no one left directly involved in taking care of it. Half-buried in the rampant vegetation, the surfaces of its polychrome marbles, originally smooth and brilliant, made opaque by gray accumulations of dust, the roof and the outer steps damaged by the baking sun and by frosts: even then it seemed transformed into that rich and wondrous thing into which any long-submerged object is transformed.

Who knows how, and why, a vocation for solitude is born? The fact is that the same isolation, the same separation with which the Finzi-Continis had surrounded their deceased, surrounded also the *other* house they possessed, the one at the end of Corso Ercole I d'Este. Immortalized by Giosuè Carducci and by Gabriele D'Annunzio, this Ferrara street is so well known to lovers of art and poetry throughout the world that any description of it would be superfluous. We are, as everyone knows, in the very heart of that northern section of the city added to the cramped medieval town during the Renaissance, and called for this reason the Addizione Erculea. Broad, straight as a sword from the Castle to the Mura degli Angeli, its entire length flanked by the dark forms of patrician dwellings, with that distant, sublime backdrop of brick-red, vegetal green, and sky, which seems to lead you, truly, to the infinite: Corso Ercole I d'Este is so beautiful, its tourist attraction is so great, that the Socialist-Communist coalition, responsible for the city government of Ferrara for more than fifteen years, has realized the necessity of leaving it untouched, defending it with all severity against any building or commercial speculation, preserving, in other words, its original aristocratic character.

The street is famous: moreover, substantially intact.

And yet, as far as the Finzi-Contini house in particular is concerned, though even today you enter it from Corso Ercole I—but to reach the house itself, you must cover more than a quarter-mile, through an immense open space, scantily cultivated or not at all—though it incorporates still those historic ruins of a sixteenth-century building, once an Este residence or "folly," bought by the same Moisè in 1850, and later transformed by his heirs, through successive remodelings and restorations, into a kind of neo-Gothic manor, English-style: despite such surviving points of interest, who knows anything about it, I wonder, who remembers it any more? The *Touring Club Guide* doesn't mention it, and so excuses the passing tourists. But in Ferrara itself, not even the few remaining Jews in the languishing Jewish community seem to recall it.

The *Touring Club Guide* doesn't mention it, and that, no doubt, is too bad. Still, we must be fair: the garden, or, to be more precise, the vast park that surrounded the Finzi-Contini house before the war, and spread over almost twenty-five acres to the foot of the Mura degli Angeli on one side, and as far as the Barrier of Porta San Benedetto on the other, representing in itself something rare, exceptional (the Touring Club guides of the early twentieth century never failed to speak of it, in a curious tone, half-lyrical, half-snobbish), today no longer exists, literally. All the big trees, the lindens, elms, beeches, poplars, planes, horse chestnuts, pines, firs, larches, cedars of Lebanon, cypresses, oaks, ilexes, and even palms and eucalyptuses, planted by the hundreds at the orders of Josette Artom, were cut down during the last two years of war for firewood, and the terrain for some time has returned to what it was once, when Moisè Finzi-Contini bought it from the Marchese Avogli's family: one of the many big vegetable gardens enclosed within the city walls.

There would still be the house proper. But the big, singular building, severely damaged by bombs in '44, is now occupied by about fifty refugee families, belonging to that same wretched urban subproletariat, not unlike the plebs of the Roman slums, that continues to huddle especially in the entrances of the Palazzone on Via Mortara: hard, wild people, intolerant (a few months ago, I was told, they received the city health inspector with a hail of stones, when he went there on his bicycle for an inspection); and to discourage any eviction plan of the Fine Arts Commission of Emilia and Romagna, they have apparently had the fine idea of scraping from the walls anything that was left of the ancient paintings.

Now, why put poor tourists in jeopardy?—I imagine the compilers of the latest edition of the *Touring Club Guide* asked themselves. And, to see what, after all?

# II

If the tomb of the Finzi-Contini family could be called a "horror," and smiled at, their house, isolated down there among the mosquitoes and frogs of the Panfilio Canal and the outlets of the sewers, and nicknamed enviously the *magna domus*, at that, no, not even after fifty years could anyone manage to smile. Oh, it still took very little to feel offended by it! It was enough, say, to pass along the endless outside wall of the garden along Corso Ercole I d'Este, a wall interrupted, at about the halfway point, by a solemn door of dark oak, without any kind of knob; or else, in the other direction, from the top of the Mura degli Angeli, overlooking the park, to peer through the forestlike tangle of trunks, boughs, and foliage below, until you could glimpse the strange, sharp outline of the lordly dwelling, and behind it, much farther on, at the edge of a clearing, the tan patch of the tennis court: and the ancient offense of rejection and separation would smart once more, burning almost as it had at the beginning.

What a typical nouveau riche idea, what an outlandish idea!—my father used to repeat, with a kind of impassioned bitterness, every time he happened to mention the subject.

True, true—he admitted—the former owners of the place, the Marchese Avogli family, had "the bluest" blood in their veins; vegetable garden and ruins *ab antiquo* had boasted the highly decorative name of Barchetto del Duca: all excellent things, yes, indeed! and the more so since Moisè Finzi-Contini, who had to be granted the undoubted merit of having "seen" a good deal, in concluding that same deal must not have spent more than the proverbial pittance. But what of that?—he would add immediately. Was it really necessary, for this reason, that Moisè's son, Menotti, called, not without reason, *al matt mugnàga*, the apricot madman, after the color of his eccentric, marten-lined overcoat, to decide to move his wife, Josette, and himself into such an out-of-the-way part of the city, unhealthy even today, so imagine then! and moreover deserted, melancholy, and, especially, unsuitable?

You could even excuse the parents, who belonged to a different age, and after all could afford the luxury of investing all the money they liked in some old stones. You could especially excuse her, Josette Artom, descendant of the Artom barons of the Treviso branch (a magnificent woman in her day: blond, ample bosom, blue eyes, and in fact her mother had come from Berlin, an Olschky); besides being mad about the House of Savoy, to such a degree that in May of '98, shortly before her death, she had taken the initiative of sending a congratulatory telegram to General Bava Beccaris, who had turned his cannon on those poor devils, the Socialists and anarchists of Milan, she was also a fanatical admirer of Bismarck's studded-helmeted Germany, and had never troubled, since her husband, Menotti, eternally at her feet, had settled her in her Valhalla, to dissimulate her own aversion towards Ferrara's Jewish circles, too narrow for her—as she said—not to mention, in effect, though it was a fairly grotesque matter, *her own basic anti-Semitism.* Professor Ermanno and Signora Olga, nevertheless (he a scholar, she a Herrera from Venice: and therefore born of a western Sephardic family, *very* good, beyond a doubt, but somewhat badly off, however devout): what sort of people did they think they had become, the two of them as well? Real nobility? Oh, yes, it was comprehensible, yes: the loss of their son Guido, their first-born, who died in 1914 at the age of only six, after an attack of infantile paralysis, the American kind, galloping, against which even Dr. Corcos had been helpless, must have been a very hard blow for them: especially for her, for Signora Olga, who after that had never put off her mourning. But apart from this, wasn't it possible that, as time passed, living apart, they had got swelled heads, falling into the same absurd notions of Menotti Finzi-Contini and his worthy spouse? Aristocracy, indeed! Instead of giving themselves so many airs, they would have done much better, they at least, to remember who they were, where they came from, for it's a fact that Jews—Sephardic and Ashkenazic, western and Levantine, Tunisian, Berber, Yemenite, and even Ethiopian —in whatever part of the earth, under whatever sky History scattered them, are and always will be Jews, that is to say, close relatives. Old Moisè didn't give himself airs, not him! He didn't have any aristocratic fancies in his brain! When he was living in the ghetto, at number 24 Via Vignatagliata, in the house where, resisting the pressure of his haughty Treviso daughter-in-law, impatient as she was to move as quickly as possible to the Barchetto del Duca, he was determined at all costs to die, he would go out himself every morning to do the shopping in Piazza delle Erbe with his faithful shopping bag over his arm: he, who for this same reason, was nicknamed *al gatt*, the cat, had brought them up from nothing, *his* family. Yes, while there was no doubt that "la Josette" had come down to Ferrara, accompanied by a large dowry, consisting of a villa in the Treviso region frescoed by Tiepolo, a large check, and jewels obviously, many jewels, which at the opening nights of the Teatro Comunale, against the red-velvet background of their private box, attracted the eyes of the whole theatre to her, to her splendid décolletage, there was also no doubt that it had been *al gatt*, and he alone, who had put together, in the Ferrara plain, between Codigoro, Massa Fiscaglia, and Jolanda di Savoia, the thousands of acres on which the bulk of the family patrimony was still based today. The monumental tomb in the cemetery: that was the only mistake, the only sin (against taste, especially) of which Moisè Finzi-Contini could be accused. But apart from that, nothing.

So said my father: at Passover, especially, during the long suppers that continued to be held in our house even after the death of Grandfather Raffaello, at which about twenty friends and relations were present; but also at Kippur, when the same friends and relatives came back to our house to end the fast.

I remember, however, one Passover supper in the course of which, to the usual criticisms—bitter, generic, always the same, and expressed chiefly for the pleasure of summoning up the old tales of the community—my father added some new and surprising ones.

It was in 1933, the year of the notorious *infornata del Decennale*, Fascism's tenth-anniversary membership campaign. Thanks to the "clemency" of the Duce, who all of a sudden, as if inspired, had decided to open his arms to every "agnostic or adversary of yesterday," in the circle of our community the number of party members had also risen abruptly to 90 percent. And my father, sitting down there in his usual place at the head of the table, in the same place from which Grandfather Raffaello had pontificated for long decades with quite different authority and severity, had not failed to express his satisfaction at the event. The rabbi, Dr. Levi, had been quite right—he said—to mention it in the speech he had recently made at the Italian synagogue when, in the presence of the leading authorities of the city—prefect, provincial party secretary, mayor, the brigadier general in command of the garrison—he had commemorated the Fascist Statute!

And yet he was not wholly pleased, Papà. In his boyish blue eyes, filled with patriotic ardor, I could read a shadow of chagrin. He must have discerned a stumbling block, a little obstacle, unforeseen and unpleasant.

And in fact, having begun at a certain point to count on his fingers how many of us, us Ferrarese *judìm*, had still remained "outside," when he came at last to Ermanno Finzi-Contini, who had never taken out a party card, true, and after all, considering also the substantial agricultural holdings of which he was proprietor, it had never been quite clear why, suddenly, as if irked at himself and his own discretion, my father decided to reveal two curious events: perhaps unrelated—he premised—but no less significant for that.

First: that the lawyer Geremia Tabet, when in his position as a *Sansepolcrista*, a Fascist of the first days, and intimate friend of the party secretary, had gone to the Barchetto del Duca expressly to offer the Professor a card, already made out in his name, he had not only seen it handed back to him, but also a little later, very politely of course, but equally firmly, had been shown the door.

"And on what pretext?" someone asked, in a faint voice. "Ermanno Finzi-Contini has never been considered a lion."

"On what pretext did he refuse?" My father laughed violently. "Oh, one of the usual things: that he's a scholar (I'd like to know what subject!), that he's too old, that in his whole life he has never concerned himself with politics, et cetera, et cetera. For that matter he was sly, our friend. He must have noticed Tabet's grim expression, so then, *wham!* he slipped five thousand-lire bills into his pocket!"

"Five thousand lire!"

"That's right! To be contributed to the Seaside and Mountain Summer Camps of the Young Fascists. A nice thought, wasn't it? But now listen to the latest."

And he went on to inform the company that a few days ago, with a letter sent to the council of the community through the lawyer Renzo Galassi-Tarabini (could he have chosen a more stiff-necked, more obsequious, more "*halto*" lawyer than that?), the Professor had asked permission to restore, at his own expense, "for the use of his family and of anyone interested," the ancient, little Spanish synagogue on Via Mazzini, which had not been used for religious functions for at least three centuries and had long served as a storeroom

# III

In 1914, when little Guido died, Professor Ermanno was forty-nine, Signora Olga twenty-four. The child felt ill, was put to bed with a very high temperature, and sank at once into a deep drowsiness.

Dr. Corcos was urgently summoned. After a silent, endless examination, performed with a frown, Corcos abruptly raised his head, and stared, gravely, first at the father, then the mother. The doctor's gaze was long, severe, oddly scornful; meanwhile, beneath his thick, Umberto-style mustache, already completely gray, his lips curled in the bitter, almost vituperative grimace of desperate cases.

"Nothing can be done," Dr. Corcos meant, with that gaze and that grimace. But perhaps also something further. That he, too, ten years earlier (and who knows if he spoke of it that very day, before taking his leave, or else, as certainly happened, only five days later, addressing Grandfather Raffaello, while they both slowly followed the impressive funeral?), he, too, had lost a child, his Ruben.

"I too have known this suffering, I also know well what it means to see a five-year-old son die," Elia Corcos had said abruptly.

Head bowed, his hands resting on the handlebar of his bicycle, Grandfather Raffaello was walking beside him. He seemed to be counting, one by one, the cobblestones of Corso Ercole I d'Este. At those words, truly unusual on the lips of his skeptical friend, he turned, amazed, to look at him.

And, in fact, what did Elia Corcos himself know? He had examined at length the child's inert body, decreed to himself the grim prognosis, and then, having raised his eyes, fixed them on the petrified eyes of the two parents: the father, an old man; the mother, still a girl. By what paths could he have descended, to read those two hearts? And who else could, ever, in the future? The epigraph dedicated to the dead child, on the monumental tomb of the Jewish cemetery (seven lines lightly carved and inked in a humble rectangle of white marble), was to say only:

Mourn
GUIDO FINZI-CONTINI
(1908–1914)
of exceptional form and spirit
your parents thought
to love you always more
not to mourn you

Always more. A subdued sob, and that was all. A weight upon the heart to be shared with no other person in the world.

Alberto was born in '15, Micòl in '16: more or less the same age as me. They were sent neither to the Jewish elementary school on Via Vignatagliata, where Guido had attended, without finishing, the first grade, nor, later, to the public Liceo-Ginnasio G. B. Guarini, the early crucible of the city's finer society, Jewish and non-Jewish, and therefore at least as sacramental. They studied together privately, both Alberto and Micòl, as Professor Ermanno interrupted from time to time his solitary studies of agronomy, physics, and history of the Jewish communities of Italy, to supervise closely their progress. These were the mad but, in their own way, generous years of early Fascism in Emilia. All action, all behavior was judged—even by those who, like my father, happily quoted Horace and his *aurea mediocritas*—by the crude yardstick of patriotism or defeatism. To send one's children to the public schools was considered, in general, patriotic. Not to send them, defeatist: and therefore, towards all those who did send their children there, somehow offensive.

All the same, even in their segregation, Alberto and Micòl Finzi-Contini always maintained a fragile relationship with the outside world, with the young people, like us, who went to the public schools.

There were two professors of the Guarini whom we had in common, who acted as links.

Professor Meldolesi, for example, in the fourth year of *ginnasio* taught us Italian, Latin, Greek, History, and Geography; and every other afternoon he took his bicycle, and from the neighborhood of little villas, built in those years outside Porta San Benedetto, where he lived alone in a house he rented furnished, whose view and exposure he was accustomed to extol, he ventured all the way to the Barchetto del Duca, remaining there at times for three full hours. Signora Fabiani, our mathematics teacher, did the same.

From la Fabiani, to tell the truth, nothing had ever leaked. Bolognese by birth, a childless widow in her fifties, very devout, she would become preoccupied during question period, as she muttered to herself, constantly widening her sky-blue Flemish eyes, as if about to go into a trance. She was praying. For us, poor things, surely without any talent in algebra, almost all of us; but also, perhaps, to hasten the conversion to Catholicism of the Jewish family to whose house—and what a house theirs was!—she went twice a week. The conversion of Professor Ermanno, of Signora Olga, and especially of the two children, Alberto, so intelligent, and Micòl, so lively and pretty, must have seemed to her too important, too urgent a matter for her to risk compromising its probabilities of success through banal scholastic gossip.

Professor Meldolesi, on the contrary, did not remain silent at all. Born in Comacchio of a peasant family, educated in a seminary through the *liceo* years (and he much resembled a priest, a little, clever, almost feminine country priest), he had then moved on to study literature in Bologna, in time to attend the last lectures of Giosuè Carducci, whose "humble pupil" he boasted of being. The afternoons spent at the Barchetto del Duca, in an atmosphere steeped in Renaissance memories, with five o'clock tea taken in the company of the whole family—and Signora Olga often came in from the park at that hour, her arms filled with flowers—and then later, perhaps, up in the library, relishing until dark Professor Ermanno's learned conversation: those extraordinary afternoons obviously represented, for him, something too precious not to be made the subject, even with us, of constant discussion and digression.

And ever since one evening when Professor Ermanno had revealed to him how Carducci, in 1875, had been his parents' guest for about ten consecutive days, showing him then the room the poet had occupied, and letting him touch the bed where he had slept, and finally allowing him to take home, to examine at his convenience, a little "sheaf" of autograph letters sent his mother by the poet, Professor Meldolesi's agitation, his enthusiasm had known no limit. He had gone so far as to convince himself, and he tried to convince us as well, that the famous verse in the *Canzone di Legnano*:

O blond, O beautiful empress, O trusted one

which clearly heralded the even more famous verses:

Whence did you come? What centuries handed you down,
So mild and beautiful, to us . . .

and, at the same time, the sensational conversion of the great son of Maremma to the "eternal royal feminine" of Savoy, had been in fact inspired by the paternal grandmother of his private pupils, Alberto and Micòl Finzi-Contini. Oh, what a magnificent subject this would have been—Professor Meldolesi, once, in class, had sighed—for an article to send to that same *Nuova Antologia* where Alfredo Grilli, his friend and colleague Grilli, has been publishing for some time his acute notes on Serra! One of these days, naturally, with all the delicacy demanded by the situation, he would take care to mention this to the letters' owner. And heaven grant that, considering how many years had passed, and given the importance and, obviously, the perfect propriety of a correspondence in which Carducci addressed the lady only in such terms as "charming Baroness" or "most kind hostess" or the like, heaven grant that the owner would not say no! In the happy hypothesis of a yes, he, Giulio Meldolesi, would immediately take care—provided, also in this instance, that he was given explicit consent by the person who had every right to give it or deny it—to copy out the letters one by one, complementing later those sacred shards, those venerated sparks from the great forge, with a minimum commentary. What, in fact, did the text of the correspondence demand? No more than an introduction of a general nature, integrated, perhaps, with a few sober, historical-philological footnotes . . .

But besides the teachers we had in common, there were also the examinations reserved for private students—examinations held in June, at the same time as the other examinations, national and local—which at least once a year brought us in direct contact with Alberto and Micòl.

For us regular students, especially if we were promoted, there were perhaps no days more beautiful. As if, all of a sudden, we regretted the just-ended hours of lessons and assignments, we could usually find no better place to meet than the entrance hall of the school. We would linger in the vast passage, cool and dark as a crypt, clustering in front of the big white sheets announcing the final grades, fascinated by our names and our companions', which, read there, written in handsome calligraphy and exposed behind glass, beyond a fine wire grille, never ceased to amaze us. It was beautiful to have nothing more to fear from school, beautiful to be able to go outside a moment later into the clear, blue light of ten o'clock in the morning, beckoning, there, through the postern of the front door, beautiful to have before us long hours of idleness and freedom, to spend as we liked best. Everything beautiful, everything stupendous, in those first days of vacation. And what happiness at the ever-current thought of our imminent departure for the sea or the mountains, when studying, which still burdened and tormented so many others, would be for us almost forgotten!

And there, among these *others* (rough boys from the country, for the most part, sons of peasants, prepared for their examinations by the village priest, who, before crossing the threshold of the Guarini, looked around bewildered, like calves led to the slaughterhouse), there were Alberto and Micòl Finzi-Contini, in fact: not at all bewildered, not they, accustomed as they were for years, to present themselves and triumph. Slightly ironic perhaps, especially towards me, when, crossing the hall, they glimpsed me among my companions and greeted me from the distance with a nod or a smile. But always polite, even too polite, and well behaved: like guests.

They never came on foot, or, still less, on bicycles. In a carriage: a dark-blue brougham with large rubber wheels, red shafts, all glistening in fresh paint, crystal, nickel.

The carriage would wait there, outside the door of the Guarini, for hours and hours, never moving, not even to seek shade. And it must be said that examining the equipage more closely, in all its details, from the great, heavy horse, with his bobbed tail and his cropped mane, calmly stamping a hoof from time to time, to the tiny, aristocratic crown that stood out, in silver, against the blue background of the doors, even obtaining, sometimes, from the indulgent coachman in summer uniform, permission to climb on one of the side steps, so that we could contemplate at our leisure, noses pressed against the crystal, the interior, all gray, padded, and in semidarkness (it seemed a drawing room: in one corner there were even some flowers in a slender oblong vase, like a chalice): all this could be another delight, indeed it certainly was, one of the many adventurous delights with which, then, for us, those marvelous adolescent mornings of late spring were prodigal

# IV

As far as I personally am concerned, there had always been something more intimate, in any case, about my relations with Alberto and Micòl. The knowing looks, the confidential nods that brother and sister addressed to me, every time we met around the Guarini, alluded only to this, I well knew; something regarding us and only us.

Something more intimate. But what, exactly?

It's obvious: in the first place we were Jews, and this, in itself, would have been more than enough. Let me explain: between us there might have been nothing in common, not even the scant communion derived from having occasionally exchanged a few words. The fact, however, that we were what we were, that twice a year at least, at Passover and Kippur, we appeared with our respective parents and close relations at the same doorway on Via Mazzini—and it often happened that, having passed the door all together, the narrow hall that followed, half-dark, forced the grownups to hat-doffings, hand-clasps, obsequious bows, such as they would have no other occasion to exchange for the rest of the year—this would have been enough to ensure that when we young people met elsewhere, and especially in the presence of outsiders, there would immediately appear in our eyes the shadow or the smile of a certain special complicity and connivance.

That we were Jews, nevertheless, and inscribed in the ledgers of the same Jewish community, still counted fairly little in our case. For what on earth did the word "Jew" mean, basically? What meaning could there be, for us, in terms like "community" or "Hebrew university," for they were totally distinct from the existence of that further intimacy—secret, its value calculable only by those who shared it—derived from the fact that our two families, not through choice, but thanks to a tradition older than any possible memory, belonged to the same religious rite, or rather to the same "school"? When we met on the threshold of the entrance to the temple, as a rule at dusk, after the embarrassed formalities exchanged by our parents in the gloom of the porch, in the end we almost always climbed, still a group, the steep stairs that led to the third floor, where, crowded with a mixed throng, wide, echoing with sounds of organ and singing like a church—and so high, among the rooftops, that on some May evenings, with the big side windows flung open towards the setting sun, at a certain point we found ourselves bathed in a kind of golden mist—that was the Italian synagogue. So only we, Jews, to be sure, but also brought up in the observance of a same rite, could realize actually what it meant to have the same family bench in the Italian synagogue, up there on the third floor, instead of on the second, in the German one, so different in its severe, almost Lutheran assemblage of wealthy, bourgeois bowler hats. And this was not all: because, even taking for granted, outside the strictly Jewish world, an Italian synagogue's being different from a German one, with everything in particular that such distinction involved on the social and the psychological planes, who, besides us, would have been able to provide specific information about "the Via Vittoria people," just to give one example? This expression regularly referred to members of the four or five families who had the right to attend the separate little Levantine synagogue, also known as the Fano synagogue, situated on the fourth floor of an old house on Via Vittoria: the Da Fano family of Vià Scienze, in fact, the Cohens of Via Gioco del Pallone, the Levis of Piazza Ariostea, the Levi-Minzis of Viale Cavour, and I forget what other isolated family groups: all slightly odd people in any case, characters always a bit ambiguous and elusive, for whom religion in the Italian school had taken on too popular, theatrical a form, almost Catholic, with evident effect also on the character of the people, open and optimistic, for the most part, very "Po Valley," whereas religion for those others had remained essentially worship to be performed in a small group, in semiclandestine chapels to which it was best to go at night, slipping along the darkest and most infamous alleyways of the ghetto. No, no: only we, born and brought up *intra muros*, so to speak, could know, could really understand these things: very subtle, practically unimportant, but nonetheless real. It was futile to think that others, all the others, without excluding from the roster even school companions, childhood friends, playmates incomparably more beloved (at least by me), could be informed of such a private subject. Poor souls! In this respect, they were to be considered, all of them, only simple crude beings, sentenced for life, basically, to irreparable gaps of ignorance, or—as even my father would call them, with a benign grin—*goyishe blacks*.

And so, on occasion, we climbed the stairs together, and together we made our entrance into the synagogue.

And since our benches were neighboring, down front near the semicircular enclosure, marked all round by a marble railing, at the center of which stood the *tevá*, or reader's lectern, and both in excellent view of the black carved wooden cupboard that contained the scrolls of the Law, the so-called *sefarìm*, we crossed together also the great hall's resounding pavement of white and pink rhombohedrons. Mothers, wives, aunts, and sisters had separated from us men in the vestibule. Vanishing in single file through a little door in the wall, which led into a closet, from there, by a circular stair, they had climbed even higher, into the women's section, and in a little while we would see them again, peering from above, from their coop set just below the ceiling, through the holes in the grille. But even in this way, reduced to males only—namely, me, my brother, Ernesto, Professor Ermanno, Alberto, as well as, now and then, Signora Olga's two bachelor brothers, the engineer and Dr. Herrera, who would come especially from Venice—even in this way we formed a fairly numerous group. Significant and important, at least: for, at whatever moment of the function we might appear, we were never able to reach our seats without arousing the liveliest curiosity around us.

As I said, our benches were neighboring, one behind the other. My family occupied the bench in front, in the first row, and the Finzi-Continis the one behind, in the second. And so, even if we had wanted to, it would have been difficult to ignore one another.

For my part, attracted by their diversity to the same degree my father was repelled by it, I was always very alert to any movement or murmur from the bench behind ours. I was never still a moment. Whether I chattered in whispers with Alberto, who was two years older than I, true, but still had to "enter the *mignàn*," and nevertheless, hastened, as soon as he arrived, to enfold himself in the large *talèd* of white wool with black stripes that had once belonged to "Grandpa Moisè," or whether Professor Ermanno, smiling at me kindly through his thick glasses, invited me with a gesture to observe the copper engravings that illustrated an ancient Bible, which he had taken especially for me from the drawer; or whether, fascinated, I listened, open-mouthed, to Signora Olga's brothers, the railway engineer and the phthisiologist, chatting among themselves half in Venetian dialect and half in Spanish ("What is it? *Cossa stas meldando*? Come, Giulio, *alevantate, ajde!* And see that *el chico* also stands up"), only to stop then, suddenly, and join very loudly, in Hebrew, in the rabbi's chants; for one reason or another my head was almost always turned. In a row, on their bench, the two Finzi-Continis and the two Herreras were there, just a few feet away, and yet very remote, unattainable: as if they were protected all around by a wall of crystal. They did not resemble one another. Tall, thin, bald, with long pale faces shadowed by a growth of beard, dressed always in blue or black, and accustomed, moreover, to inject into their devotion an intensity, a fanatical ardor of which their brother-in-law and nephew—you only had to look at them—would never have been capable, the Venetian relations seemed to belong to a civilization completely alien to Alberto's sweaters and tobacco-colored long stockings, to Professor Ermanno's English woolens and tan cottons, a scholar's, a country gentleman's. And yet, different as they were, I felt a deep solidarity among them. What was there in common—all four seemed to say to themselves— between them and the distracted, whispering floor below, so *Italian*, which even in the temple, before the opened Ark of the Lord, continued to concern itself with all the pettiness of common life, business, politics, even sport, but never the soul and God? I was a boy then: between ten and twelve years old. An intuition, confused, yes, but substantially correct, was mingled with irritation and humiliation in me, equally confused, but searing, the intuition that I was part of the downstairs, the vulgar throng to be avoided. And my father? At the glass wall beyond which the Finzi-Continis and the Herreras, polite always, but distant, continued basically to ignore him, he behaved in a manner the opposite of mine. Instead of attempting approaches, as I did, I saw him react—he, with his doctorate in medicine, a freethinker, a war volunteer, a Fascist with a 1919 party card, an impassioned sports fan, he, a modern Jew, in other words—by exaggerating his own healthy intolerance of any excessively servile, shameless exhibition of devotion.

When there passed along the benches the happy procession of *sefarìm* (wrapped in rich short mantles of embroidered silk, with silver crowns askew and tinkling little bells, they seemed, the sacred scrolls of the Torah, an array of royal infants displayed to the populace to shore up a tottering monarchy), the doctor and the engineer Herrera were prompt to lean forward impetuously beyond the bench, kissing as many mantle hems as they could, with an almost indecent eagerness, greed. What did it matter that Professor Ermanno, imitated by his son, simply covered his eyes with a corner of the *talèd* and murmured a prayer with his lips?

"What a fuss, what *haltud!*" my father would comment later, at table: not that this prevented him, perhaps immediately afterwards, from returning once more to the hereditary pride of the Finzi-Continis, the absurd isolation in which they lived, as aristocrats, or even to their subterranean, persistent anti-Semitism. But for the moment, having no one else at hand, it was I that he took it out on.

As usual, I had turned to look.

"Would you do me the great favor of sitting properly?" he hissed at me, his teeth clenched, as his irate blue eyes glared at me in exasperation. "You don't know how to behave even in temple. Look at your brother here: four years younger than you, but he could teach you manners!"

I didn't hear. A little later, there I was again, turning my back to Dr. Levi's chanting, heedless of every prohibition.

Now, to have me again for some moments in his control—physical, mind you, only physical—my father could only wait for the solemn blessing, when all the sons would be gathered under the paternal *taletòd*, like so many tents. And there, finally (the sexton Carpanetti had already gone round with his pole, lighting one by one the synagogue's thirty candelabra of silver and ormolu: the hall blazed with light) there, awesomely awaited, Dr. Levi's voice, usually so colorless, suddenly assumed the prophetic tone suited to the supreme, and final, moment of the *berahà*.

"*Jevarehehà Adonài veishmerèha . . .*" the rabbi began solemnly, bent, almost prostrate, over the *tevà*, after having covered his towering white cap with the *talèd*.

"Now, boys," my father said then, happy and brisk, snapping his fingers, "come under here!"

In reality, even in that situation, escape was always possible. It was all very well for Papà to press his hard, athletic hands on our collars, on mine in particular. Though vast as a tablecloth, Grandfather Raffaello's *talèd*, which Papà used, was too worn and full of holes to guarantee the hermetic cloistering he dreamed of. And in fact, through the holes and rips produced by the years in the very fragile cloth, which smelled of age and must, it was not hard, for me at least, to observe Professor Ermanno as, there beside me, his hands placed on Alberto's dark hair and on the fine, light, blond hair of Micòl, who had rushed down from the women's section, he also said, one after the other, following Dr. Levi, the words of the *berahà*. Over our heads, my father, who knew no more than twenty words of Hebrew, the usual ones of family conversation—and moreover he would never have bent—kept silent. I imagined the suddenly embarrassed expression of his face, his eyes, at once sardonic and shy, raised towards the modest stucco decorations of the ceiling or towards the women's section. But meanwhile, from where I was, I looked up, with always renewed amazement and envy, at Professor Ermanno's wrinkled, keen face, as if transfigured at that moment, I looked at his eyes, which, behind his glasses, I would have said were filled with tears. His voice was faint and chanting, with perfect pitch: his Hebrew pronunciation, frequently doubling the consonants, and with the z, the s, and the h much more Tuscan than Ferrarese, could be heard, filtered through the double distinction of culture and rank. . . .

I looked at him. Below him, for the entire duration of the blessing, Alberto and Micòl never stopped exploring, they too, the gaps in their tent. And they smiled at me and winked at me, both curiously inviting: especially Micòl.

# V

One time, however, in June of '29, the day when the final *ginnasio* examination results were posted in the entrance of the Guarini, something unusual happened.

During the orals I hadn't shone, and I knew it.

Though Professor Meldolesi had done his best to favor me, even managing, against all regulations, to have himself chosen to question me, nevertheless at the famous *pons asinorum* I had not by any means been at the high level of the numerous sevens and eights that dotted my report card. Even in the literary examinations I should have done much better. Questioned, in Latin, on the *consecutio temporum*, I had stumbled in a hypothetical sentence of the third type, namely the "contrary to fact." I also had trouble responding in Greek, on a passage of the *Anabasis*. It is true that later I regained some ground with Italian, history, and geography. In Italian, for example, I had done very well, both on *I promessi sposi* and on *Le ricordanze*. I had then recited from memory the first three octaves of *Orlando furioso*, without missing a word; and Meldolesi promptly rewarded me with a "bravo!" so ringing that it brought smiles not only from the rest of the examining board but also from me. In general, however, I repeat, my performance, even in the field of literature, had not been up to the reputation I enjoyed.

Even the year before, in the fourth year of *ginnasio*, algebra had refused to enter my head. Moreover, with Signora Fabiani, the teacher, my behavior had always been fairly despicable. I would study the minimum necessary to get a six out of her; and often, not even that minimum, as I was relying on the unfailing support I would receive, in the finals, from Professor Meldolesi. What importance could mathematics have anyway for someone, like me, who had declared more than once that, at the university, he was going to study literature?—I kept saying to myself, even that morning, as I rode on my bicycle up Corso Giovecca, towards the Guarini. In algebra and also in geometry, I had hardly opened my mouth, unfortunately. But what of it? Poor Signora Fabiani, who had never dared, during the past two years, give me less than six in the council of professors, would never do so now. And as I avoided uttering even mentally the word "flunked," the very idea of flunking, with its consequent wake of the tiresome and depressing private lessons I would be subjected to in Riccione through the whole summer, seemed absurd, in my case. I, yes I, who had never suffered the humiliation of October make-up exams, and indeed, in the first, second, and third years of *ginnasio*, had been honored "for good studies and conduct" with the sought-after title of "Guard of Honor at the Monument to the Fallen and the Memorial Park," I, flunked, reduced to mediocrity, confused with the masses! And what about Papà? If, hypothetically speaking, la Fabiani had given me a temporary failure till October (she taught math also at the *liceo*, Signora Fabiani: for this reason she had questioned me, it was her right!), where would I find the courage, in a few hours' time, to go home, to sit at the table opposite Papà, and start eating? He, Papà, would perhaps beat me: and it would have been better, after all. Any punishment would have been preferable to the reproach that would come to me from his silent, terrible blue eyes. . . .

I entered the hall of the Guarini. A group of youngsters, among whom I immediately noticed various friends, was calmly standing in front of the results of the middle grades. I propped my bicycle against the wall, beside the front door, and I approached, trembling. Nobody seemed to notice my arrival.

I looked from behind a hedge of stubbornly turned backs. My eyesight blurred. I looked again: and the red five, the only number in red ink in a long row of black numbers, was impressed on my spirit with the violence and burning pain of a fiery brand.

"Well, what's wrong with you?" Sergio Pavani asked me, giving me a friendly tap on the back. "You're not going to make a tragedy out of a five in math, I hope! Look at me," he laughed. "Latin and Greek."

"Cheer up," Otello Forti added. "I failed a subject, too: English."

I stared at him, in a daze. We had been classmates, deskmates in the first grade, accustomed since then to studying together, one day at his house, the next at mine, and both of us convinced of my superiority. No year passed without my being promoted in June, while he, Otello, always had to make up some subject: English one time, Latin another, or math, or Italian.

And now, suddenly, to hear myself compared to *an* Otello Forti: and by

Otello himself, what's more! To find myself hurled suddenly down to his level!

It is not worth narrating at length what I did, what I thought, during the next four or five hours, beginning with the effect, as I was coming out of the Guarini, of my meeting Professor Meldolesi (smiling, he was, without hat and tie, the collar of his striped shirt turned up, à la Robespierre, and quick to confirm, as if there had been any need, la Fabiani's "doggedness" in my case, her categorical refusal to "close an eye one more time"), and then to continue with the description of the long, desperate, aimless wandering to which I abandoned myself once I had received, from the same Professor Meldolesi, a friendly pat on the cheek of dismissal and encouragement. Suffice it to say that around two in the afternoon I was still roaming, on my bicycle, along the Mura degli Angeli, in the vicinity of Corso Ercole I d'Este. I hadn't even telephoned home. My face streaked with tears, my heart brimming with an immense self-pity, I rode along almost not knowing where I was, meditating vague suicide plans.

I stopped under a tree: one of those ancient trees—lindens, elms, planes, chestnuts—that a dozen years later, in the icy winter of Stalingrad, would be sacrificed to make firewood, but which in '29 still held high, over the city bastions, their great umbrellas of leaves.

Around me, absolute emptiness. The packed-dirt path that, like a sleep-walker, I had covered from Porta San Giovanni to here, went on winding among the age-old trunks towards Porta San Benedetto and the railway station. I stretched out in the grass, prone beside the bicycle, my face, which was burning, hidden in the crook of my elbow. Warm, breezy air around the outstretched body, desire only to lie like this, eyes closed. In the hypnotic chorus of the cicadas, only an occasional isolated sound stood out: a cock's crowing from the nearby gardens, a slamming of clothes perhaps made by a washerwoman lingering to do her laundry in the greenish water of the Panfilio Canal, and finally, very close, inches from my ear, the clicking, slower and slower, of the bicycle's rear wheel, still seeking the point of immobility.

By now, surely—I thought—at home they had already heard the news: from Otello Forti, no doubt. Had they sat down to dinner? Yes, probably, acting as if nothing had happened: even if then, unable to continue, they had been forced to interrupt the meal. Perhaps they were looking for me.

Perhaps they had unleashed Otello himself, the good friend, the inseparable friend, giving him the task of searching on his bicycle the entire city, Montagnone and walls included, so it was possible that I might see him turn up at any moment, Otello, with a saddened face assumed for the occasion, but overjoyed, as I would clearly realize, at having flunked only English. But no: perhaps, seized with anxiety, my parents had not been satisfied only with Otello, they had even set the police in motion. My father had gone there, to the Castle, to speak with the chief. I could see him: stammering, distraught, frightfully aged, the shadow of himself. He was crying. Ah, but if he had been able to see me, two hours ago, at Pontelagoscuro, while I stared at the current of the Po from the height of the iron bridge (I had stayed there quite a while, looking down! How long? At the very least, twenty minutes .   . ), then he would really have been frightened . . . then he would really have understood . . . then he really . . .

"Psst."

I woke with a start, but I didn't open my eyes at once.

"Psst!" I heard again.

I slowly raised my head, turning it to the left, against the sun. Who was calling me? It couldn't be Otello. Who then?

I was about halfway along that stretch of the city walls which runs for a mile or so, from the end of Corso Ercole I to Porta San Benedetto, opposite the station. The place has always been particularly solitary. It was thirty years ago, and it still is today, despite the fact that, to the right especially, towards the Industrial Zone, that is, since '45, dozens and dozens of varicolored little workers' houses have sprung up, against which, and against the smokestacks and warehouses that are their background, the dark, bushy, wild, half-ruined spur of the fifteenth-century bastion seems every day more absurd.

I looked, I sought, half closing my eyes against the glare. At my feet (I realized only now), the crowns of its noble trees swollen with the noon light like those of a tropical forest, there stretched the Barchetto del Duca: immense, really endless, with the little towers and pinnacles of the *magna domus* in the center, half-hidden in the green, and bounded, for its whole perimeter, by a wall interrupted only about fifty yards farther on, to allow the Panfilio Canal to empty.

"Hey, you're really blind!" a girl's merry voice said.

From the blond hair, that special blond, streaked with Nordic locks, which was hers alone, like a *fille aux cheveux de lin*, I immediately recognized Micòl Finzi-Contini. She was leaning over the park wall, thrusting her shoulders forward, her folded arms resting on the top. She must have been no more than twenty meters away. She was looking up at me, observing me: close enough for me to be able to see her eyes, which were pale, big (too big, perhaps, then, in her thin little-girl's face).

"What are you doing up there? I've been watching you for ten minutes. If you were sleeping and I've waked you up, I'm sorry. And . . . sincere condolences!"

"Condolences? What? Why?" I stammered, feeling my face covered with blushes.

I had pulled myself up.

"What time is it?" I asked, raising my voice.

She glanced at her wristwatch.

"I have three o'clock," she said, with a pretty grimace. And then:

"I imagine you must be hungry."

I had lost my bearings. So they also knew! I even thought, for a moment, that the news of my disappearance had reached them directly from my father or my mother: by telephone, as, surely, it had reached countless other people. But it was Micòl who immediately set me straight.

"This morning I went to the Guarini with Alberto. We went to look at the grades. It hit you hard, eh?"

"And you? Were you promoted?"

"We don't know yet. Maybe they're waiting, to post our grades, until the other private students have *also* finished. But why don't you come down? Come closer, so I won't have to yell."

It was the first time she had spoken to me. Moreover: it was the first time, practically, that I had heard her speak. And at once I noticed how her speech resembled Alberto's. They both spoke in the same way: slowly, as a rule, underlining certain trivial words, whose true meaning, true weight, only they seemed to know, and skipping, in a bizarre way, over other words that one would have thought far more important. They considered this their *real* language: their special, inimitable, completely private distortion of Italian. They even gave it a name: Finzi-Continian.

Letting myself slide down the grassy bank, I approached the bottom of the wall. Despite the shade—a shade that smelled sharply of nettles and of dung—it was hotter, there. And now she was looking at me from above, her blond head in the sun, calm, as if our meeting had not been a casual encounter, entirely accidental, but as if, since the days perhaps when we were little children, the times we had made appointments to meet in that place were beyond counting.

"You're exaggerating, all the same," she said. "What does a make-up exam in October in one subject count?"

But she was teasing me, that was clear, and she also felt a slight contempt for me. It was fairly normal, after all, that such a thing should have happened to a character like me, son of people so common, so "assimilated": a quasi-*goy*, in short. What right did I have to make such a fuss?

"I think you have some rather strange notions," I answered.

"Do I?" she grinned. "Then explain to me, please, the reason why you didn't go home to dinner today."

"How do you know?" The question escaped from me.

"We know, we know. We also have our informers."

It had been Meldolesi—I thought—it could only have been he (in fact, I was not mistaken). But what did it matter? Suddenly I realized that the question of being flunked had become secondary, a childish matter that would work itself out.

"How can you manage," I asked, "to stay up there? You look as if you were at a window."

"My feet are on my faithful ladder," she answered, separating the syllables of "my faithful," in her usual, proud way.

From beyond the wall, at this point, a deep barking rose. Micòl looked around, giving a rapid glance behind her, filled at once with annoyance and affection. She pouted at the dog, then looked my way again.

"Uff!" she sighed calmly. "It's Jor."

"What breed is he?"

"A Great Dane. He's only a year old, but he weighs about two hundred pounds. He's always following me. Lots of times I try to cover my tracks, but after a while, he's sure to find me. He's *terrible*."

Then, almost without a pause:

"Want me to let you in?" she added. "If you want, I'll show you right away what you must do."

# VI

How many years have gone by since that far-off afternoon in June? More than thirty. Nevertheless, if I close my eyes, Micòl Finzi-Contini is still there, leaning over the wall of her garden, looking at me, and speaking to me. She was hardly more than a child, in 1929, a thirteen-year-old, thin and blond, with great, pale, magnetic eyes. I, a little boy in short pants, very bourgeois and very vain, whom a minor scholastic mishap was enough to plunge into the most childish desperation. We stared at each other. Above her, the sky was a uniform blue, a warm sky, already of summer, without the slightest cloud. Nothing could change it, and nothing has changed it, in fact, in my memory.

"Well, do you want to or not?" Micòl insisted.

"Um . . . I don't know . . ." I began saying, with a nod at the wall. "It seems very high to me."

"That's because you haven't taken a good look," she replied impatiently. "See there . . . and there . . . and there," and she pointed her finger, for me to observe. "There are lots of notches, and even a spike, up here. I drove it in myself."

"Yes, there would be footholds, for that matter," I murmured, hesitant, "but . . ."

"Footholds!" she interrupted me, at once, bursting out laughing. "I call them notches myself."

"You're wong. They're called footholds," I insisted, stubborn and sharp. "Obviously you've never been in the mountains."

I have always suffered from vertigo, since childhood, and, slight as it was, the climb made me stop and think. As a child, when my mother, with Ernesto in her arms (Fanny was not yet born), took me up on the Montagnone, and she sat in the grass of the broad lawn facing Via Scandiana, from which you could just glimpse the roof of our house, barely discernible in the sea of roofs around the great bulk of the church of Santa Maria in Vado, it was with some fear, I remember, that I eluded Mamma's vigilance and went to lean over the parapet that bounded the lawn towards the country, where I would look down, into the abyss a hundred feet deep. Almost always, along the sheer wall, someone was climbing up or down: young masons, peasants, laborers, each with a bicycle over his shoulder, and old men, too, mustachioed fishermen of frogs and catfish, loaded with rods and creels: all people from Quacchio, from Ponte della Gradella, from Coccomaro, from Coccomarino, from Focomorto, who were in a hurry, and rather than come around by Porta San Giorgio or Porta San Giovanni (because at that period the bastions were intact on that side, with no breaches for a length of almost three miles), they preferred to take, as they said, the "wall road." Some were leaving the city: in this case, having crossed the lawn, they passed by, without looking at me, climbing over the parapet and slipping down until the tip of their foot touched the first outcrop or niche in the decrepit wall, until they reached, in a few minutes, the meadow below. Or they were arriving from the country: and then they came up with widened eyes that seemed to me fixed in mine, as those eyes timidly peered over the edge of the parapet. But on the contrary, I was mistaken; obviously they were alert only to select the best foothold. In any case, while they were there like that, suspended over the abyss—in pairs, as a rule: one behind the other—I could hear them chatting calmly, in dialect, exactly as if they were walking along a path among the fields. How calm they were, strong, and brave—I said to myself. After they had come to within inches of my face, so that often, besides mirroring me in their own flushed faces, they struck me with the wine-stink of their breath; their thick, callused fingers grasping the inner edge of the parapet, they emerged from the void with their whole body, and, *allez-oop*, they were home safe. I would never have been capable of doing such a thing—I repeated to myself each time, watching them go off: full of admiration, but also of revulsion.

Well, I was feeling something similar again, before the wall to whose summit Micòl Finzi-Contini was inviting me to climb. The wall certainly did not appear as high as that of the Montagnone bastions. Still it was smoother, far less eroded by the years and the weather; and the indentations that Micòl pointed out to me were bare scratches. What if—I thought—after climbing up there, I were to feel dizzy and fall? I might be killed all the same.

And yet, it was not so much for this reason that I still hesitated. I was held back by a repugnance different from the purely physical one of vertigo: similar, but different, and stronger. For a moment I even regretted my desperation of a moment before, my foolish, puerile tears of a flunked schoolboy.

"And besides, I don't see any reason," I continued, "why I should start mountain climbing here, of all places. If I am to come into *your fami-ly's* house, thank you very much, I'm delighted: however, frankly, it seems far more comfortable to come in that way"—and with this, I raised my arm in the direction of Corso Ercole I—"by the front door. It would only take a minute. With my bicycle, I can cover the distance in no time."

I realized at once that she didn't welcome my suggestion.

"Oh no, no . . ." she said, distorting her face in an expression of in-tense annoyance, "if you come that way, Perotti is bound to see you, and then it's all over, there's no fun then."

"Perotti. Who's he?"

"The gatekeeper. You know. You may have noticed him; he's our coachman and chauffeur, too. . . . If he sees you—and he can't help but see you, because, except for when he goes out with the carriage or the car, he's always there on guard, the beast—afterwards, then I'd absolutely have to take you into the house . . . and I ask you if . . . You see?"

She looked me straight in the eyes: grave, now, though quite calm.

"All right," I answered, turning my head, and pointing with my chin to-wards the embankment, "but what about my bicycle? Where can I put it? I can't leave it there, after all, by itself! It's new, a Wolsit: with an electric headlight, a tool kit, pump. . . . Imagine! . . . I'm not going to let them steal my bicycle *too.* . . ."

And I said nothing more, suddenly gripped again by the anguish of the inevitable meeting with my father. That very evening, at the latest, I would have to go home. I had no other choice.

I turned my eyes again towards Micòl. Without saying anything, while I talked, she sat on the wall, her back to me; and now she sharply raised one leg, to sit astride.

"What are you up to?" I said, surprised.

"I've had an idea, for the bicycle. And, at the same time, I can show you the best places to put your feet. Now watch where I put mine. Look!"

She spun around, up there on the top, with great nonchalance, then, her right hand grasping the big rusty spike she had pointed out to me a little earlier, she began to climb down. She descended slowly, but sure of herself, seeking the footholds with the tips of her little tennis shoes, first one, then the other, and always finding them without much effort. She climbed down well. Still, before touching the ground, she missed a hold and slipped. She landed on her feet. But she had hurt her fingers; and, scraping against the wall, her little pink cotton dress, a beach-dress, had torn slightly beneath one arm.

"Stupid me," she grumbled, putting her hand to her mouth and blowing on it. "This is the first time that's happened to me."

She had also skinned one knee. She pulled up the hem of her dress, baring her thigh, strangely white and strong, already a woman's, and she bent to examine the bruise. Two long blond locks, the paler ones, escaping the little ring which held her hair in place, fell down, hiding her forehead and her eyes.

"How stupid," she repeated.

"You should put alcohol on it," I said mechanically, without approaching her, in the slightly whining tone that all of us, in my family, assumed in such situations.

"Alcohol, my foot."

She rapidly licked the wound: a kind of affectionate little kiss; and promptly she straightened up.

"Come on," she said, all flushed and disheveled.

She turned and began to climb up obliquely along the sunny slope of the embankment. She helped herself with her right hand, grabbing the clumps of grass; meanwhile, the left, at her head, was removing and replacing the little band that held her hair. She repeated the maneuver several times, as rapidly as if she were using a comb.

"You see that hole, there?" she said to me then, as soon as we had reached the top. "You can hide your bicycle inside there. It's perfect."

She was pointing out, perhaps fifty yards away, one of those little grassy conical mounds, no more than five feet high, the entrance almost always sunk in the ground, that you come upon fairly frequently as you make the circle of the walls of Ferrara. At first sight, they resemble somewhat the Etruscan *montarozzi* of the Roman Campagna, on a much smaller scale, of course. But the subterranean room, often vast, to which some of them still allow access, never served as the home for any dead person. The ancient defenders of the walls kept their weapons there: culverins, harquebuses, gunpowder, and so on. And perhaps also those strange cannon balls, of precious marble, that in the fifteenth and sixteenth centuries made the Ferrara artillery so feared in Europe, and of which you can still see some examples in the Castle, placed as ornaments in the central courtyard and on the terraces.

"Who would ever guess there's a brand-new Wolsit down there? They would have to know in advance. Have you ever been down?"

I shook my head.

"No? I have. Lots of times. It's *magnificent.*"

She moved with decision, and picking up the Wolsit from the ground, I followed her in silence.

I overtook her on the threshold of the opening. It was a kind of vertical fissure, cut sharply in the blanket of grass that, compact, covered the mound: so narrow that only one person could pass through it at a time. Just beyond the threshold the descent began, and you could see eight or ten yards ahead, no more. Farther, there were only shadows. As if the passage ended against a black curtain.

She leaned forward to look, then turned.

"You go down," she whispered, and she smiled faintly, embarrassed. "I'd rather wait for you up here."

She stood aside, clasping her hands behind her back, and leaning against the grass wall, beside the entrance.

"You're not scared, are you?" she asked, still in a low voice.

"No, no," I lied; and I bent to raise the bicycle and hoist it to my shoulder.

Without another word, I stepped past her, entering the passage.

I had to proceed slowly, also because of the bicycle, whose right pedal kept banging against the wall; and at first, for five or six feet at least, I was virtually blind; I could see nothing, absolutely nothing. At about ten yards from the entrance opening, however ("Be careful," the already distant voice of Micòl, behind my back, shouted at this point: "watch out for the steps!") I began to discern something. The passage ended a little farther on: there were only a few more yards of descent. And it was there, in fact, starting from a kind of landing, around which, even before arriving there, I guessed a completely different space existed, it was there that the steps announced by Micòl began.

When I had reached the landing, I paused briefly.

The childish fear of the dark and the unknown, which I had felt the moment I left Micòl, had gradually been replaced, in me, as I advanced in the underground passage, by a feeling, no less childish, of relief: as if, having saved myself in time from Micòl's company, I had escaped a great danger, the greatest danger a boy of my age ("a boy of your age" was one of my father's favorite expressions) could encounter. Ah, yes—I was thinking now—tonight, when I go home, Papà may even beat me. But now I can face his blows with serenity. One subject to make up by October: she was right, Micòl, to laugh at it. What was one examination in October compared to the rest (and I trembled) that there, in the darkness, might have happened between us? Perhaps I would have found the courage to give Micòl a kiss: a kiss on the lips. And then? What would have happened, then? In the movies I had seen, and in novels, it was all very well for kisses to be long and impassioned! In reality, compared to the *rest*, they represented only a brief instant, a moment actually negligible, if after the lips had met and the mouths almost penetrated each other, the thread of the story could most of the time be picked up only the next morning, or even several days later. Yes, but if Micòl and I had reached the point of kissing like that—and the darkness would surely have fostered it—after the kiss time would have continued to flow calmly, with no outside, providential intervention to help us suddenly reach the harbor of the following morning. What would I have had to do, then, to fill the minutes and the hours? Ah, but this hadn't happened. Thank goodness I had saved myself.

I began to go down the steps. Into the passage a few weak rays of light penetrated: now I was aware of them. And a bit by sight, a bit with my hearing (a trifle sufficed: for the bicycle to bump against the wall, or a heel to skid down from the step, and immediately the echo enlarged and multiplied the sound, measuring spaces and distances), I soon realized how vast the place was. It must have been a chamber about a hundred feet in diameter—I calculated—round, with a high domed ceiling at least the same height: a kind of upside-down funnel. Who knows, perhaps, through a system of secret corridors, it communicated with other underground rooms of the same sort, nesting by the dozens in the body of the bastions. Nothing could be more likely.

The floor was of packed earth, smooth, hard, and damp. I stumbled over a brick, then, groping my way along the curve of the wall, I trampled on some straw. Propping the bicycle against the wall, I sat down, remaining with one hand gripping the wheel of the Wolsit, and an arm around my knees. The silence was broken only by some rustling, an occasional squeak: rats, perhaps, or bats. . . .

And if, on the other hand, it had happened—I thought—would it have been so terrible, if it had happened?

Almost certainly I would not have gone home, and my parents, and Otello Forti, and Sergio Pavani, and all the others, police included, would have hunted for me in vain! The first days they would have breathlessly searched everywhere. The papers would have talked about it too, dragging out the usual hypotheses: kidnaping, accident, suicide, illegal expatriation. Little by little, things would have calmed down, all the same. My parents would have consoled themselves (after all, they still had Ernesto and Fanny), the search would have stopped. And the one who would really pay, in the end, would have been that stupid humbug, la Fabiani, who, in punishment, would have been transferred to "another educational institution," as Professor Meldolesi would put it. Where? Sicily or Sardinia, no doubt. And it would serve her right! She would learn, at her own expense, to be less mean and treacherous.

As for me, seeing that the others consoled themselves, I would do the same. I would count on Micòl, outside: she would take care of supplying me with food and anything I might need. And she would come to me every day, climbing over the wall of her garden, summer and winter. And every day we would kiss each other, in the darkness: because I was her man, and she, my woman.

And anyway this didn't mean I could never come out into the open again! During the day I would sleep, obviously, breaking off only when I felt Micòl's lips graze mine, and, later, dozing off again with her in my arms. At night, however, at night I could very well make long sorties, especially if I chose the hours after one or two in the morning, when everyone is in bed, and nobody, practically speaking, is in the streets of the city. Strange and terrible, but actually also amusing, to pass along Via Scandiana; to see our house again, the window of my bedroom, by now turned into a sitting room; to hide in the shadows and from afar glimpse my father, coming home, just at this hour, from the Merchants Club, and it never crosses his mind that I am alive and am watching him. In fact, he takes the key from his pocket, opens the door, enters, and then, calmly, just as if I, his older son, had never existed, shuts the door again with a single thud.

And Mamma? One day or another couldn't I try to inform her (through

Micòl, perhaps) at least that I wasn't dead? And see her, too, before, weary of my subterranean life, I left Ferrara and disappeared definitely? Why not? Of course I could!

I don't know how long I stayed there. Ten minutes, perhaps; perhaps less. I recall precisely, in any case, that as I was climbing up the steps and entering once more the passage (relieved of the burden of the bicycle, I moved quickly now), I continued to think, to let my imagination range. And Mamma—I asked myself—would she also forget me, like all the others?

In the end I found myself outside again; and Micòl was no longer there waiting for me where I had left her a little while before; instead, as I saw almost immediately, shielding my eyes with my hand against the sunlight, she was up there again, seated astride the garden wall of the Barchetto del Duca.

She was arguing and parleying with someone waiting for her at the foot of the ladder, on the other side of the wall: the coachman Perotti, probably, or even Professor Ermanno himself. It was clear: having noticed the ladder against the wall, they had immediately become aware of her brief escape. Now they were telling her to come down. And she couldn't make up her mind to obey.

Suddenly she turned, and saw me at the top of the embankment. Then she puffed out her cheeks, as if to say:

"Uff! Finally!"

And her last look, before she vanished behind the wall (a look accompanied by a smiling wink: just as when, in temple, she peeped at me from beneath her father's *talèd*), had been for me.

# Part
# Two

# I

When I did finally manage to pass it, to pass beyond the wall of the Barchetto del Duca and venture among the trees and glades of the great private forest, reaching the *magna domus* and the tennis court, it was much later, almost ten years afterwards.

It was in 1938, about two months after the promulgation of the racial laws. I remember well: one afternoon, towards the end of October, a few minutes after we had got up from the table, I received a telephone call from Alberto Finzi-Contini. Was it or wasn't it true—he promptly asked me, forgetting any preamble (mind you, we had had no occasion to exchange a word for more than five years)—was it or wasn't it true that I and "all the others," receiving letters signed by the vice president–secretary of the Eleonora D'Este Tennis Club, Marchese Barbacinti, had been forced to resign from the club in a body: "kicked out," in other words?

I denied this, firmly: it was not true. I had received no letter of that sort, not I, at least.

But immediately, as if he considered my denial worthless, or as if he weren't even listening, he invited me to come over without fail, to play at their house. If I was content with a court of white earth—he repeated—with a narrow out-of-bounds zone; and if, above all, since I was surely a much better player, I would "condescend to volley a bit" with him and with Micòl: they, both of them, would be very happy and "honored." And any afternoon was fine, if I was interested—he added. Today, tomorrow, the next day: I could come when I liked, bring anyone I liked, Saturday as well, of course. He would be staying in Ferrara at least another month or so, since the courses at the Milan Polytechnic wouldn't begin before November 20 (Micòl always took things more calmly: and this year, as she was not officially enrolled any more and didn't have to stay there and beg for signatures on attendance reports, who knows if she would ever set foot again in Ca' Foscari, in the University of Venice) and, besides, had I ever seen such splendid days? While this weather lasted, it would be a real crime not to make the most of it.

He spoke these last words with less conviction: it seemed as if, all at once, a less happy thought had crossed his mind, grazed him, or else a feeling of boredom, as sudden as it was unmotivated, had made him wish I wouldn't come, wouldn't take his invitation seriously.

I thanked him, not making any specific promise. Why that telephone call?—I asked myself, not without amazement, as I hung up. After all, since he and his sister had been sent to study outside of Ferrara (Alberto in '33, Micòl in '34: about the time that Professor Ermanno had received permission from the community to restore "for the use of his family and anyone interested" the former Spanish synagogue incorporated in the temple building on Via Mazzini, so the bench behind ours, in the Italian synagogue, had always remained empty after that), we had really seen each other only very rarely and fleetingly, those few times, at a distance. During that whole period we had become, in other words, so alien to one another that one morning in '35, at the Bologna station (I was already in my second year of literature: and I went back and forth on the train practically every day), when I was violently jostled, on the platform of track 1, by a tall, dark-haired, pale young man, with a laprobe under his arm, and with a porter laden with suitcases at his heels, as he strode towards the express to Milan, about to leave, I hadn't at first recognized this person as Alberto Finzi-Contini. On reaching the end of the train, he had turned to hurry the porter, jostling me at the same time, and I had swung around to protest, as, with an absent glance, he vanished that moment inside the car. That time—I went on thinking—he hadn't even felt obliged to greet me. And now, why all this insinuating courtesy?

"Who was it?" my father asked, once I had come back into the breakfast room.

He was the only one left there. He was sitting in an armchair beside the little table with the radio, in his usual anxious waiting for the two o'clock news.

"Alberto Finzi-Contini."

"Who? The boy? What condescension! And what did he want?"

He was examining me with his bewildered blue eyes, which had long ago lost all hope of imposing anything on me, now, of managing to guess what was passing through my head. He well knew—his eyes were telling me—that his questions irked me, that his constant insistence on meddling in my life was indiscreet, unjustified. But, good heavens, wasn't he my father? And couldn't I see how he had aged this past year? There was no question of his confiding in Mamma or in Fanny: they were women. Nor even with Ernesto: he was too young, a *putìn*. With whom was he to talk, then? Couldn't I possibly understand that I was the one he needed?

I reported, teeth clenched, what the call was about.

"Well? Are you going?"

He didn't give me time to answer him. Continuing, with the warmth that I saw enliven him every time he had a chance to draw me into some sort of conversation, especially if the subject was politics, he plunged headlong into a "summing up of the situation."

Unfortunately it was true—he began recapitulating, tirelessly—last September 22, after the first official announcement of the ninth of the month, all the newspapers had published that additional notice of the secretary of the party that spoke of various "practical measures" which the Fascist provincial offices were to apply immediately towards us. In the future, "while the prohibition of mixed marriages remains in effect, with the exclusion of any young person recognized as belonging to the Hebrew race from all State schools of whatever order and rank," as well as the exemption, for the same, from the "highly honored" obligation of military service, we "Israelites" were not to be allowed to insert death notices in the papers, appear in the telephone directories, employ domestic servants of the Aryan race, frequent "recreational clubs" of any kind, And yet, in spite of that . . .

"I hope you're not going to repeat the same old story," I interrupted him at that point, shaking my head.

"What story?"

"That Mussolini is more *good* than Hitler."

"All right, all right," he said. "Still you have to admit it. Hitler is a bloodthirsty madman, whereas Mussolini may be what you like, Machiavellian and turncoat, as you please, but . . ."

Again I interrupted him, unable to restrain a gesture of impatience. Was he, or was he not, in agreement—I asked him, rather curtly—with the thesis of the essay by Leo Trotsky that I had "passed" on to him a few days before?

I was referring to an article published in an old number of the *Nouvelle Revue Française,* a magazine of which I jealously preserved in my bedroom several years' complete runs. What had happened was this: I don't remember for what reason, I had been rude to my father. He took offense, became grouchy, so that, anxious to re-establish normal relations as quickly as possible, I had found no better solution than to share with him my most recent reading. Flattered by this sign of esteem, my father hadn't needed to be asked twice. He had immediately read, indeed devoured, the article, underlining many passages with his pencil and covering the margins of the pages with copious notes. In effect—and he had declared this to me explicitly—the article by "that rogue, the old bosom pal of Lenin" had been a genuine revelation for him.

"Of course I'm in agreement!" he exclaimed, pleased at seeing me willing to start a discussion, and dismayed at the same time. "There's no doubt Trotsky is a magnificent debater. So lively! The language! Quite capable of having written the article directly in French. Of course," and he smiled with pride, "Russian and Polish Jews may not be very likable, but they have a real gift for languages. It's in their blood."

"Never mind the language, let's stick to the ideas," I cut him off, with a slight professorial harshness, which I promptly repented.

The article was clear—I went on, in a more tranquil tone. Capitalism, in the phase of industrial expansion, cannot help but be intolerant of all national minorities, and of the Jews, in particular, who are *the* minority by antonomasia. Now, in light of this general theory (Trotsky's essay dated from '31, we had to remember: the year in which Hitler's real rise had begun), what did it matter that Mussolini, as a man, was better than Hitler? And was he really better, Mussolini, even as a man?

"Yes, yes, I understand . . ." my father continued repeating, softly, as I spoke.

His eyelids were lowered, his face contracted in a grimace of painful tolerance. Finally, when he was quite sure I had nothing else to add, he placed his hand on my knee.

He understood—he repeated yet another time, slowly raising his eyelids.

Still, if I would allow him to say so: in his opinion, I took too black a view of things, I was too catastrophic.

Why wouldn't I admit, in fact, that after the communiqué of September 9, and even after the supplementary notice of the twenty-second, things, at least in Ferrara, had gone on almost as before? True—he agreed, smiling sadly—during that month, among the seven hundred and fifty members of our community there had been no death of such importance as to make it worthwhile to print the news in the *Corriere ferrarese* (only two old women in the Home on Via Vittoria had died, unless he was mistaken: a Saralvo and a Rietti; and the latter not even Ferrarese: she was from some town in the province of Mantua: Sabbioneta, Viadana, Pomponesco, somewhere of the sort). But we had to be fair: the telephone directory hadn't been withdrawn, in order to be replaced by a purged one; there hadn't yet been a single *havertà*, maid, cook, nurse, or old housekeeper. employed by any of our families, who had suddenly discovered a "racial conscience" and had really thought of packing her bags; the Merchants Club, where for more than ten years the position of vice president had been occupied by the lawyer Lattes—and which he himself, as I ought to know, continued to visit undisturbed almost every day—had, until today, not demanded any resignations. And had Bruno Lattes, the son of Leone Lattes, perhaps been expelled from the tennis club? With no consideration for my brother, Ernesto, who, poor thing, was always there staring at me, gaping, and imitating me as if I were who knows what sort of great *hahàm*, I had stopped going to the club; and I was making a mistake, if I didn't mind his saying so; I was making a great mistake to shut myself up, to segregate myself, not seeing anyone, only, with the excuse of the university and the railway season ticket, slipping off to Bologna three or four times a week. I didn't even see Nino Bottecchiari, Sergio Pavani, and Otello Forti any more, my bosom friends here in Ferrara till a year ago; (and they, after all, one one day, the other another, you might say, never let a month pass without phoning me, poor boys!). I should look instead at young Lattes, if you please. According to the sports page of the *Corriere ferrarese*, he had not only been able take part normally in the annual final tournament, still in progress; but in the mixed doubles, playing with that beautiful Adriana Trentini, the daughter of the chief engineer of the province, he was doing very well: they had won three rounds, and were now about to play in the semi-finals. Ah, no: you could say what you liked about old Barbacinti, that he set too much store by his own (modest) quartering of nobility, for example, and too little by the grammar of the articles propagandizing tennis that the provincial party secretary made him write every now and then for the *Corriere ferrarese*. But that he was a gentleman, all the same, not at all hostile to the Jews, quite mildly Fascist—and at the word "Fascist," my father's voice quavered, a little quaver of timidity—about this there could be no doubt or argument.

And as for Alberto's invitation and the behavior of the Finzi-Continis in general, what was, suddenly, all this agitation on their part, all this frantic need for contact?

What had happened last week at the temple, for Rosh Hashana, had already been fairly odd (I had refused to go, as usual: and once again, if I would allow him to say so, I had made a mistake). Yes, it had been fairly odd, just when the service was at its climax, and the benches appeared most crowded, to see all of a sudden the whole Finzi-Contini tribe, with no distinctions between males and females—Professor Ermanno, his wife, his mother-in-law, followed, not only by the boy and the girl but by the two inevitable Herrera brothers from Venice—make its solemn re-entry into the Italian synagogue after a good five years of haughty isolation in the Spanish one, and with such faces, too, smug and benign, as if, with their very presence, they meant to reward and to *pardon* not only those present, but the entire community. This, in any case, hadn't been enough, obviously. Now they had reached the limit, inviting people to their house, to the Barchetto del Duca, if you please, where, since the time of Josette Artom, no fellow citizen or foreigner had set foot, except on occasions of extreme emergency. And did I want to know why? Why, because they were content, obviously, with what was happening! Because they, *halti* as they had always been (opposed to Fascism, yes, but most of all *halti*), *were pleased with the racial laws!* And if only they were good Zionists, at least! Then, seeing that here, in Italy, and in Ferrara, they had always found themselves so ill-at-ease, so out of things, if only they would exploit the situation to move once and for all to *Eretz!* But no. Beyond coughing up a bit of money every now and then, for *Eretz*—nothing exceptional, in any case—they hadn't wanted to do a thing. They had always preferred to spend their real money for aristocratic trivialities; like when, in '33, to find an *ehàl* and a *parochèt* worthy of their personal synagogue (genuine Sephardic articles, for heaven's sake, they mustn't be Portuguese, or Catalan, or Provençal, but Spanish, and of proper dimensions!), they had journeyed by car, with a Carnera following them, all the way to Cherasco, in the province of Cuneo, a village that until 1910, or around then, had been the headquarters of a little Jewish community, now extinct, and where only the cemetery had remained in operation, simply because some families in Turin, which had originally lived in the place, Debenedetti, Momigliano, Terracini, et cetera, continued to bury their dead there. And Josette Artom, too, the grandmother of Alberto and Micòl, in her day constantly importing palms and eucalyptus trees from the Rome Botanical Garden, the one at the foot of the Janiculum: and for this reason, so that the wagons could pass comfortably, but also for reasons of prestige, needless to say, she had made her husband, that poor Menotti, at least double the width of the already broad entrance of the park that opened on to Corso Ercole I d'Este. Actually, if you have a mania for collecting—things, plants, everything—you end up wanting also to collect people. Ah, but if they, the Finzi-Continis, regretted the ghetto (it was in the ghetto, obviously, that they dreamed of seeing everyone shut up: prepared, perhaps, in view of that fine ideal, to divide the Barchetto del Duca into lots, turning it into a kind of *kibbùtz* subject to their lofty patronage): they were quite, quite free to do so. He, in any event, would always have preferred Palestine. And, even better than Palestine, Alaska, Tierra del Fuego, or Madagascar . . .

It was a Tuesday. I couldn't say why, a few days later, the Saturday of the same week, I resolved to do exactly the opposite of what my father wished. I don't believe the usual mechanism of contradiction that leads sons to disobedience had anything to do with it. What made me suddenly dig out my racket and my tennis clothes, which had been lying in a drawer for more than a year, was perhaps only the radiant day, the light, caressing air of an extraordinarily sunny early autumn afternoon.

True, in the meanwhile various things had happened.

First of all, two days, I believe, after Alberto's call, on Thursday then, the letter that "accepted" my resignation as member of the Eleonora d'Este Tennis Club had in fact reached me. Typewritten, but with the full signature, at the bottom, of the Marchese Ippolito Barbacinti, the special-delivery registered letter did not waste space on personal and particular considerations. In a few, very curt lines, echoing not without some clumsiness the bureaucratic style, it came straight to the point: it confined itself to referring to the "precise instructions imparted by the provincial party secretary," declaring promptly that any further "attendence" (sic) at the club on the part of my "distinguished self" was "unacceptible." (Could Marchese Barbacinti ever refrain from enlivening his prose with spelling errors? Obviously not. But to note it, and laugh at it, was a little more difficult, this time, than before).

In the second place, it seems to me that the next day, Friday, there had been another telephone call for me, from the *magna domus*; and not from Alberto this time, but from Micòl.

The result was a long, indeed, very long conversation: whose tone remained, thanks especially to Micòl, that of a normal, ironic, digressive chat between two seasoned university students, between whom, as youngsters, there might also have been a hint of a crush, but which now, after something like ten years, is meant only to achieve a straightforward renewal of friendship.

"How long can it be since we saw each other?"

"Five years, at least."

"And what are you like, now?"

"Ugly. An old maid with a red nose. And you? By the way: I read, I read . . ."

"Read what?"

"Yes, in the papers, that you took part in the Youth Competition of Culture and Art, in Venice, two years ago. Getting ahead in the world, aren't we? Congratulations! But, of course, you were always very good in Italian, even back in the *ginnasio*. Meldolesi was really *enchanted* with some of the compositions you wrote in class. I believe he actually brought some of them to us, to read."

"It's nothing to tease about. And you, what are you doing?"

"Nothing. I was supposed to take a degree in English at Ca' Foscari, last June. And then, instead, I didn't. I hope to make it this year, laziness permitting. Do you think they'll let outside students finish *all the same*?"

"I realize I'm causing you great sorrow, but I haven't the slightest doubt of it. Have you already chosen your thesis?"

"Oh, as far as choosing it goes, yes. Emily Dickinson. You know? That nineteenth-century American poetess, that terrible woman . . . But how can I manage? I ought to dog the professor's heels, spend week after week in Venice, but for me, the Pearl of the Adriatic, after a while . . . In all these years I've never stayed there more than the bare minimum. Besides, frankly, studying has never been my strong point.''

"You're a liar. A liar and a snob.''

"No, no, I *swear*. And this autumn, I feel less than ever like sitting there, nice and quiet. You know what I'd like to do, my friend, instead of burying myself in the library?''

"What?''

"Play tennis, dance, and flirt—imagine!''

"Healthy pastimes, tennis and dancing included, which, if you liked, you could easily indulge also in Venice.''

"Of course . . . with the housekeeper of Uncle Giulio and Uncle Federico always after me!''

"Well, the tennis at least: don't tell me you couldn't manage that. I do, for example; whenever I can, I grab a train and slip off to Bologna. . . .''

"You slip off to your girl friend, go on. Confess.''

"No, no. I have to take my degree next year, too: I still don't know whether it'll be in art history or Italian, but I suppose Italian, by now. And when I feel like it, I allow myself an hour of tennis. I reserve a court, paying for it, on Via del Cestello or at the Littorale (they're red courts, believe me: with hot showers, bar, and all modern conveniences) and nobody says a thing. Why don't you do the same, in Venice?''

"The point is that to play tennis and to dance you need a *partner*, and in Venice I don't know anybody who would do. And besides, I tell you: Venice may be very beautiful, I won't say it isn't, but I don't feel at home there. I feel temporary, cut off . . . as if I were abroad.''

"You live at your uncles' house?''

"That's right. Room and meals.''

"I understand. Anyway, two years ago, when there was the Fascist Youth Competition at Ca' Foscari, thanks for not coming. I mean it. I consider it the blackest page of my life.''

"Why? After all . . . For that matter, I'll tell you that, at one point, knowing you were going to compete, I harbored the sweet notion of rushing there to be your claque . . . rallying to the flag. . . . But listen, another thing: you remember that time on the Mura degli Angeli, outside here, the year you failed math? You must have cried like a ewe lamb, poor thing: your eyes! I wanted to console you. I had even had the idea of making you climb the wall and letting you into the garden. And why didn't you come in, then? I know you *didn't* come, but I can't remember why not.''

"Because someone caught us just at the wrong moment.''

"Oh, of course, Perotti, that *dog* Perotti, the gardener.''

"Gardener? I thought he was the coachman.''

"Gardener, coachman, chauffeur, gatekeeper, everything.''

"Is he still alive?''

"I'll say he is!''

"And the dog, the real dog, the one that barked?''

"Who? Jor?''

"Yes, the Great Dane.''

"He's flourishing, too.''

She had repeated her brother's invitation ("I don't know whether Alberto called you or not, but why don't you come and bat a few balls around at our house?''), without insisting, however, and, unlike him, without any reference to Marchese Barbacinti's letter. She referred to nothing except the pure pleasure of our meeting again after such a long time, and enjoying together, despite all prohibitions, what beauty there was left to enjoy of the season.

# II

I wasn't the only one who had been invited.

That Saturday afternoon, when I turned up at the end of Corso Ercole I (having avoided Corso Giovecca and the center of town, I was coming from Piazza della Certosa), I immediately noticed, outside the entrance of the Finzi-Contini house, a little group of tennis players standing in the shade. There were five of them, also with bicycles: four boys, and a girl. Who were they?—I wondered. Except for one, whom I didn't know even by sight—an older boy, about twenty-five, with long white linen trousers, and with a brown corduroy jacket—there was no doubt that the others, all in bright sweaters and shorts, were habitual visitors of the Eleonora d'Este. They were waiting, clearly. While they waited to be admitted, they must already have pressed the button of the entrance bell several times. And since the door hadn't yet been opened, now, in merry protest, not caring if the rare passersby noticed them, every so often they stopped their loud talking and laughing, to ring, together, rhythmically, the bells of their bicycles.

I braked, tempted to turn back. Too late! They had already stopped ringing their bells, a pair of them, and were looking at me, curious. One, then, whom, as I came closer, I suddenly recognized as Bruno Lattes, was actually signaling to me with his racket, brandished at the end of a long and very thin arm. He wanted to make me recognize him (we had never been friends: he was two years younger than I, and even in Bologna, in the literature department, we had seldom run into each other), and, at the same time, to urge me to come forward.

I came and stopped directly in front of him.

"Good afternoon." I grinned. "Why such a gathering around these parts today? Has the tournament finished? Or am I in the presence of a host of the eliminated?"

I hadn't addressed anyone in particular, my left arm resting against the smooth oak of the doorway, my feet still on the pedals. In the meanwhile, I observed them one by one: Adriana Trentini, with her beautiful blond hair loose over her shoulders, and with her long legs, magnificent, to be sure, but the skin too white, dotted with strange red patches that she always got when she was overheated; the taciturn young man in the linen trousers and brown jacket (who was he? Not surely a Ferrarese!—I said to myself at once); the other two boys, much younger than he and even than Adriana: still at the *liceo,* perhaps, or at the *Istituto tecnico,* and for that reason, as they had "come up" during the last year, while I had gradually cut myself off from every circle of the city, half-strangers to me; and finally Bruno, there facing me, taller and skinnier than ever, and with his dark skin, more than ever like a young Negro, vibrant and apprehensive: in the grip of such nervous agitation, that day too, that he managed to transmit it through the faint contact of the front tires of our two bicycles.

Rapidly, between him and me, there passed the inevitable glance of Jewish complicity that, with anxiety and disgust, I had already foreseen. Then I added, looking at him meaningfully:

"I trust that before daring to come and play in a different place you have all asked permission of *Signor* Barbacinti."

The non-Ferrarese stranger, whether he was amazed at my sarcastic tone, or whether he was uneasy, made a small movement beside me. Instead of restraining me, the action aroused me still further.

"Come, now, reassure me," I insisted. "Is this an allowed transgression on your part, or is it an escape?"

"What!" Adriana blurted, with her usual thoughtlessness: innocent, but none the less offensive. "Don't you know what happened last Thursday, during the finals of the mixed doubles? Don't tell me you weren't there! Come on! And drop those airs of yours, always acting like something out of Vittorio Alfieri! While we were playing, I saw you in the stands. I saw you very distinctly."

"I wasn't there at all," I replied. "I haven't darkened those parts for at least a year."

"And why not?"

"Because I was sure that one day or another I'd be kicked out anyway. I was right, in fact: here's my letter of dismissal."

I took the envelope from the pocket of my jacket.

"I imagine you've received one, too," I continued, addressing Bruno.

At this point Adriana finally seemed to remember that I was also in the same position as her doubles partner. She was visibly upset; but the prospect of being able to communicate something important to me, something about which I was obviously uninformed, promptly swept any other thought from her head.

Something very "nasty" had happened—she began telling me, while one of the younger boys again pressed the doorbell's little pointed button of black horn. Perhaps I didn't know it, but she and Bruno, in the club tournament, had actually reached the finals: a result that they would never, never have dreamed of hoping for, neither she nor Bruno. Well: the decisive game was in full swing, and once again, things had begun to take the most incredible turn (it was enough to make your eyes pop, honestly: Désirée Baggioli and Claudio Montemezzo, two aces, put on the defensive by a couple of weekend players: they had actually lost the first set ten to eight, and were doing badly also in the second), when, all of a sudden, thanks to the unexpected initiative of Marchese Barbacinti, the tournament referee, the game had been called. It was six o'clock, and, true, you couldn't see very well. But not so badly, in any case, that it wouldn't have been possible to keep on for at least another two games! Is that any way to act, really?

At four games to two of the second set of an important contest, unless she was mistaken, nobody has the right to start yelling suddenly "stop!" to come onto the court, arms in the air, proclaiming the game suspended "because of impending darkness," and postponing the continuation and conclusion to the afternoon of of the following day. Anyway, he hadn't been at all honest, the Marchese hadn't, this was obvious. As if she, Adriana, hadn't seen him, already at the end of the first set, conferring heatedly with that villain Gino Cariani, secretary of the Fascist University Students Association, the GUF (they had moved away from the crowd a bit, near the little dressing-rooms building); and Cariani, perhaps to be less conspicuous, kept his back turned to the court, as if to signify: "Play, go on playing, we're not talking about you": for her the Marchese's face at the moment when he had bent over to open the gate: so pale and distraught, she had never seen the like—a coward's face, that's what it was!—was enough for her to guess that the darkness was only a pretext, a weak excuse. Could there be any doubt about it, for that matter? There had been no further mention of the interrupted game, because Bruno, too, the next morning, had received the same special-delivery letter that I had: Q.E.D. And she, Adriana, was so disgusted by this whole thing—so outraged, above all, that they had had the bad taste of mixing politics with sport—that she had sworn never to set foot there again, at the Eleonora d'Este. Did they have something against Bruno? If so, they could easily have forbidden his entering the tournament. Say to him frankly: "As things are thus and so, sorry, we can't accept your application." But, once the tournament had begun, or rather, almost ended, moreover, with his winning, by a hair, one of the competitions, they should never have behaved the way they had. Four to two! What a lousy trick! A lousy thing like that was worthy of savages, not of well-brought-up, civilized people!

Adriana Trentini talked heatedly, growing gradually more animated; and Bruno also spoke now and then, adding details.

In his opinion, the game had been interrupted mostly because of Cariani, from whom, if you only knew him, nothing else was to be expected. It was all too obvious: dimwit that he was, with a consumptive chest and bird's bones, his sole thought, from the first moment he had entered the GUF, had been to make a career, and for this reason he never overlooked an opportunity, in public or in private, to lick the feet of the provincial secretary (had I never seen him, at the Caffè della Borsa, the rare times he managed to sit down at the table of the "old snakes of *The Hand-Grenade* Gang"? He swelled up, cursed, paraded obscenities bigger than he was, but the moment the Consul Bolognesi, or "Sciagura," or some other big shot of the group put him in his place, he promptly tucked his tail between his legs, capable, to win forgiveness and be restored to favor, of even the most humble services: running to the tobacconists's to buy the secretary's pack of Giubeks, or telephoning to Sciagura's house, to herald the great man's imminent return to his wife, the former laundress): a worm of that sort, Bruno could have sworn, surely hadn't missed the opportunity to show off, once again, for the party officials! Marchese Barbacinti was what he was: a distinguished gentleman, no doubt, but rather lacking "when it came to independence of action," and far from a hero. They kept him there to run the tennis club, because he was presentable, and, mostly, because of his name, which in their minds they no doubt dreamed was some kind of lure for trapping the innocent. Now it must have been child's play, for Cariani, to fill the poor nobleman with fear and trembling. Perhaps he had said to him: "What about tomorrow? Have you thought about tomorrow evening, Signor Marchese, when the party secretary will come here, for the dance, and will find himself forced to give the prize to a . . . Lattes, silver cup and everything and the proper Roman salute? If you ask me, I foresee a huge scandal. And problems; no end of problems. In your place, as it's beginning to grow dark, I wouldn't think twice about calling the game." That had been all it took, "100 percent guaranteed," to lead the Marchese to his grotesque and painful intrusion.

Before Adriana and Bruno had finished informing me of these events (at a certain point Adriana also found the opportunity to introduce me to the stranger: a certain Malnate, Giampiero Malnate, Milanese, a young chemist just appointed to a position with one of the new synthetic rubber factories in the Industrial Zone), the door had finally been opened. On the threshold a man of about sixty had appeared, burly, squat, with close-cropped gray hair from which the rays of the two-thirty sun, pouring through the vertical opening of the entrance, struck reflections of metallic luminosity, and with an equally short and gray mustache beneath the fleshy, purplish nose: a bit Hitlerian—I was led to think—nose and mustache. It was really he, old Perotti, gardener, coachman, chauffeur, gatekeeper, everything, as Micòl had said: not in the least changed, for the most part, since the Guarini days, when, seated on the box, he waited, impassive, outside the dark and menacing cavern, which had swallowed up his "young master and mistress," fearless, a smile on their lips, until they finally decided to return, no less serene and self-confident, to the vehicle, all crystal, fresh paint, nickel, padded upholstery, rare woods—similar, really, to a precious glass case—whose maintenance and driving were his responsibility. The little eyes, for example, also gray and piercing, sparkling with hard, Veneto peasant shrewdness, laughed kindly beneath the thick, almost black eyebrows: just as in the old days. But at what, now? At us, left there waiting for at least ten minutes? or at himself, who had turned up in striped jacket and white cotton gloves: brand new, the latter, perhaps inaugurated for the occasion?

We entered then, beyond the door, promptly closed after us with a loud bang by the alert Perotti, to be received by deep barks of Jor, the black and white "Harlequin." He was coming down the driveway, the Great Dane, trotting wearily towards us with an anything but threatening manner. All the same, Bruno and Adriana were abruptly silent.

"He doesn't bite, does he?" Adriana asked, frightened.

"Don't worry, signorina," Perotti answered. "With the two or three teeth he has left, what could he be up to biting now? Except polenta . . ."

And while the decrepit Jor, stopping in the midst of the drive in a statuesque pose, stared at us with his two icy, expressionless eyes, one dark and one pale blue, Perotti began apologizing. He was sorry to have kept us waiting—he said—but it wasn't his fault. It was the electricity that failed every now and then (luckily Signorina Micòl had noticed and had immediately sent him to see if by chance we had already arrived), and also the distance, a quarter of a mile, unfortunately. He didn't know how to ride a bicycle; but when Signorina Micòl got a thing into her head . . .

He sighed, raising his eyes to heaven, smiled once again, for some reason, revealing between his thin lips two rows of teeth far more compact and strong than the Great Dane's; and meanwhile, with his arm raised, he pointed out to us the path that, after a hundred yards, entered a clump of flowering canna. Even though we could use our bicycles—he warned us—to reach the *palazzo* we still had to allow three or four minutes.

# III

We were really very lucky with the season. For ten or twelve days the perfect weather lasted, held in that kind of magic suspension, of sweetly glassy and luminous immobility peculiar to certain autumns of ours. It was hot in the garden: almost like summertime. Those who wanted could go on playing till five thirty and even later, with no fear that the evening dampness, already so heavy towards November, would damage the gut of the rackets. At that hour, naturally, you could hardly see on the court any longer. But the light, which in the distance still gilded the grassy slopes of the Mura degli Angeli, filled, especially on Sunday, with a far-off crowd (boys chasing a football, wet nurses seated knitting beside baby carriages, soldiers on passes, pairs of lovers looking for places where they could embrace), that last light invited you to insist, to continue volleying no matter if the play was almost blind. The day was not ended, it was worth lingering a little longer.

We went back every afternoon, at first telephoning beforehand, then not even bothering; and always the same ones, except for the occasional absence of Giampiero Malnate, who had met Alberto in '33 in Milan, and, contrary to what I had thought that first day, encountering him outside the door of the Finzi-Contini house, had not only never seen any of the four young people with him before, but had no connection either with the Eleonora d'Este or with its vice president and secretary, Marchese Ippolito Barbacinti. The days seemed too beautiful and, at the same time, too threatened by the now imminent winter. To miss even one was a downright crime. Without making an appointment, we always arrived around two o'clock, just after lunch. Often, at the beginning, it would again happen that all of us would be gathered in a group at the entrance, waiting for Perotti to come and open the door. Later, however, after about a week, when an intercom and a remote-control lock had been installed, entering the garden no longer represented a problem, so we arrived casually, one or two at a time. As for me, I never missed an afternoon; not even for one of my usual dashes to Bologna. But neither did the others, if I remember rightly: not Bruno Lattes, or Adriana Trentini, or Carletto Sani, or Tonino Collevatti, later joined by my brother, Ernesto, as well as three or four other boys and girls. The only one who, as I said, came with less regularity was Giampiero, "il Malnate" (it was Micòl who began to call him that: and soon it was general usage). He had to contend with the factory hours—he once confided—not a very strict schedule, true, since the Montecatini factory, where he worked, had not produced, till now, so much as one pound of synthetic rubber, but still, the schedule existed. His absences, in any case, never lasted more than two days in a row. For that matter he was the only one, besides me, who didn't seem to care excessively about playing tennis (to tell the truth, he was a fairly poor player), often content, when he appeared on his bicycle around five, coming from his laboratory, to referee a game, or to sit off to one side with Alberto, smoking his pipe and conversing.

In any event, our host and hostess were even more assiduous than we. You could turn up very early, when the distant clock in the square still hadn't struck two: no matter how early you arrived, you were sure to find them already on the court, and never playing against each other, as on that first Saturday when we had turned up in the clearing behind the house where the court was located, but checking, now, to make sure all was in order, the net in position, the ground well rolled and sprinkled, the balls in good shape, or else they would be lying in two deck chairs with great straw hats on their heads, motionless, sunning themselves. As hosts, they could not have been better. Though it was clear that, for them, tennis as a purely physical exercise, as a sport, was of only limited interest, nevertheless they stayed there until after the game—almost always both of them, one or the other always—never saying good-bye ahead of time with the excuse of an engagement, things to do, a headache. They were the ones, indeed, who sometimes insisted in the almost total darkness, that we have "one more volley, the last!" and they would push back onto the court those who were already coming off.

The court, as Carletto Sani and Tonino Collevatti had remarked at once, wasn't really up to much.

Experienced fifteen-years-olds, too young ever to have trod playing fields different from those that filled Marchese Barbacinti with rightful pride, they had immediately begun, not lowering their voices at all, to make up the list of defects of that sort of "potato patch" (so one of them had expressed himself, curling his lips in a sneer of contempt). And these were: hardly any out-of-bounds area, especially behind the base lines; white earth, and also badly drained, which therefore at the slightest rain, would turn into a marsh; no evergreen hedge against the metal fences.

But, as soon as they had ended their game (Micòl hadn't managed to prevent her brother's catching up with her at five–all: and at this point they had dropped it), Alberto and Micòl, as if continuing their competition, had hastened to denounce the same defects, without a shred of reticence, I would actually say with a kind of mocking, masochistic enthusiasm. Ah, yes—Micòl had said gaily, while she was still rubbing her flushed face with a Turkish towel—for people like us, accustomed to the red courts of the Eleonora d'Este, it would be very hard to feel at ease on this dusty "potato patch" of theirs! And the out-of-bounds? How would we manage to play with so little room behind us? Alas: in what an abyss of decadence we had fallen, poor things! Personally, however, her conscience was clean. She had told him again and again, her papà, that they should make up their minds and extend the metal nets at the back at least three meters, and the side fences at least two. But, naturally, he, Papà, thought like a typical farmer; land, for them, if it isn't used to plant things, seems wasted; and so he had always shilly-shallied, calculating also the fact that she and Alberto had always played on a dreadful court like this since they were children, and they could very well go on playing there as grownups. Now, at last, things were different; now they had guests, "illustrious guests": hence she would take up the cause again with renewed energy, vexing and tormenting her "silver-haired parent" so much, that for the next spring, ninety-nine chances out of a hundred, she and Alberto would be in a position to offer us "something decent." She grinned, openly, meanwhile. So we, in chorus, could do nothing but contradict, assure that everything, court included, was fine, praising in addition the green setting of the park, compared to which (it was Bruno Lattes who declared it: just at the moment when, interrupting their "duel to the death," Micòl and Alberto had come towards us), the remaining private parks of the city, including that of Duke Massari, faded to the level of little neatly combed bourgeois gardens.

But the tennis court, really, was not "decent," and moreover, since there was only the one, it imposed over-long turns of rest. So, at four o'clock sharp every afternoon, especially for the purpose, perhaps, of keeping the two fifteen-year-olds of our heterogeneous company from regretting the far more intense hours, athletically speaking, that they would have spent under the wing of Marchese Barbacinti, Perotti invariably appeared, his bull neck taut and red from the effort of carrying a great silver tray in his gloved hands.

The tray was heavily laden: with buttered sandwiches of anchovy paste, smoked salmon, caviar, *pâté de foie gras,* ham; with little *vol-au-vents* filled with minced chicken in béchamel; with tiny *buricchi,* which had surely come from the prestigious little kosher shop Signora Betsabea, the celebrated Signora Betsabea (Da Fano) had run for decades on Via Mazzini, to the delight and glory of the entire population of the city. And that wasn't all. Before Perotti had finished settling the contents of the tray on the little wicker table especially prepared at the side entrance to the court, under a broad umbrella of red and blue stripes, he was joined by one of his daughters, either Dirce or Gina, both about Micòl's age, and both in service "in the house," Dirce as housemaid, Gina as cook (the two boys, Titta and Bepi, the former about thirty, the latter eighteen, tended the park, in the double position of flower gardeners and truck farmers: and we never managed to see more than an occasional glimpse of them in the distance, bent over their work, but quick to direct at us, as we passed on our bicycles, the flash of their ironic blue eyes). She, the daughter, had drawn after her, down the path from the *magna domus* to the court, a rubber-wheeled trolley, also laden with carafes, pots, glasses, and cups. And inside the porcelain and pewter pots there was tea, milk, coffee; inside the beaded Bohemian crystal carafes, lemonade, fruit juice, *Skiwasser:* a thirst-quenching drink, this—composed, in equal parts, of water and raspberry syrup, with a slice of lemon added and a few grapes—which Micòl preferred above all else, and in which she displayed a special pride.

Ah, that *Skiwasser*! During the breaks between games, besides biting into a sandwich, which, not without some ostentation of religious anti-conformism, she always chose from those with ham, Micòl often gulped down an entire glass of her dear "beverage," constantly urging us also to take some, "in homage"—she would say, laughing—"to the defunct Austro-Hungarian Empire." The recipe—she had told us—had been given to her in Austria, in fact, at Offgastein, in the winter of '34: the only winter she and Alberto, "in coalition," had managed to go off for a fortnight on their own, to ski. And though *Skiwasser,* as its name indicated, was a winter drink, and thus should be served boiling hot, still, in Austria too, there were people who continued to drink it in summer, like this, in the iced "version" and without the lemon slice; and they called it *Himbeerwasser,* in this case.

In any event we were to note carefully—she added with comic emphasis, raising one finger—the grapes, "very, very important," had been her initiative, she herself had introduced them into the classic Tyrolean recipe. It was her idea, and it meant a great deal to her: there was nothing to laugh about. They represented, those grapes, the special Italian contribution to the holy and noble cause of *Skiwasser,* or rather to this, more exactly, the special "Italian variant, or rather Ferrarese, or rather . . . et cetera, et cetera."

# IV

A little time went by before the other members of the household began to be seen.

In this respect, in fact, something curious happened the first day, so curious that I remembered it towards the middle of the next week, when neither Professor Ermanno nor Signora Olga had yet appeared, and I was beginning to suspect, on the part of all those whom Adriana Trentini called, in a body, the "*côté* old folks," a unanimous decision to stay clear of the tennis court: perhaps not to cause embarrassment, who knows, to avoid altering with their presence parties that, basically, were not parties, but simple gatherings of boys and girls in the garden.

The curious event occurred at the start, shortly after we had taken our leave of Perotti and Jor, who remained there watching us while we rode off on our bicycles along the drive. After passing the Panfilio Canal, over a strange, massive bridge of black beams, our bicycle patrol had then come to within a hundred yards of the lonely neo-Gothic bulk of the *magna domus,* or, to be more precise, of the graveled, sad space, entirely in the shade, which opened in front of it, when the attention of us all was attracted by two people, unmoving, in the very center of that space: an old lady seated in an armchair, with a pile of cushions supporting her back, and a blond, buxom young girl, apparently a maid, standing erect behind her. As soon as she saw us coming forward, the lady made a kind of start. After which she immediately began making great signals with her arms, to indicate no, we shouldn't come any further, not towards the space where she was, because beyond there was nothing but the house; instead we were to turn left, along the path covered by a tunnel of little climbing roses which she pointed out to us, at the end of which (Micòl and Alberto were already playing: couldn't we hear, from where we were, the regular sounds that their rackets made, sending the ball back and forth?), we would automatically come upon the tennis court. It was Signora Regina Herrera, Signora Olga's mother. I had recognized her at once from the special, intense whiteness of her thick hair, gathered in a bun on her neck, hair that I had always admired whenever at temple, as a child, I had happened to glimpse it through the grille of the women's section. She waved her arms and hands with willful energy, signaling at the same time to the girl, Dirce as it happened, to help her up: she was tired of staying there, she wanted to go back inside. And the maid carried out the instructions with immediate haste.

One evening, however, contrary to all expectation, it was Professor Ermanno and Signora Olga who showed up. They seemed to have come upon the court by chance, returning from a long stroll in the park. They were arm in arm. Shorter than his wife, and more bent, much more than he had been ten years earlier, at the time of our whispered dialogues in the Italian synagogue, from one bench to the other, he was wearing one of his usual light linen suits, with a black-ribboned Panama, its brim pulled down to the thick lenses of his pince-nez, and leaning, as he walked, on a bamboo cane. She, the signora, all in black, was carrying a big bunch of chrysanthemums in her arms, obviously picked in some remote part of the garden, in the course of their walk. She held them tight to her bosom, obliquely, cradling her right arm around them in a tenderly possessive gesture, almost maternal. Though still erect, a full head taller than her husband, she also seemed greatly aged. Her hair had turned completely gray: an ugly, gloomy gray. Beneath her bony, protruding forehead, her eyes, very black, gleamed with the fanatic and suffering ardor they had always had.

Those of us sitting around the umbrella stood up; the players stopped their game.

"No, no," the Professor said, in his polite, musical voice. "Please, don't let us disturb you. Do go on playing."

He was not obeyed. Micòl and Alberto took care at once to introduce us:

Micòl especially. Besides saying first and last names, she went on to illustrate whatever there was about each of us that she presumed might arouse her father's interest: studies and occupations, first of all. She began with me and with Bruno Lattes, speaking of us both in a detached tone, markedly objective: as if to restrain her father, on that particular occasion, from any possible sign of special recognition or preference. We were "the two literary men of the band," two "very smart" characters. Then she went on to Malnate, joking on his "rare" passion for chemistry, which had impelled him to leave a metropolis as full of resources as Milan ("_Milàn l'è on gran Milàn!_"), to come and bury himself in a "backwater" like Ferrara.

"He works in the Industrial Zone," Alberto explained, simply and seriously. "In a Montecatini plant."

"They ought to be producing synthetic rubber," Micòl resumed, "but they don't seem to have succeeded so far."

Afraid perhaps that his daughter's ironies might have wounded the doctor of chemistry from out of town, the Professor quickly spoke up.

"You were at the university with Alberto, weren't you?" he asked, addressing Malnate.

"Well, yes, in a way," the latter confirmed. "To tell the truth, I was three years ahead of him, and in a different department. But we were excellent company for each other, all the same."

"I know, I know. My son has often spoken to us about you. He also told us he has been many times to your home, and that your parents, on numerous occasions, were very kind and thoughtful. Will you thank them for us, when you see them again? We are very happy to have you here now, at our house. And do come back, you understand . . . come whenever you like."

He turned to Micòl, and asked her, indicating Adriana:

"And this young lady? Who is she? If I'm not mistaken, she's a Zanardi? Or am I wrong?"

The conversation went on like this, until the introductions had been completely exhausted, including those of Carletto Sani and Tonino Collevatti, defined by Micòl as the two "white hopes" of Ferrarese tennis. In the end Professor Ermanno and Signora Olga, who had remained at her husband's side the whole time without saying anything, merely smiling kindly every now and then, went off, still arm in arm, towards the house.

Though the Professor had taken his leave with a cordial "I hope to see you again," nobody would have thought of taking that promise into great account.

Yet, on the contrary, the following Sunday, while, on the court, Adriana Trentini and Bruno Lattes on one side, and Désirée Baggioli and Claudio Montemezzo on the other, were battling with great commitment in a game whose result, according to the declared intentions of Adriana, who had promoted and organized it, was to compensate her and Bruno, "at least morally," for the nasty trick played on them by Marchese Barbacinti (but the matter, this time, didn't seem to be taking the same turn: Adriana and Bruno were losing, and fairly definitely): suddenly, towards the end of the match, there appeared from the path under the climbing roses, the entire "*côté* old folks," one after the other. They actually made up a little procession. At the head, Professor Ermanno and the signora. At a distance, there followed the Herrera uncles from Venice: one, a cigarette between his thick, protruding lips, his hands clasped behind his back, looking around in the somewhat embarrassed manner of the city man who has reluctantly ventured into the country; the other, a few yards farther back, with Signora Regina on his arm, adapting his pace to the very slow pace of his mother. If the phthisiologist and the engineer were in Ferrara—I said to myself—they must be here because of some religious solemnity. But which? After Rosh Hashana, which had fallen in October, I couldn't remember what other holiday there was, in autumn. Succoth, perhaps? Probably. Unless it had been the equally probable dismissal of the engineer, Federico, from the state railways to prompt the calling of a special meeting . . .

They sat down, composed, hardly making any sound at all. With one exception: Signora Regina. At the moment when she was settled into a chaise longue, she uttered, in a loud, deaf person's voice, two or three words in the patois of the house. She complained, I believe, about the "*mucha* dampness" of the garden. But beside her, her son Federico was always alert, and he, in a voice no less loud (but toneless, his voice: a voice that my father also produced now and then, in *mixed* surroundings, when he wanted to communicate with some member of the family, and with that one alone), was prompt to silence her. He told her to remain "*callàda,*" quiet, that is. Couldn't she see that there was the "*musafìr*"?

I bent to Micòl's ear.

"Instead of "sta' *callàda*," we say "*shadòk*" at home. But what does "*musafir*" mean?"

"Guest," she whispered back to me. "But *goy*."

And she laughed, childishly covering her mouth with one hand, and winking: Micòl 1929-style.

Later, at the end of the game, and after the "new additions," Désirée Baggioli and Claudio Montemezzo had been, in turn, introduced, I happened to find myself to one side with Professor Ermanno. In the park, the day was as usual dying in a diffuse, milk-colored shadow. I had gone off about ten paces. I could hear behind me Micòl's voice shrilly dominating all the others. I wondered with whom she was annoyed now, and why.

I was looking towards the Mura degli Angeli, still lighted by the sun.

"*Era già l'ora che volge il disìo . . .*" an ironic voice recited softly, beside me.

I turned, amazed. It was Professor Ermanno, in fact, who smiled at me good-humoredly, pleased at having given me a start. He took me gently by the arm, then, very slowly, stopping from time to time, we made together a wide turn around the tennis clearing. We had kept ourselves at a distance from the metal fence, well away from it. In the end, still, to avoid the risk of ending up anyway amidst relatives and friends, we turned back. Back, and forth: we repeated the distance several times, in the growing darkness. Meanwhile we spoke: or rather, he spoke almost always, the Professor.

He began by asking me what I thought of the tennis court, if it was really so outrageous. Micòl, for her part, was determined: she insisted the whole thing had to be done over, according to modern criteria. But he had doubts: perhaps, as usual, his "beloved earthquake" was exaggerating, perhaps it wouldn't be necessary to tear up the whole thing, as she demanded.

"In any case," he added, "in a few days it will start raining. No use deceiving ourselves. Best to postpone any sort of undertaking till next year, don't you agree?"

He then went on to ask me what I was doing, what I planned to do in the immediate future. And how my parents were.

While he was asking me about "Papà," I noted two things: first of all, that it cost him an effort to call me *tu*, and in fact, a little later, stopping abruptly, he declared as much to me explicitly, but I immediately begged him with great and sincere warmth, please, to do me a favor and not call me *lei*, otherwise I would be offended; second, that the interest and respect in his voice and his face as he inquired about my father's health (in the eyes, especially: the lens of his glasses, enlarging them, accentuated the gravity and mildness of their expression) were not at all forced, not at all hypocritical. He urged me to take his greetings to him. And his congratulations, too: for the many trees that had been planted in our cemetery since, chosen by the community, Papà had taken charge of it. Indeed: did he want any pines? Cedars of Lebanon? Firs? Weeping willows? I was to ask Papà. If by any chance they were of use (these days, with the means at the disposal of modern agriculture, transplanting big trees had become child's play), he would be happy to put at his disposal the number wanted. A stupendous idea, I had to admit: dense with big, tall trees, in time, our cemetery too would be in a position to rival that of San Niccolò del Lido, in Venice.

"Don't you know it?"

I answered no.

"Ah, but you must, you *must* try to visit it as soon as you can!" he said, with lively animation. "It's a national monument! For that matter, you who are literary, must surely remember the opening of Giovanni Prati's *Edmenegarda.*"

I was forced to declare my ignorance once again.

"Well," Professor Ermanno resumed, "Prati sets the beginning of his *Edmenegarda* just there, in the Jewish cemetery on the Lido, considered in the nineteenth century one of the most romantic places in Italy. But mind you: if and when you go, don't forget to tell the caretaker of the cemetery at once—he is the man who keeps the key to the gate—that you want to visit the old one, remember, the old cemetery, where nobody has been buried since the eighteenth century, and not the other, the modern one, adjacent to it, but separate. I discovered it in 1905. Imagine. Even though I was almost twice the age you are now, I was still a bachelor. I was living in Venice (I lived there for two whole years), and any time I didn't spend in the State Archive, in Campo dei Frari, digging among the manuscripts concerning the various so-called nations into which the Venetian community was divided in the sixteenth and seventeenth centuries—the Levantine nation, the Ponentine, the German, the Italian—I spent out there: sometimes even in winter. It's true I hardly ever went there alone"—here he smiled—"and that, in a way, deciphering one by one the gravestones of the cemetery, many dating back to the early sixteenth century, written in Spanish and Portuguese, I was continuing, in the open air, my work in the archive. Ah, delightful afternoons, those were . . . Such peace, such serenity . . . with the gate, facing the lagoon, opened only for us. We became engaged there, Olga and I.''

He remained silent a moment. I seized the opportunity to ask him what was the precise object of his research in the archive.

"At first I started out with the idea of writing a history of the Jews of Venice,'' he answered: "a subject suggested to me, in fact, by Olga, which Roth, the Englishman Cecil Roth (Jewish), dealt with about ten years later, so brilliantly. Then, as often happens with historians who are too . . . too impassioned, certain seventeenth-century documents, which I happened to come across, completely absorbed my interest, and finally led me astray. I'll tell you, I'll tell you about it, if you come back. . . . A real novel, from every point of view . . . In any event, instead of a thick historical tome, at the end of two years, I hadn't succeeded in achieving— apart from a wife, of course—anything except two slim essays: one, which I consider still useful, in which I collected all the inscriptions of the cemetery, and one in which I discussed those seventeenth-century papers I mentioned to you, but merely expounding the facts and without venturing any interpretation on the subject. Would it interest you to see them? It would. One of these days I'll take the liberty of presenting you with copies. But apart from that: do go, I insist, to the Jewish cemetery on the Lido! It's worth it, you'll see. You'll find it just as it was thirty-five years ago: identical!''

We went slowly back towards the tennis court. At first sight it seemed no one was left there. And yet, in the almost complete darkness, Micòl and Carletto Sani were still playing. Micòl was complaining: that the boy was making her run too much, that he was not being "a gentleman," that the darkness, too, was "frankly excessive.''

"Micòl tells me you still haven't decided whether to take your degree in art history or Italian,'' Professor Ermanno was saying to me meanwhile. "Or have you already made up your mind?''

I answered that I had made up my mind, deciding finally on a thesis in Italian. My hesitation—I explained—had stemmed mostly from the fact that, until a few days before, I had hoped to be able to take my degree under Professor Longhi, in art history, and instead, at the last moment,

Professor Longhi had asked for a leave from teaching for two years. The thesis I had planned to work on under his guidance concerned a group of Ferrarese painters of the second half of the sixteenth century and early seventeenth: Scarsellino, Bastianino, Bastarolo, Bonone, Caletti, Calzolaretto. Working on such a subject, I might have produced something worthwhile, only with Longhi guiding me. But now, as Longhi had been granted the two years' leave by the ministry, I had preferred to fall back on an ordinary thesis, in Italian.

He listened to me, thoughtfully.

"Longhi?" he asked finally, twisting his lip, dubiously. "What? Have they *already* named the new full professor of art history?"

I didn't understand.

"Yes," he insisted. "The professor of art history, in Bologna, I always heard, is Igino Benvenuto Supino, one of the leading figures of Italian Jewry. So . . ."

He had been—I interrupted—he had been: until 1933. Afterwards, in Supino's place, when he had been retired, having reached the maximum age, Roberto Longhi had been called. Didn't he know—I went on, pleased also, to catch him out, uninformed—didn't he know the fundamental essay by Roberto Longhi on Piero della Francesca? And his others, on Caravaggio and his school? And his *Officina ferrarese,* a work that had aroused so much discussion, in '33, at the time of the Ferrarese Renaissance Exhibition held in Ferrara that same year, at the Palazzo dei Diamanti? To write my thesis, I would have based my work on the last pages of the *Officina,* where the book's theme confined itself merely to touching on the subject: masterfully, but without exploring it deeply.

I spoke, and Professor Ermanno, more bent than ever, stood listening to me in silence. What was he thinking about? About the number of academic "figures" which Italian Jewry had boasted from the unification down to our own time? It was probable.

But suddenly I saw him become animated.

Looking around and dropping his voice to a muffled whisper, just as if he were confiding in me a state secret, he told me the big news: that he owned a group of unpublished letters of Carducci, letters written by the poet to his mother, in '75. Would I be interested in seeing them?—he asked. If, by chance, I were to consider them a suitable subject for a thesis in Italian, he was quite ready to place them at my disposal.

Thinking of Meldolesi, I couldn't help smiling. And the essay to be sent to the *Nuova Antologia*? After so much talk about it, had he then never produced anything? Poor Meldolesi. Some years back he had been transferred to the Minghetti in Bologna: to his great satisfaction, naturally! One of these days I really should go and call on him. . . .

Despite the darkness, Professor Ermanno noticed, all the same, that I was smiling.

"Ah, I know, I know," he said, "You young people, for some time now, take him lightly, Giosuè Carducci! I know you prefer a Pascoli or a D'Annunzio to him."

It was easy for me to persuade him that I had smiled for quite another reason, and that is to say, regret. If I had only known, that there existed in Ferrara some unpublished Carducci letters. Instead of proposing to Professor Calcaterra, as unfortunately I already had, a thesis on Panzacchi, I could easily have proposed to him a "Carducci Ferrarese," beyond doubt of greater interest. But who knows? Perhaps, if I spoke of the matter frankly with Professor Calcaterra, who was an excellent man, perhaps I could still manage to shift from Panzacchi to Carducci without too much loss of dignity.

"When do you expect to take your degree?" Professor Ermanno asked me finally.

"Ah, I should hope next year, in June. Don't forget that I am *also* an outside student."

He nodded several times, silently.

"Outside student?" he sighed, at last. "Well, it's not serious."

And he made a vague gesture with his hand, as if to say that, with what was happening, we had time ahead of us, both I and his children: all too much time.

But my father was right: at heart he didn't seem too grieved by this. Quite the contrary.

# V

Micòl wanted to show me the garden herself. She insisted on that. "I have a certain right, I'd say!" She grinned, looking at me.

Not the first day. I played tennis late, and it was Alberto who, when he had stopped playing with his sister, accompanied me to a kind of Alpine refuge, about a hundred yards from the court (the *Hütte*, he and Micòl called it), in which refuge, or *Hütte*, outfitted as a dressing room, I could change, and then, at dusk, have a hot shower and dress again.

The next day, however, things were different. A doubles game, with Adriana Trentini and Bruno Lattes opposite the two fifteen-year-olds (with Malnate, sitting at the top of the referee's chair, playing the role of patient scorekeeper), soon took on the character of those games that never end.

"What shall we do?" Micòl said to me at a certain point, springing to her feet. "Before we can take over from this quartet, I have the impression that you, I, Alberto, and our Milanese friend will have a good hour to wait. Listen: why don't we go off, the two of us, on a preliminary reconnaissance of the garden?" As soon as the court was free—she added—Alberto would surely think to call us. He would stick three fingers in his mouth, and produce one of his famous whistles.

She turned towards Alberto, dozing nearby in the sun on a third deck chair, his face hidden under a reaper's straw hat.

"Won't you, Monsieur le Pashà?"

Without changing position, Alberto nodded.

We set off. Yes, her brother was amazing—Micòl continued explaining. When required, he could emit certain blasts so powerful that the whistling of shepherds, in comparison, was ridiculous. Funny, wasn't it? From a character like that. To look at him, you wouldn't bet two cents on him. And instead . . . God only knew where he got all that breath!

And so, almost always to pass the time between one game and another, our long excursions began, the two of us. The first few times we took our bicycles. The bicycle was indispensable—my guide decided at once—the garden was large, "a" twenty acres, and the paths, broad and narrow, amounted in all to about four miles. But aside from that: without bicycles, how, for example, would we ever reach the bottom there, towards the west, where she and Alberto, as children, had often gone to watch the trains being shunted in the station? If we were to go that far on foot, we risked being caught there by Alberto's "oliphant," unable to get back then with the necessary promptness.

So that first day we went to see the trains being shunted in the station yards. And afterwards? Afterwards we came back. We skirted the tennis court, crossed the open area in front of the *magna domus* (the space, deserted as always, sadder than ever), repeating in the opposite direction, beyond the black wooden bridge over the Panfilio Canal, the entrance drive: and this as far as the tunnel of flowering canna and the entrance at Corso Ercole I. On arriving there, Micòl insisted we turn left, along a winding path that followed the entire perimeter of the outer walls: first towards the Mura degli Angeli, so that in a quarter-hour we had again reached the side of the park from which the station was seen; and then in the opposite direction, much more wooded, rather grim and melancholy, flanking the entire length of the deserted Via Arianuova. We were there, in fact, making our way through the clumps of ferns, nettles, and brambles, when, suddenly, from beyond the thick barrier of trunks, Alberto's shepherd's whistle arose, very distant, to summon us swiftly back to "hard labor."

With only a few variations of the route, these wide-ranging explorations were repeated other times, three or four, on the afternoons that followed.

When the width of the alleys and the paths allowed it, we rode abreast. Often I steered with one hand, the other resting on the handlebar of her bicycle. Meanwhile we talked: about trees, especially, at least in the beginning.

I knew nothing, or almost, on the subject, and this fact never ceased to amaze Micòl. She looked at me as if I were a monster.

"How can you possibly be so ignorant?" she would exclaim. "You must surely have studied a bit of botany at the *liceo!*"

"Listen," she would then ask, already prepared to raise her eyebrows at some new absurdity. "May I inquire, if you please, what kind of tree you think that one is, the one over there?"

She could be referring to anything: to honest elms and lindens from our region, or to the most rare exotic plants, African, Asiatic, American, which only a specialist would have been able to identify: because there was everything, in the Barchetto del Duca, really everything. In any case, I always answered at random: partly because I really couldn't tell an elm from a linden, and partly, too, because I realized she enjoyed nothing more than hearing me blunder.

It seemed absurd, to her, that there could exist in the world someone like me, who did not feel for trees, "for the great, calm, strong, pensive" trees, her own sentiments of impassioned admiration. How could I fail to *understand?* How could I go on living, without *feeling?* At the edge of the tennis clearing, for example, to the west of the court, there was a group of seven very tall, slender *Washingtoniae graciles,* or desert palms, isolated from the surrounding vegetation (dark, thick trees, that might have come from a European forest: oaks, ilexes, planes, horse chestnuts) with a fine stretch of lawn around them. Well, every time we went near them, on our bicycles, Micòl had always new words of tenderness for the solitary group of *Washingtoniae.*

"There they are, my seven old men," she might say. "Look at their venerable beards!"

Really—she would insist—didn't they seem, also to me, seven hermits of the Thebaid, seared by the sun and fasting? What elegance, what "holiness" in those trunks of theirs, dark, dry, curved, scaly! They looked like so many John the Baptists, honestly, nourished only by locusts.

Her affection was not, however, limited to exotic trees: to the palms of various species, to the *Howaeniae dulces,* which produced deformed little tubers filled with a honey-flavored pulp, to the agaves formed like candelabra, like the *"menoràh,"* which—she explained to me—flower only once every twenty, twenty-five years, and then die, or to the eucalyptuses, the *Zelkoviae sinicae,* with their little green trunks dotted with gold (towards the eucalyptuses, in fact, though she never told me why, she felt a kind of strange mistrust: as if between her and *"them,"* in distant years, something unpleasant had occurred, not to be dwelt on).

For one enormous plane tree, in fact, with a whitish gnarled trunk, thicker than that of any other in the garden and, I believe, of the entire province, her admiration bordered on reverence. Naturally it had not been "Grandmother Josette" who had planted it, but Ercole I d'Este in person, perhaps, or Lucrezia Borgia.

"You understand? It's almost five hundred years old!" she would murmur, her eyes wide. "Imagine what it must have seen, how many things, since it came into the world."

And it seemed as if it, too, had eyes and ears, the great beast, the gigantic plane: eyes to see us and ears to hear us.

For the fruit trees, which had a broad strip of ground to themselves just against the Mura degli Angeli and, hence, not only exposed to the sun but well sheltered from the north winds, Micòl felt an affection very similar—I noticed—to that she showed towards Perotti and all the members of his family. She spoke of them, of those humble domestic trees, with the same good humor, the same patience; and, very often, in dialect: the dialect that, in her relations with people, she used only when dealing with Perotti, in fact, or with Titta and Bepi, if we happened to run into them and stopped to exchange a few words. Every time, ritually, we had to stop before a great plum tree, whose trunk was as massive as an oak's: her favorite. *Il brógn sèrbi,* the green plums, that this tree produced—she told me—used to seem extraordinary to her, as a child. In those days she preferred them to the best Lindt chocolate. Then, when she was about sixteen, she had suddenly lost all taste for them; she didn't like them any more, and now, to *brógn* she preferred chocolates, Lindt and non-Lindt (the bitter kind, though, only the bitter kind!) . And so apples were *i pum,* figs *i figh,* apricots *il mugnàgh,* peaches *il pèrsagh.* There could only be dialect for speaking of these things. Only the dialect word allowed her, naming trees and fruits, to curl her lips in the grimace, half-tender, half-scornful, that her heart prompted.

Later, when our reconnaissance missions had ended, our "pious pilgrimages" began. And since all pilgrimages, according to Micòl, had to be made on foot (otherwise, what sort of pilgrimages would they be?), we gave up our bicycles. We went on foot, then, almost always accompanied by Jor every step of the way.

To begin with, I was taken to see a little solitary dock on the Panfilio Canal, hidden amidst thick vegetation of willows, white poplars, and callas. From that minuscule harbor, all bounded by a mossy bench of red tile, it was probable that, in the old days, they could sail off to reach either the Po or the moat of the Castle. And she and Alberto—Micòl told me—used to set off, too, when they were little, on long trips in a double-paddled canoe. They had never reached the foot of the towers of the Castle, right in the heart of the city, with their little craft (as I well knew, the Panfilio nowadays communicated with the Castle moat through an underground channel). But as far as the Po, yes, right opposite Isola Bianca, they had gone there, and how! Did I like this place? she asked me finally. At present there could be no thought of using the canoe: half stove in, covered with dust, reduced to a kind of "ghost canoe"; one of these days I would be able to see its carcass in the coach house, if she remembered to take me there. She had continued to visit the dock's bench regularly, in any case, always, always. It remained her secret refuge. An ideal place, for that matter, to come and study for exams in peace, when the hot weather began.

Another time we ended up at the Perottis', an authentic farmhouse with barn and hayloft, halfway between the main house and the orchard area.

We were received by old Perotti's wife, Vittorina, a wan *arzdóra* of indefinable age, sad, thin, emaciated, and by Italia, the wife of the older son, Titta, a woman of thirty from Codigoro, fat and sturdy, with watery blue eyes and red hair. Sitting at the door of the house on a straw chair, surrounded by a crowd of hens, she was nursing a baby, and Micòl bent over to pat it.

"Now, when are you going to invite me back to eat bean soup again?" she was asking Vittorina meanwhile, in dialect.

"Whenever you like, *sgnurina*. If you're content with that . . ."

"One of these days we really must. You know," she added, addressing me, "Vittorina makes a positively *monstre* bean soup. With crackling, of course . . ."

She laughed, and then said:

"Would you like to have a look at the barn? We have *all of* six cows."

Preceded by Vittorina, we headed for the cow barn. The *arzdóra* opened its door with a heavy key, which she kept in the pocket of her black apron, then she stepped aside to allow us to enter. As we crossed the threshold of the barn, I noticed a furtive look of hers, taking us in: full of concern, it seemed to me, but also of secret satisfaction.

A third pilgrimage was devoted to the sacred place, to the "*vert paradis des amours enfantins.*"

We had gone by there several times, in the previous days; but on our bicycles, without stopping. There, there was the exact spot on the outer wall—Micòl was saying to me now, pointing a finger—where she had always set the ladder; and there were the "notches" ("yes, sir, notches!") which she used when, and it happened, the ladder was not available.

"Don't you think it wold be only fitting to place a commemorative plaque here?" she asked me.

"I suppose you already have the inscription in mind."

"More or less. 'Over this wall—eluding the vigilance of two huge brutes of dogs . . .'"

"Stop. You were talking about a plaque. But at this rate I'm afraid you'll need a marble slab like the ones with the Victory Bulletin. The second line is too long."

A quarrel started. I played the role of the stubborn heckler, and she, for her part, raising her voice and with a babyish whine, accused me of my "usual prissiness." It was obvious—she shouted—I *must* have sensed her intention of not even mentioning me in her inscription, and so, out of sheer jealousy, I was refusing to listen to her.

Then we became calm. She began talking once again about when she and Alberto were children. If I really wanted to know the truth, both she and Alberto had always felt a huge envy of those who, like me, were lucky enough to study in a public school. Would I believe it? They even reached the point of eagerly awaiting the exam period every year, only for the pleasure of going to school too.

"But if you liked going to school so much, why did you study at home?" I asked.

"Papà and Mamma, especially Mamma, absolutely insisted. Mamma has always had an obsession about germs. She used to say that schools existed for the specific purpose of spreading the most horrible diseases; and it was never any good for Uncle Giulio, every time he came here, to try to make her understand it's not true. Uncle Giulio used to tease her; but even though he's a doctor, he doesn't much believe in medicine. Actually, he believes in in the inevitability and the usefulness of diseases. Imagine him convincing Mamma; since the tragedy of Guido, our little older brother who died, in '14, before Alberto and I were born, she hasn't stuck her nose out of the house, you might say! Later we rebelled a bit, naturally: we both managed to go to the university, and even to Austria skiing, one winter, as I believe I've already told you. But when we were little, what could we do? I used to run away a lot (not Alberto; he's always been much quieter than me, much more obedient). But then, one day I stayed out a bit too long, on the city walls, riding on the handlebars of the bikes of a bunch of kids I had made friends with, and when I came home, I saw they were so desperate,

Mamma and Papà, that afterwards (because Micòl is goodhearted, a real dear!), afterwards I decided to behave, and I didn't run off any more. My only lapse was in June of '29, in your honor, sir!''

"And I, who thought I was the only one!" I sighed.

"Well, if not the only one, surely the last. And besides: I never invited anybody else to come into the garden!"

"Can that be true?"

"Absolutely true. I always used to look in your direction, at temple . . . When you turned around, to speak with Papà and Alberto, your eyes were so blue! Celestial! Secretly I had even given you a nickname.''

"A nickname? What?"

"Blue Eyes, Celestino."

"Who from cowardice made The Great Refusal . . .'' I mumbled.

"Exactly!" she cried, laughing. "In any case, I really believe that for a certain time I had a little crush on you!"

"And then?"

"Then life came between us."

"What an idea, though, to rig up a temple all for yourselves. What was it? Fear of germs again?''

She waved a hand.

"Well . . . almost . . .'' she said.

"What do you mean, almost?''

But there was no persuading her to confess the truth. I knew well the reason why Professor Ermanno, in '33, had asked to restore the Spanish synagogue for himself and his family: it had been the shameful *infornata del Decennale*, the Fascist tenth-anniversary party membership drive, shameful and grotesque, that had prompted his decision. She, however, insisted that, once again, Mamma's wish had been decisive. The Herreras, in Venice, belonged to the Spanish school. Mamma, Grandmother Regina, and the uncles, Giulio and Federico, had always been greatly attached to the family traditions. And so Papà, to make Mamma happy . .

"But now, tell me, why have you come back to the Italian synagogue?" I rebutted. "I wasn't there, at temple, on the night of Rosh Hashana. I haven't set foot in temple for at least three years. But my father was there, he told me the whole scene in detail.''

"Oh, never fear, your absence was greatly noticed, Mr. Freethinker!" she answered. "Also by me."

She became serious again, then said:

"You know how it is. . . . Now we're all in the same boat. With the situation we're in, I also feel it would be rather ridiculous to go on making so many distinctions."

Another day, the last, it started to rain, and while the others sought shelter in the *Hütte,* to play rummy and Ping-Pong, the two of us, not caring about getting soaked, ran halfway across the park to take refuge in the coach house. The coach house now was used only as storeroom—Micòl had told me—once, however, a good half of the inside space had been equipped as a gymnasium, with bars, ropes, seesaws, rings, ladder, et cetera; and all this only so that she and Alberto could present themselves well prepared for the annual physical education exam, too. The lessons they received from Professor Anacleto Zaccarini were surely not very serious; he was over eighty, and had long been pensioned off, when he came to them once a week. But they were amusing: perhaps the most amusing of all. She, Micòl, never forgot to bring a bottle of Bosco wine to the gym. And old Zaccarini, his normally red nose and cheeks gradually turning purple, drank it very slowly, till the last drop had been drained. On certain winter evenings, when he went off, he seemed to glow with a light of his own.

It was a dark brick building, low and long, with two side windows protected by strong grilles, a sloping tile roof, and the outer walls almost entirely hidden by ivy. Not far from Perotti's hayloft, and from the glassy parallelepiped of a greenhouse, it was entered through a wide main door, painted green, facing away from the Mura degli Angeli, towards the big house.

We stayed a moment on the threshold, huddled against the door. The rain was pouring down in long, oblique stripes of water, on the lawns, on the great dark masses of the trees, on everything. It was cold. Our teeth chattering, we both looked straight ahead. The spell in which, till then, the season had been suspended was now irreparably broken.

"Shall we go inside?" I suggested finally. "It'll be warmer in there."

Inside the vast room, at the end of which, in the semidarkness, there glowed the tops of two shiny blond gym poles, reaching the ceiling. A strange smell hovered: a mixture of gasoline, lubricating oil, old dust, citrus fruits. The smell was really good—Micòl said at once, noticing how I sniffed, my curiosity aroused—she also liked it very much. And she pointed to some tall shelves of dark wood, against one of the side walls, crammed with heavy fruits, yellow and round, bigger than oranges and lemons, which I had never seen before. They were grapefruit, placed there to ripen—she explained to me—produced in the greenhouse. Hadn't I ever eaten one? she asked then, taking one and holding it out for me to smell. Too bad she didn't have a knife with her, to cut it into two "hemispheres." The taste of the juice was hybrid: it resembled an orange's and a lemon's. With, in addition, a hint of a bitterness all its own.

The center of the coach house was occupied by two vehicles, side by side: a long gray Dilambda, and a blue carriage, whose shafts, raised, were only a bit lower than the gym poles behind them.

"We don't use the carriage any more," Micòl was saying meanwhile. "The few times Papà has to go out in the country, he has himself driven in the car. And Alberto and I do the same when we have to leave: he for Milan, I for Venice. The eternal Perotti takes us to the station. In our house the only ones who know how to drive are he (he drives dreadfully) and Alberto. Not I, I've never got my license. But I will, I really must make put my mind to it next spring, provided . . . The trouble is, it consumes so much gas, this great car!"

She approached the carriage, its appearance no less shiny and efficient than the automobile's.

"You recognize it?" she asked.

She opened a door, climbed in, sat down; finally, patting the cloth of the seat beside her, she invited me to do the same.

I got in and sat down, too, at her left. And I had barely taken my place when, turning slowly on its hinges through the force of inertia, the door closed on its own, with the sharp, precise click of a trap.

Now the pelting of the rain on the coach house roof had ceased to be audible. It was really like being in a little salon: a stifling little room.

"How well you keep it," I said, unable to master a sudden emotion, reflected in a slight quaver in my voice. "It seems new still. Only the flowers in the vase are missing."

"Oh, as for the flowers, Perotti puts them in too, when he goes out with Grandmother."

"So you do still use it!"

"No more than two or three times a year, and only for a few turns around the garden."

"And the horse? Is it still the same one?"

"Still old Star. He's twenty-two. Didn't you see him the other day, at the back of the barn? He's half-blind now, but when he's hitched up here, he still cuts . . . a dreadful figure."

She burst out laughing, shaking her head.

"Perotti has a downright mania about this carriage," she went on, bitterly, "and it's chiefly to please him (he hates and despises automobiles: you can't believe how deeply!) that we give him Grandmother every now and then to take out for a spin up and down the drive. Every ten or fifteen days, he comes in here with buckets of water, sponges, chamois, carpet-beaters: and that explains the miracle, that's why the carriage, best seen in the half-light, still manages to fool people fairly well."

"Fairly well?" I protested. "Why, it looks brand-new!"

She gave a bored huff.

"Don't talk nonsense, if you please!"

On an unpredictable impulse, she had moved aside brusquely, huddling in her corner. Now she was looking straight ahead, frowning, her features sharpened by an expression of curious resentment. She suddenly seemed to have aged ten years.

We remained like that for a few moments, in silence. Then, without changing position, her arms hugging her tanned knees, as if she felt a great cold (she was wearing shorts and a cotton polo shirt, with a sweater tied around her neck by its sleeves), Micòl went on speaking:

"It's useless for Perotti," she said, "to spend so much time and elbow grease on this pathetic relic! No, you listen to me: here, in this gloom, you might even say it's a miracle, but outside, in daylight, it's hopeless, a thousand little defects are immediately obvious; the paint has flaked off here and there, the axles and spokes of the wheels are all wormy, the cloth on this seat (now you can't tell, but I assure you it's so), is a downright cobweb in places. So I ask myself, what's the use of all Perotti's *struma?* Is it worth it? He, poor thing, would like to wring permission from Papà to re-paint it all, restoring it and fixing it up to suit himself; but Papà, as usual, is hesitating, and can't make up his mind. . . ."

She was silent. She shifted slightly.

"But look at the canoe, on the contrary," she went on—and, meanwhile, through the pane of the door that our breath was beginning to cloud, she pointed to a gray form, oblong and skeletal, propped against the wall opposite the one occupied by the shelves of grapefruit—"Look instead at the canoe, I beg you, and observe its honesty, dignity, and moral courage; it's drawn all the necessary conclusions from its own total loss of function. Objects also die, my friend. And if they also must die, then that's it, better to let them go. It shows far more style, above all. Don't you agree?"

# Part Three

Countless times, in the course of the following winter, spring, and summer, I went back to what had happened (or rather, had not happened) between me and Micòl inside old Perotti's beloved carriage. If on that rainy afternoon, when the radiant Indian summer of '38 suddenly ended, I had at least managed to speak to her—I told myself bitterly—perhaps things between us would have gone differently from the way they went. Speak to her, kiss her: it was then, when everything was still possible—I never ceased repeating to myself—that I should have done it! And I forgot to ask myself the essential question: whether in that supreme moment, unique, irrevocable—a moment, perhaps, that decided my life and hers—I had really been capable of attempting an act, a word of any sort. Did I already know, then, for example, that I was in love, *really*? Well, no, not at all: I didn't know. I didn't know then, and I wasn't to know for at least another two weeks, when the bad weather, now steady, irreparably scattered our fortuitous company.

I remember: the insistent rain, not letting up for days and days—and after, it would be winter, the severe, grim winter of the Po Valley—immediately made further visits to the garden impossible. And yet, despite the change of season, everything went on in such a way that I could have the delusion that nothing, basically, had changed.

At two thirty on the afternoon following our last visit to the Finzi-Continis'—the hour, more or less, when we could be seen appearing, one after the other, from the tunnel of climbing roses, shouting "Hi!" or "Hello there!" or "Salutations!"—the telephone bell in my house rang, and put me in contact, all the same, with the voice of Micòl. That evening I was the one, in my turn, who telephoned her; then she called again the next afternoon. We could continue talking as we had the last few days, grateful, in other words, now as then, that Bruno Lattes, Adriana Trentini, Giampiero Malnate, and all the others would leave us alone, apparently forgetting all about us. And for that matter, when had we ever given them a thought, Micòl and I, during our long excursions through the park: so long that sometimes, on our return, we no longer found a living soul, either on the court or in the *Hütte?*

Followed as usual by my parents' concerned eyes, I shut myself up in the telephone closet. I dialed the number; and often she answered the phone herself; and with such promptness, moreover, that I suspected she kept the receiver always within reach.

"Where are you talking to me from?" I tried asking her.

She broke out laughing.

"Why . . . from home, I should think."

"Thanks for the information. I only wanted to know how you always manage to answer first crack: so promptly, I mean. What is it? Do you have the phone on your desk, like a businessman? Or do you stalk around the phone from morning to night with the pace of the caged tiger in Machaty's *Nocturne?"*

From the other end of the line I seemed to sense a hesitation. She reached the phone ahead of the others—she then replied—thanks to the "legendary" efficiency of her muscular reflexes: that was all; and the intuition she possessed, naturally, her intuition which, whenever I had the idea of calling her, enabled her always to be in the vicinity of the telephone. She then changed the subject. How was my thesis on Panzacchi going? And, if only for a breath of fresh air, when was I planning to resume my usual to-ing and fro-ing with Bologna?

But at times it was the others: Alberto, or Professor Ermanno, or one of the two maids; and once, even Signora Regina, who over the telephone displayed a surprising sensitivity of hearing. In these cases I could not avoid stating my name, obviously, and saying that it was with "Signorina" Micòl that I wished to speak. Still, after a few days (at first this embarrassed me even more, but then gradually I became used to it), after a few days I had only to drop my "Hello?" into the receiver, and at the other end they immediately passed me the person I wanted. Even Alberto, when he was the one who answered, behaved in the same way. And Micòl was always there, to snatch the receiver from the hand of whoever was holding it: as if they were all collected in a single room, living room, salon, or library as it might be, each sunk in a great leather chair, with the telephone a few feet away. Seriously, you could imagine something of the sort. To alert Micòl, who, at the ring of the phone (I could almost see her) would raise her eyes abruptly, they simply pointed at the receiver from a distance, Alberto perhaps adding, for his part, a half-sardonic, half-affectionate wink.

One morning I decided to ask her for a confirmation of my suppositions; she heard me out in silence.

"Isn't that how it is?" I insisted.

But that was not how it was. Since I seemed so determined to know the truth—she said—here it was: each of them had, in his or her room, a personal extension (after she had gained one for herself, the rest of the family had finally done the same): a very useful system, highly recommended, thanks to which a person could telephone at any hour of the day or night without disturbing or being disturbed, and, at night especially, without having to move a step from bed. What an idea!—she then added, laughing—whatever had made me think that they were all together, always, as if in a hotel lobby? And for what reason, anyway? Strange, in any case, that I had never noticed the *click* of the switch, when she hadn't answered directly.

"No," she repeated, categorically. "To protect one's personal freedom, there is nothing better than a good telephone extension. I really mean it: you should have one too, in your bedroom. Imagine the hours I'd ramble on with you, especially at night!"

"So now you're calling me from your room."

"Of course. And lying in bed, what's more."

It was eleven.

"Not exactly an early riser, are you?" I remarked.

"Now don't you start too!" she complained. "It's all right for Papà, a good seventy, and with things in their present state, to get up every morning still at six thirty to set an example, as he says, and to dissuade us from wallowing in our beds of roses. *Transeat*. But if, now, even our best friends start acting pedagogical, that's really too much. You know when your friend here got up, my boy? At seven. And you dare express wonder, at eleven, on finding me back in bed again! Besides, I don't sleep. Not at all: I read, I scribble a few lines of my thesis, I look outside. I always do heaps of things, when I'm in bed. The warm blankets make me incredibly active."

"Describe your room to me."

She clicked her tongue against her teeth several times, in a sign of refusal.

"That, never. *Verboten. Privat.* I can describe, if you like, what I see when I look out of the window."

She could see through the window, in the foreground, the bearded crowns of her *Washingtoniae graciles,* which the rain and the wind were whipping "indecently"; and she wondered if the care of Titta and Bepi, who had already begun binding the trunks with the usual shirts of straw, as they did every winter, would be enough to preserve them during the coming months from the death by freezing that threatened every time the bad weather returned, and so far, luckily, had always been avoided. Then, farther on, hidden at times by wisps of passing fog, she could see the four towers of the Castle, which the downpours of rain had made as black as spent embers. And beyond the towers, so livid they made you shudder, and hidden also from time to time by the fog, the distant marble facade and the spire of the Duomo . . . Oh, the fog! When it was like this, and made her think of dirty rags, she didn't like it. But sooner or later the rain would end: and then the fog, in the morning, pierced by dim shafts of sunlight, would be transformed into something precious, delicately opalescent, with glints, in their shifting hues, just like those *làttimi* that her room was full of. Winter was a bore, yes, also because it prevented us from playing tennis. Still it had its compensations. "There is no situation, however sad or boring," she concluded, "that doesn't, basically, have some compensation, often substantial."

"*Làttimi?*" I asked. "What's that? Something to eat?"

"Oh, no, no," she whimpered, horrified as usual by my ignorance. "They're glass objects: goblets, chalices, ampoules, phials, boxes, trinkets: antique shops' refuse, as a rule. In Venice they call them *làttimi:* outside Venice, *opalines,* also *flûtes.* You can't imagine how I *adore* them, these things. On this subject, I know literally *all.* Question me and you'll see."

It had been in Venice—she went on—perhaps because of the influence of the local mists, which were so different from our grim Po Valley fogs, mists infinitely more luminous and hazy (only one painter, in the world, had been able to portray them: not so much late Monet, as "our own" De Pisis), it had been in Venice that she had begun to feel this passion for *làttimi*. She spent hours and hours combing antique shops. There were some, especially around San Samuele, around Campo Santo Stefano, or else in the ghetto, down towards the station, that sold practically nothing else. Her uncles, Giulio and Federico, lived on Calle del Cristo, near San Moisè. Towards evening, not knowing what else to do, and naturally, with the housekeeper, Signorina Blumenfeld, at her side (a distinguished *jodè* of sixty from Frankfurt-am-Main, in Italy for more than thirty years: a real pain!), she would go out into Calle XXII Marzo, on a *làttimi* hunt. Campo Santo Stefano is only a few steps away from San Moisè. But not San Geremia, where the ghetto is: if you pass San Bartolomeo and follow the Lista di Spagna, it takes at least a half hour's walk to get there, and yet it is very near, you only have to take the ferry across the Gran Canal at Palazzo Grassi, and then go down towards the Frari . . . But about *làttimi* now: she felt a thrill, like a dowser, every time she managed to dig up a new, rare one! Did I want to know how many pieces she had managed to collect? Almost two hundred.

I carefully avoided pointing out that what she was saying hardly jibed with her declared aversion to any attempt at rescuing, however temporarily, things, objects, from the inevitable death that awaited "even them," and to Perotti's mania for preservation in particular. I was eager for her to discuss her room, to forget having said, *"Verboten. Privat."*

My wish was granted. She went on talking about her *làttimi* (she had arranged them neatly in three tall, dark mahogany cases that covered almost the entire wall opposite the long one against which the bed was set), and meanwhile the room, I don't know how unconsciously on her part, was taking form, was gradually being defined in all its details.

So then: the windows were two in all. Both faced south, and they were so high from the floor that looking out from the sill, with the expanse of the park below, and with the roofs spreading beyond the park as far as the eye could see, was like looking down from the deck of an ocean liner. Between the two windows, a fourth case: shelves of English and French books. Against the left wall, a desk with a green cloth and a lamp, flanked on one side by the little typewriter table, and, on the other, by a fifth case, for books of Italian literature, classic and contemporary, and translations:

from the Russian, mostly, Pushkin, Gogol, Dostoyevsky, Chekhov. On the floor, a big Persian carpet, and in the center of the room, which was long but rather narrow, three armchairs and a Récamier, where she could stretch out and read. Two doors: the entrance, at the far end, next to the left-hand window, leading directly to the stairs and the elevator, and another a few inches from the obliquely opposite corner of the room, which led to the bath. At night she slept without ever closing the blinds completely, a tiny lamp always burning on the little table beside her bed, and also close by, the trolley with the thermos of *Skiwasser* (and with the telephone!), which she could reach simply by extending one arm. If she woke up during the night, she had only to take a sip of *Skiwasser* (it was *so* convenient to have some always at hand, "good and hot"; why didn't I get myself a thermos too?), then, flinging herself down again, she could let her gaze wander among the luminous mists of her beloved *làttimi:* and then sleep, imperceptibly, like a Venetian "high tide," would return slowly to submerge and "annihilate" her.

But these were not our only subjects of conversation.

As if she wished to give me the illusion that nothing had changed, that everything was continuing, between us, in the same way as *before*, as when, that is, we could see each other every afternoon, Micòl never overlooked an opportunity to take me back to that series of stupendous, "incredible" days.

We had always spoken of all sorts of things, then, moving around the park: of trees, plants, our childhood, our relatives. And meanwhile, Bruno Lattes, Adriana Trentini, Malnate, Carletto Sani, Tonino Collevatti, and, with them, those who had come along afterwards, were never granted more than some mention, some allusion, from time to time, lumped together, remunerated perhaps, with a brisk and fairly contemptuous "that bunch."

Now, on the contrary, over the phone, our talk returned constantly to them, and especially Bruno Lattes and Adriana Trentini, between whom, according to Micòl, there was surely a *thing*. What!—she kept saying to me—hadn't I noticed that they were a steady couple? It was so obvious! He never took his eyes off her for a moment, and she too, though she treated him like a slave, while flirting a bit with everybody, with me, with that bear Malnate, and even with Alberto, she, too, basically, went along with him. *Dear* Bruno! With his sensitivity (a bit morbid, let's be frank: to realize that, you only had to see how he literally worshiped two agreeable idiots of the caliber of little Sani, and that other one, the Collevatti boy!), with his sensitivity, there were difficult months in store for him, given the situation. Adriana surely granted him some satisfaction (one evening, in fact, in the *Hütte*, she had seen them half-sprawled on the sofa, kissing at full tilt), but whether she was the sort who could keep up such a serious *thing*, despite the racial laws and his parents and her own, this was another question. He wasn't going to have an easy winter, no, not Bruno. And it wasn't that Adriana was a bad girl, good heavens, no! Almost as tall as Bruno, blond, with her splendid skin à la Carole Lombard, under other circumstances she would perhaps have been just the right girl for Bruno, who obviously liked the ''very Aryan'' type. She was a bit giddy and empty, of course, and unconsciously cruel, ah, yes, that was undeniable. Didn't I remember how cross she had been with Bruno that time when the two of them had lost the famous return match against the Désirée Baggioli–Claudio Montemezzo pair? She had been mostly responsible for losing the match, with that ''mass'' of double faults she had piled up—at least three per game—not Bruno! But instead, shamelessly, all through the match she had done nothing but say whatever she liked to him, as if he, ''poor thing,'' were not already depressed and downcast enough on his own. It would have been laughable, honestly, if, when you thought it over, the situation hadn't been rather bitter! But so it went: as if deliberately, moralists like Bruno always go and fall in love with dimwits like Adriana, and then: jealous scenes, surprises, tears, vows, maybe slaps, and . . . unfaithfulness, yes, mind you, no end of that. No, no: in the final analysis, Bruno should light a candle to the racial laws. He had a difficult winter ahead, true. But the racial laws, not entirely unprovidential, then, would prevent him from carrying out the biggest foolishness: becoming engaged.

''Don't you agree?'' she added once. ''And besides, he too is a literary type, like you, someone who aims to write. I believe I saw some verses of his, two or three years ago, published on the literary page of the *Corriere ferrarese* under the general title *A Young Fascist's Poems*.''

''Alas!'' I sighed. ''Anyway, what are you getting at? I don't understand.''

She was silently laughing; I could feel that very well.

''Yes, yes,'' she said. ''In the end, a bit of torment won't do him any harm. 'Do not leave me yet, suffering,' Ungaretti says. He wants to write, doesn't he? So let him stew properly in his own juice, and then we'll see.

Besides, you only have to look at him: you can see with the naked eye that, basically, his only aspiration is sorrow.''

"Your cynicism is revolting; you're as bad as Adriana."

"That's where you're wrong. You're insulting, in fact. Adriana is an innocent angel. Spoiled, perhaps, but innocent like 'all—the females of all—the serene animals—that are near God.' Whereas Micòl is good, I told you and I'll repeat it, and she *always* knows what she's doing. Remember that.''

Though more rarely, she also mentioned Giàmpiero Malnate, towards whom she had always maintained a curious attitude, basically critical and sarcastic: as if she were jealous of the friendship between him and Alberto —a bit exclusive, to tell the truth—but at the same time were annoyed at admitting it, being jealous; and as if for this very reason she persisted in "demolishing the idol."

According to her, Malnate was nothing much, even "as to physique." Too big, too heavy, too much "a father," to be given serious consideration from this aspect. He was one of those excessively hairy types who, no matter how many times a day they shave, always look a bit dirty, a bit unwashed: and this would *not* do, let's be frank. Perhaps, yes, from what could be glimpsed through those awful thick eyeglasses he camouflaged his face with (they seemed to make him sweat: and you always felt like tearing them off him), perhaps his eyes were not bad: gray eyes, *steel,* a strong man's. Still, too grave and stern, those eyes. Too constitutionally matrimonial. Despite their contemptuous superficial misogyny, they threatened sentiments so eternal that they would make any girl shudder, even the most calm and proper.

He was a great grouch, that's what: and not even all that original, as he seemed to consider himself. Would I bet that, carefully questioned, at a certain point he would come out with the declaration that in city clothes he felt ill at ease, preferring to them in any situation the Windbreaker, plus fours, and ski boots of his inevitable weekends on Mottarone or Monte Rosa? The faithful pipe, in this respect, was quite revealing: it was a whole program of male, sub-Alpine austerity, a banner.

He and Alberto were friends, great friends, though Alberto, with that character of his, more passive than a punching ball, was always the friend of everybody and nobody. They had spent whole years together, in Milan: and this, to be sure, had its importance. But didn't I also find them a bit excessive, in that constant confabulation of theirs? *Pss pss pss:* they no sooner met than, right away, nobody and nothing could restrain them from going off by themselves and plunging into deep conversation. And God knows what about! Girls? Hm! Knowing Alberto, who in this field had always been rather reserved, not to say mysterious, she wouldn't risk two cents on that, honestly.

"Do you still see him?" I brought myself to ask, one day, dropping the question in the most indifferent tone I could muster.

"Oh yes . . . I think he comes now and then to visit his Alberto . . ." she answered, calmly. "They shut themselves up in his room, drink tea, smoke their pipes (Alberto has taken to smoking one, too, recently), and they talk and talk, the lucky things, nothing but talk."

She was too intelligent, too sensitive, not to have guessed what I was hiding behind my indifference: namely, the suddenly acute—and symptomatic—desire to see her again. She behaved, on the other hand, as if she hadn't understood, without referring even indirectly to the possibility that sooner or later I, too, might be invited there, to the house.

# II

I spent the following night in great agitation. I fell asleep, woke, fell asleep again. And I always resumed dreaming of her.

I dreamed, for example, that I was watching her as she played tennis with Alberto, just like the very first day I set foot in the garden. Now too, as I was dreaming, I didn't take my eyes off her for a single moment. I told myself once more that she was splendid, that I liked her as she was, sweating and flushed, with that almost fierce furrow of commitment and determination that vertically divided her brow, while she was all tensed in the effort of defeating her smiling, somewhat sluggish, bored older brother. Now, however, I felt oppressed by an uneasiness, a bitterness, a sadness, almost unbearable. Of the girl of ten years before—I asked myself desperately—what had remained in this Micòl of twenty-two, in shorts and cotton jersey, in this Micòl who seemed so free, athletic, modern (but free, especially), as to make me think that she had spent the past years making the rounds of the Meccas of international tennis: London, Paris, Côte d'Azur,

Forest Hills? Yes—I made the comparison—there was still the child's blond hair, still, light, streaked with almost white locks, and the blue, Scandinavian irises, the honey-colored skin, and on her breast, perhaps, every now and then popping from the round neck of the jersey, the little golden disk of the *shaddai*. But what else?

Then we were closed in the carriage, in that gray and stagnant shadow: with Perotti outside, seated on the box, motionless, mute, looming. If Perotti, up there—I reasoned—was turning his back stubbornly on us, he was certainly doing it so as not to see what happened, or could happen, inside the carriage: in short out of a servant's discretion. And yet he was informed, all the same, of *everything*, the old boor, indeed he was! His wife, the colorless Vittorina, peeping through the half-closed door of the coach house (every now and then I glimpsed the woman's little reptile head, glistening with smooth black hair, jutting cautiously beyond the panel of the door: and I could also discern an eye of the same color, with a discontented and worried expression), his wife was there, on guard, half inside and half outside the doorway, stealthily signaling to him with gestures and grimaces.

And we were even in her room, Micòl and I, but not alone there either, "encumbered"—she whispered—by the "inevitable" alien presence: which, this time, was Jor, crouched in the center of the room like an enormous, granitic idol, Jor who stared at us with his icy eyes, one black and one blue. The room was long and narrow, just like the coach house; like the coach house full of edible things: grapefruit, oranges, tangerines, and especially of *làttimi*, lined up in rows like books on the shelves of the great black cases, austere and churchly, high as the ceiling: because the *làttimi* were not at all objects of glass, as she, Micòl, had tried to make me believe, but on the contrary, just as I had supposed, cheeses, small dripping forms of a whitish cheese, bottle-shaped. Laughing, Micòl insisted I should taste one of her cheeses; and there, she stood on tiptoe, there she was, about to touch with her fingers one of the highest (the ones up there were the best—she explained to me—the most fresh), but no, I absolutely refused to accept, distressed not only by the dog's presence, but by the awareness that outside, as we were arguing, the lagoon's tide was rapidly rising. If I delayed a little longer, the high tide would block me, would prevent me from leaving her room unnoticed. In fact I had entered at night and in secret, into Micòl's bedroom: a secret from Alberto, from Professor Ermanno, from Signora Olga, from Grandmother Regina, from the uncles, Giulio and Federico, from the innocent Signorina Blumenfeld. And Jor, who was the only one to know, the only witness to the *thing* that there was *also* between us, Jor could not report.

I dreamed also that we spoke, and finally without pretense, finally with our cards on the table.

We quarreled a bit, as usual: Micòl insisting that the *thing* between us had begun the first day, when she and I, both of us still filled with the surprise of meeting again and recognizing each other, had run off to see the park, and I protesting this wasn't so at all, in my opinion the *thing* had begun even earlier, on the telephone, when she had announced that she had become "ugly, an "old maid with a red nose." In my heart of hearts I hadn't really believed her, of course. And yet she couldn't begin to imagine—I said, with a lump in my throat—how those words of her had made me suffer. In the hours that followed, before I saw her again, I had thought about them constantly, unable to resign myself.

"Well, maybe you're right," Micòl agreed at this point, pitying, putting a hand on mine. "If the thought of me being ugly and with a red nose immediately upset you, then I surrender, you really must be right. But now, in any event, what's to be done? Tennis is no longer a good excuse, and at home, on the other hand, with the risk of being blocked by the high tide (you see what Venice is like?), at home it's not fitting or convenient for me to let you in."

"What's the need?" I answered. "You could come out, after all."

"Me? Out?" she exclaimed, her eyes wide. "And just tell me, *cher ami*, where would we go?

"I . . . I don't know . . ." I answered, stammering. "To the Montagnone, for example, or the Parade Ground, or towards the Aqueduct, or else, if you're afraid of being compromised, to Piazza della Certosa, on the Via Borso side. That's where *they all* go, to be alone, you know that. I don't know about your parents, but mine, in their day, went there too. And after all, what's wrong with being together a bit? It's not the same as making love! You're on the first step, on the edge of the abyss. But from there to touching the bottom of the abyss, it's a long descent!"

And I was about to add that if, as it seemed, not even Piazza della Certosa suited her, well, we could also, if desired, take separate trains and meet in Bologna. But I was silent, lacking courage even in a dream. And for that matter, she was shaking her head and smiling, already declaring that it was useless, impossible, *"verboten"*: she would never go anywhere with me, outside the house and the garden. What was all this?—she winked, amused—after she had allowed herself to be led around all the usual *"plein air"* places dear to the "eros of the savage native town," was it to Bologna that I was already plotting to lead her? To Bologna, yes, she could just imagine some "immense hotel," no doubt the sort preferred by Grandmother Josette, like the Brun or the Baglioni, where, in any case, we would have to present at the *réception*, our suitably homologous racial credentials.

The next evening, as soon as I came back from a quick trip to Bologna, to the university, I rushed to the phone.

Alberto answered.

"How's everything?" he chanted, ironically, showing for once that he recognized my voice. "It's ages since we've seen each other. How are you? What are you doing?"

Disconcerted, my heart pounding, I started speaking all in a rush. I piled up all sorts of things: news about the thesis, which (it was true) was looming before me like an unscalable wall, considerations on the season, which, after those last two weeks of bad weather, that morning had seemed to promise a break (but it wasn't to be trusted too much: the pungent air was eloquent, by now we were plunged into winter, and the fine days of the past October were to be forgotten), adding moreover an extremely detailed report on what I called my rapid "tour of duty on Via Zamboni," as if he, Alberto, who was studying in Milan, were supposed to know Bologna as well as I did.

That morning—I reported—I had been to the university, where I had to settle some things in the secretary's office, and then up to the library, to check a certain number of entries in the Panzacchi bibliography I was preparing. At one, I had eaten at Il Pappagallo: not at the so-called pasta Pappagallo at the foot of the Asinelli towers, which, besides being terribly expensive, seemed to me, as to cuisine, decidedly inferior to its reputation, but at the other, the soup Pappagallo, which was on a sidestreet off Via Galliera, and was in fact famous for its boiled meats and its broths, and for its prices, too, which were really cheap. In the afternoon I had seen some friends, made the rounds of the bookshops downtown, had a cup of tea at

Zanarini's, the one in Piazza Galvani, at the end of the Pavaglione: in short I had had a rather good day—I concluded—much like the times when I was in regular attendance.

"And just think: before going back to the station," I added at this point, inventing out of the whole cloth, and God knows what devil had suddenly prompted me to tell a story of the sort, "I even found time to have a look in at Via dell'Oca."

"Via dell'Oca?" Alberto asked, immediately animated, and yet somehow shy.

That was all I needed to discover suddenly, in myself, the same sharp pleasure that drove my father, when discussing the Finzi-Continis, to appear much more crude and *goyishe* than he really was.

"What!" I exclaimed. "Haven't you ever heard about Via dell'Oca? Why, it's one of the most famous . . . rooming houses . . . in Italy!"

He cleared his throat, embarrassed.

"No, I didn't know it."

Then, curtly changing tone and subject, he said that he, too, in a few days' time, would have to leave for Milan, and stay there at least a week. June, after all, was nearer than it seemed, and he still hadn't found a professor who would allow him to "patch together some kind of thesis"; to tell the truth, he hadn't even looked for one.

After which, skipping again to a different subject (in the meanwhile his voice had recovered its usual bored, mocking tone), he asked me if, a little while ago, I hadn't happened to pass by, on my bicycle, along the Mura degli Angeli. At that moment, he had been in the garden: he had gone out to see what shape the rain had left the tennis court in. But because of the distance, and also because it was almost dark, he hadn't been sure I was that person who, without getting off his bicycle, and with one hand against a tree trunk, was standing up there, motionless, looking down. Ah, so it had been I?—he continued, after I had admitted, not without hesitation, that, coming home from the station, I had indeed taken the road along the walls: and this, I explained, because of the inner revulsion I felt every time I tried to pass in front of certain ugly characters gathered opposite the Caffè della Borsa, on Corso Roma, or spread out along Corso Giovecca. Ah, it was I?—he repeated. He had been sure! But in that case, if it had been I, why hadn't I answered his shouts, his whistles? Hadn't I heard them?

I hadn't heard them—I lied, once more—in fact, I hadn't even noticed him in the garden. And now we really had nothing else to say to each other, nothing to fill the sudden silence that yawned between us.

"But you . . . you wanted Micòl, didn't you?" he said, finally, as if remembering.

"Yes," I answered. "Would you mind getting her for me?"

He would have been glad to get her for me—he answered—but (and it was *very* strange that, apparently, "that angel" hadn't let me know), Micòl had left in the early afternoon for Venice, with the intention, also, of "wringing the neck" of her thesis. She had come down to lunch all dressed for the journey, with suitcases and everything, announcing to "her dismayed family" what she was planning to do. She was fed up, she declared, with drawing out her "homework." Instead of June, therefore, she was going to take her degree in February: something which, in Venice, with the Marciana and the Querini-Stampalia libraries at hand, would be very easy for her, whereas in Ferrara it wouldn't; here, for a thousand reasons, her thesis on Dickinson would never be able to progress with the necessary speed (this, at least, was what she had said). But who knew how long she would hold out, Micòl, in the depressing atmosphere of Venice, and of a house, their uncles', that she didn't love? Nothing was more likely than that, in a week or two, we would see her "return shamefaced to her lair." To him it would seem like a dream if, for once, Micòl managed to stay away from Ferrara for more than three weeks, for a whole month. . . .

"Well, we'll see," he concluded. "In any case, what would you say (not this week, it's impossible, and next week too, but the following one, I think it would really be possible), what would you say to arranging a dash to Venice in the car? It would be fun to drop in on the baby sister: you, me, and Giampiero Malnate, for example!"

"It's an idea," I answered. "Why not? We can talk about it."

"In the meanwhile," he went on, with an effort in which I sensed a great desire on his part to offer me an immediate compensation for the news he had just given me, "in the meanwhile, really, if you have nothing better to do, of course, why don't you come and see me here at the house? Say, tomorrow, about five? Malnate will be here too, I think. . . . I don't know if you, who are a literary man, feel like spending time with an engineer (namely, me) and an industrial chemist. However, if you care to *condescend,* no formalities: just come, and we'll be really delighted."

We continued a little longer, Alberto more and more fervent and enthusiastic about his plan, which seemed extemporaneous, of having me at his house, and I, attracted but also repelled. It was quite true—I remembered—that a little earlier, from the top of the Mura degli Angeli, I had stood looking for almost half an hour at the garden, and the house, especially, which, from where I was, and through the almost bare limbs of the trees, I saw engraved against the evening sky, from the foundation to the pinnacled roof, slender and unfurled, like a heraldic device. Two windows of the mezzanine, at the level of the terrace from which you went down into the park, were already illuminated, and electric light filtered also from up above, from the single, very high window that opened just below the top of the final turret. At length, my eyeballs aching in their sockets, I had remained staring at the little light of the upper window—a calm, tremulous glow, suspended like a star's in the gradually darkening air—and only the distant whistles and Tyrolean shouts of Alberto, arousing in me, along with the fear of being recognized, the eagerness to hear again, immediately, Micòl's voice on the telephone, had been able at a certain point to drive me away from there. . . .

But now—I asked myself, disconsolate—what did it matter to me, to go to *their* house, now, if I would not find Micòl there any more?

But the news I received from my mother as I was coming out of the telephone closet, namely, that, around noon, Micòl Finzi-Contini had telephoned, for me ("She asked me to tell you that she had to leave for Venice, and to say good-bye, and that she'll write," Mamma added, looking away), was enough to make me suddenly change my mind. From that moment on, in fact, the time that separated me from five o'clock the next day began to pass with extreme slowness.

# III

It was in that period, then, that I began to be received, almost daily you might say, in Alberto's little private apartment (he called it his study; and a study it was, in fact; the bedroom and bath adjoined it): in that famous "chamber," beyond the double door from which, moving along the corridor beside it, Micòl could only hear the confused voices of her brother and his friend Malnate resound, and where, except for the maids, when they arrived with the tea trolley, in the course of the winter I never chanced to meet another member of the family. Oh, the winter of '38/39! I remember those long months, immobile, as if suspended above time and despair (in February it snowed, Micòl kept postponing her return from Venice), and even now, for me, at a distance of almost twenty years, the four walls of Alberto Finzi-Contini's study become once again the daily vice of those times, the drug as necessary as it was unconscious. . . .

To be sure, I didn't feel the least despair that first December evening, when, on my bicycle, I crossed the Barchetto del Duca. Micòl had left: and yet I rode along the drive, in the darkness and in the fog, as if, in a little while, I were expecting to see her again, and only her. I was excited, in a good humor: almost happy. I looked ahead of me, aiming my headlight at the places of a past that seemed to me remote, but still recoverable. Not yet lost. And there was the little wood of flowering canna; there, farther on, to the right, the hazy outline of the Perotti farmhouse, from one of whose windows, on the upper floor, a bit of yellowish light leaked; and there, still farther, the ghostly scaffolding of the Panfilio bridge was coming towards me: and there, finally, heralded for a brief stretch by the crunch of my tires on the gravel of the clearing, the gigantic bulk of the *magna domus,* impervious as an isolated cliff, all dark except for the white, vivid light that came, in spurts, from a little ground-floor door, obviously opened to receive me.

I got off my bicycle, standing for a moment to look at the deserted threshold. I could glimpse, sliced obliquely by the black wing of the door's left-hand panel, still closed, a steep stairway covered with a strip of red carpet: a bright red, scarlet, sanguine. At each step, a brass rod, shiny and sparkling as if it were of gold.

I propped the bicycle against the wall, leaning over to apply the padlock. And I was still there, in the shadow, bent next to the door through which, besides the light, there came a good warmth of radiators (in the darkness I couldn't make the lock work, so I was already thinking of striking a match to see better), when the familiar voice of Professor Ermanno resounded suddenly near.

"What are you doing there? Locking it?" the Professor said, standing in the doorway. "Good for you. You never can tell. Better safe than sorry."

Without understanding, as usual, whether he was covertly teasing me with his somewhat querulous politeness, I promptly straightened up.

"Good evening," I said, taking off my hat and holding out my hand.

"Good evening, my boy," he answered. "But keep your hat on. Please!"

I felt his small, fat hand inserted, almost limp, in mine, and immediately withdrawn. He was without an overcoat, an old hunting cap pulled down to his eyeglasses, a wool scarf wrapped around his neck.

He peered obliquely, suspiciously, towards the bicycle.

"You've locked it, haven't you?"

I answered no. And then, vexed, he insisted I should go back, do him the favor of locking it, because—he repeated—you never can tell. A theft was unlikely—he went on, from the doorway, as I was again trying to loop the padlock through the spokes of the rear wheel—but the fact was that you could only trust the garden walls up to a point. Along its length, especially towards the Mura degli Angeli, there were at least ten places where a fairly quick boy would find no difficulty climbing over. Slipping off afterwards, even burdened by the weight of a bicycle on his shoulder, would be, for the same boy, an almost equally easy operation.

I finally managed to snap the lock. I raised my eyes, but the threshold was again deserted.

The Professor was waiting for me in the little vestibule, at the foot of the stairs. I entered, taking care to close the door behind me, and only then did I realize that he was looking at me, puzzled, repentant.

"I'm wondering," he said, "if it wouldn't have been better actually to bring the bicycle inside. . . . Yes, the next time you come, do as I say: bring the bicycle in with you. If you put it there, under the stairs, it won't be in anyone's way."

He turned and began to climb, preceding me up the stairs. He went slowly, more hunched than ever, the cap still on his head and the scarf around his neck, while he held on to the railing. Meanwhile he was talking, or rather mumbling: as if he were addressing not so much me as himself.

Alberto had told him I would be coming to call today, So, as Perotti had been in bed since that morning with a bit of fever (it was only a "touch of bronchitis": but it had to be treated, all the same, to avoid contagion) and since Alberto, always so forgetful, absent, his head in the clouds, simply could not be relied on, for once he himself had taken on the assignment of "keeping watch." Micòl was the person they needed, to be sure. If Micòl had been here, he wouldn't have had any reason for anxiety, because Micòl, somehow, always found time to deal with everything, not only pursuing her own studies, but also handling the general running of the house, and even the kitchen, to be sure, for which—a great thing, this, in a woman!—she nourished a passion almost as great as her passion for literature (it was she who went over the accounts at the end of the week with Gina and Vittorina, and she who, when necessary, took care to *shacht* the poultry with her own hands: and this despite the fact that she was so fond of animals, poor child!). But Micòl, unfortunately, was not at home today (had Alberto told me, that Micòl was not home?); she had had to leave yesterday afternoon for Venice; and that explained why, in the absence of their "guardian angel," and with Perotti indisposed "into the bargain," he had been obliged, temporarily, to act also as doorkeeper.

He spoke of other things too, which I don't remember. I do remember, however, that in the end he came back to Micòl, and this time not to express pride in her, but to complain of a certain "recent restlessness" of hers—these were his very words, and he sighed—a restlessness due, in his opinion, unquestionably to "many factors," of course, but chiefly . . . Here he fell silent, abruptly, adding nothing further. And during all this time we had not only climbed to the top of the stairway, but had turned and walked the length of two corridors, entered and left various rooms, Professor Ermanno always leading the way, never allowing me to pass him, except as he switched off the lights, along our route.

Absorbed as I was by what I was learning about Micòl (the detail that it was she who, with her own hands, cut the throats of the chickens in the kitchen, had strangely fascinated me), I looked around, but almost without seeing. We were passing, for that matter, through rooms not too different from those of other houses of Ferrara society, Jewish and Gentile, these also invaded by the usual furnishing: monumental wardrobes, heavy seventeenth-century chests with lion's feet, refectory-style tables, "Savonarola" chairs of leather with bronze studs, overstuffed chairs, complicated glass or wrought-iron lamps hanging from the center of coffered ceilings, as well as, spread everywhere on the darkly polished parquet floors, thick carpets, tobacco-colored, or carrot-orange, or ox-blood. Here, perhaps, there was a greater quantity of nineteenth-century paintings, landscapes and portraits, and rows of books, mostly bound, behind the panes of massive dark mahogany bookcases. From the big radiators, moreover, a warmth was released that at our house, for example, my father would have considered insane (I could almost hear him!): a heat more like a grand hotel's than a private house's, so intense that, in fact, almost at once I began to sweat, I felt the need to take off my overcoat.

He ahead and I behind, we crossed at least a dozen rooms of various sizes, some vast as real salons, others small, even tiny, and connected at times with one another by corridors not always straight or on the same level. Finally, halfway along one of these corridors, Professor Ermanno stopped at a door.

"Here we are," he said.

He pointed at the door with his thumb, and winked.

He apologized for not being able to come in with me, but—he explained—he had to go over some accounts from the country; he promised he would immediately send "one of the girls with something hot"; after which, having shaken my hand and received my assurance that I would come back again (he was still saving for me the copies of his little essays on Venetian history, I was not to forget; and besides, it was a *great* pleasure for him, from time to time, to have a talk with "intelligent young people"), he turned his back on me, continuing down the corridor and rapidly disappearing at the end of it.

"Ah, you're here!" Alberto greeted me, seeing me enter.

He was sprawled in an armchair. Pressing both hands on the arms, he pulled himself to his feet, set down the book he was reading, open, with the spine up, on a little low table next to him, and finally came towards me.

He was wearing a pair of gray flannel pants, one of his handsome sweaters, the color of a dry leaf, brown English shoes (they were genuine Dawsons—he told me later—he found them in Milan, in a little shop near San Babila), a flannel shirt unbuttoned at the throat, no tie, and his pipe between his teeth. He shook my hand without excessive cordiality. Meanwhile he was starting at a spot beyond my shoulder. What was attracting his attention? I didn't understand.

"Excuse me," he murmured.

He pushed me away, stepped around me, bending his long back sideways, and, at the moment he passed me, I realized I had left the double door half-open. Alberto was already there, however, to attend to it personally. He grasped the knob of the outer door, but before pulling it to himself, he stuck his head out to have a look, into the corridor.

"What about Malnate?" I asked. "Hasn't he come yet?"

"No, not yet," he answered, returning.

He took my hat, scarf, and overcoat and disappeared into the adjoining room. Of this, now, through the communicating door, I was already allowed to know something: part of the bed, with a red-and-blue-checked wool blanket on it, very sporting; at the foot of the bed a leather hassock; and hanging on the wall beside the little flush door to the bath, also half-open, a little male nude by De Pisis, mounted in a simple blond strip-frame.

"Sit down," Alberto was saying meanwhile. "I'll be right there."

In fact, he reappeared at once, and now, sitting in front of me, in the chair from which I had seen him pull himself up a little earlier with a slight display of effort, perhaps of boredom, he was examining me with the strange expression of detached, objective liking that I knew was, for him, the sign of the greatest interest in others he could muster. He smiled at me, baring his big incisors, characteristic of his mother's family: too big and strong for that long, pale face of his, and even for the gums above them, no less pale than his face.

"Would you like to hear some music?" he proposed, nodding towards a radio-gramophone set in a corner of the study beside the door. "It's a Philips, really excellent."

He started to rise from the chair again, but I stopped him.

"No, wait," I said. "Maybe later."

I was looking around, observing the room.

"What records do you have?"

"Oh, a bit of everything: Monteverdi, Scarlatti, Bach, Mozart, Beethoven. Don't be alarmed, though, I also have quite a lot of jazz: Armstrong, Duke Ellington, Fats Waller, Benny Goodman, Charlie Kunz. . . ."

He continued listing names and titles, polite and even-tempered as usual, but with indifference: exactly as if he were inviting me to choose from a list of foods which he, for his part, would certainly not touch. He became animated only, moderately, in illustrating to me the merits of *his* Philips. It was—he said to me—a "fairly exceptional" set, and this was thanks to certain special "gadgets" that, conceived by himself, had then been worked out by a very good Milanese technician. These modifications concerned most of all the quality of sound, which was transmitted not just by a single loudspeaker, but by four distinct "sources." There was, in fact, the loudspeaker for the bass, one for the middle sounds, one for the treble, and one for the very high sounds: so that, for example, through the loudspeaker meant for the very high sounds, even whistles—and he chuckled—"came out" perfectly. And I wasn't to think that all four were jammed in there side by side, oh, no! Inside the cabinet itself, there were only two loudspeakers: the one for the medium sounds, and the one for the treble. The very high one, he had thought to conceal over there, by the window; while the fourth, the bass, he had set right under the sofa where I was sitting: and all in order to achieve a certain stereophonic effect.

At that moment Dirce came in, in a blue cotton smock, white apron around her waist, drawing the tea trolley after her.

I saw immediately an expression of slight annoyance on Alberto's face. The girl must also have noticed.

"It was the Professor," she explained, "he told me to bring it right away."

"That's all right. We'll have a cup in the *meanwhile*."

Blond and curly-haired, with the flushed cheeks of the girls from the Veneto pre-Alps, Perotti's daughter, in silence, her lashes lowered, prepared the cups, set them on the little table, then withdrew. In the air of the room there remained a good smell of soap and talcum. The tea also, so it seemed to me, tasted of them faintly.

I sipped from my cup, and continued looking around. I admired the furnishing of the room, so rational, functional, modern, so different from that of the rest of the house; and yet I couldn't understand why I was gradually overcome with a mounting sense of uneasiness, of oppression.

"You like the way I've done the study?" Alberto asked.

He seemed suddenly anxious for my approval: which I did not stint him, naturally, expanding in praise of the furniture's simplicity, rising from the sofa to go and examine more closely a large drafting table, set obliquely near the window, with an adjustable metal lamp attached, and finally expressing my particular admiration for the indirect lighting which—I said—I found very restful and, at the same time, ideal for working.

He let me speak and seemed pleased.

"Did you design the furniture yourself?"

"Well, no. I copied a bit from *Domus* and from *Casabella*, and a bit also from *The Studio*, you know, the English magazine. . . . Then I had it all made, here in Ferrara, by a carpenter on Via Coperta."

He was very pleased—he added—to hear I approved of his furniture. To live in a room or to work there, in fact, why did one have to be surrounded by ugly things, or by antique junk? As for Giampi Malnate (he blushed slightly, saying the name), as for Giampi Malnate, it was all very well for him to insinuate that the study, furnished like this, looked more like a *garçonnière* than a study, insisting further, like the good Communist he was, that *things*, in themselves, can offer at most palliatives, surrogates, for he, on principle, was opposed to surrogates and palliatives of any sort, and opposed even to technology, whenever technology seems to consider a drawer that closes perfectly, just to take an example, the resolution of all the individual's problems, moral and political included. He, in any case— and he tapped his chest with his hand—was of a different opinion. Though he respected Giampi's views (yes, he was a Communist: didn't I know that?), he, Alberto, felt that life was already sufficiently confused and tiresome without also having confused and tiresome furniture and bric-a-brac as our silent and faithful roommates.

This was the first and last time I saw him become heated, defend certain ideas against certain others. We drank a second cup of tea, but the conversation now was languishing, so it was necessary to fall back on music.

We listened to a couple of records. Dirce came back, bringing a platter of pastries; then around seven, the telephone, on a desk beside the drafting table, began to ring.

"I'll bet it's Giampi," Alberto muttered, rushing to it.

Before picking up the receiver, he hesitated an instant: like the gambler who, having received his cards, delays the moment when he has to look his luck in the face.

But it was Malnate, all right, as I realized at once.

"So what are you going to do? You're not coming?" Alberto was saying, disappointed, with an almost childish whine in his voice.

Malnate spoke a fairly long time. From the sofa, though I couldn't hear what he was saying, I could hear the receiver vibrate at the impact of his heavy, calm, Lombard voice. Finally I made out a "ciao," and the line went dead.

"He's not coming," Alberto said.

He went slowly back to his chair, sank into it, stretched, and yawned.

"Apparently he's been held up at the plant," he continued, "and has another two or three hours there. He's sorry, and he asked me to say hello to you too."

# IV

More than the vague "see you soon" exchanged with Alberto on taking my leave, it was a letter from Micòl, a few days later, that persuaded me to return.

The letter was witty, neither too long nor too short, written on the four sides of two sheets of blue paper, which an impetuous and, at the same time, light hand had filled rapidly, without hesitation or correction. Micòl began with an apology: she had left suddenly, she hadn't even said goodbye to me, and this had not been nice of her, she was ready to admit. Before leaving, however—she added—she had tried to phone me, but unfortunately I was out; moreover, she had urged Alberto, in the possible eventuality that I didn't call them, to dig me out. Had this actually happened, had Alberto, after all, lived up to his oath to recover me "at the cost of his life"? With that famous inertia of his, Alberto always ended by losing all contact, and yet he needed contacts so much, the wretch! The letter went on for two and a half pages, discussing her thesis "now under full sail towards the final goal," mentioning Venice, which in winter, was "simply enough to make you cry," and ending with a surprise, a verse translation of a poem by Emily Dickinson:

It went:

> *Morii per la Bellezza; e da poco ero*
> *discesa nell'avello,*
> *che, caduto pel Vero, uno fu messo*
> *nell'attiguo sacello.*
>
> *"Perché sei morta?" me chiese sommesso.*
> *Dissi: "Morii pel Bello."*
> *"Io, per la Verità: dunque è lo stesso.*
> *—disse,—son tuo fratello."*

*Da tomba a tomba, come due congiunti*
*incontratisi a notte,*
*parlavamo così; finché raggiunti*
*l'erba ebbe nomi e bocche.*

[I died for beauty, but was scarce
Adjusted in the tomb,
When one who died for truth was lain
In an adjoining room.

He questioned softly why I failed?
"For beauty," I replied.
"And I for truth,—the two are one;
We brethren are," he said.

And so, as kinsmen met a night,
We talked between the rooms,
Until the moss had reached our lips,
And covered up our names.]

A postscript followed, which began, in English: "*Alas, poor Emily.*
This is the kind of compensation vile spinsterhood is forced to hope for!"

I liked the translation, but I was particularly struck by the postscript. To
whom was I supposed to apply it? To "poor Emily," really, or perhaps to
a Micòl in a depressed, self-pitying state?

In my answer, I carefully hid once more behind a thick smoke screen.
After mentioning my first visit to the house, omitting what had been to me
disappointing about it, and promising I would soon return, I prudently
stuck to literature. The Dickinson poem was stupendous—I wrote—but her
translation of it was excellent. It interested me precisely because of its
slightly passé flavor, in the style of Carducci. I had then gone on to compare it with the English text, dictionary in hand: with the result of finding it
impeccable except on one point, perhaps, where she had translated the
word "*moss*," which to be strict meant, in Italian, *muschio, muffa, bor-
raccina,* with the word *erba,* or "*grass.*" Mind you—I went on—in its
present state the translation worked perfectly, since in these matters a beautiful freedom was always preferable to ugly fidelity. In any case, the fault I
was pointing out to her could easily be remedied, simply by revising the
last stanza in this way:

> *Da tomba a tomba, come due congiunti*
> *incontratisi a notte,*
> *parlavamo; finché il muschio raggiunti*
> *ebbe i nomi, le bocche*

Micòl answered, two days later, with an extraordinarily effusive telegram thanking me for my literary counsels, and then, the following day, with a letter containing two new typewritten versions of the translation. With a reply of about ten pages, I confuted the note, word by word. All things considered, by letter we were far more awkward and lifeless than by telephone, so after a while we stopped writing. In the meantime, however, I resumed my visits to Alberto's study, and now I went regularly, almost every day.

Giampiero Malnate also came, almost as regularly and punctually as I did. Conversing, discussing, often quarreling—hating each other and also loving each other, in short, from the first moment—in this way we soon came to know each other profoundly, and began using the *tu* form.

I remembered how Micòl had expressed herself on the subject of his "physique." I also found him heavy and oppressive; in me, too, Malnate very often inspired a kind of genuine intolerance, because of his sincerity, his honesty, that eternal protestation of manly frankness, that serene confidence in a future that would be Lombard and Communist, which glowed in his too-human gray eyes. All the same, from the first time I sat facing him in Alberto's study, I had only one desire: that he should admire me, and not consider me an intruder between himself and Alberto, that, finally, he not judge ill-assorted this daily trio in which, surely through no initiative of his own, he found himself involved. I believe it was at this time I began smoking a pipe.

We discussed many things, the two of us (Alberto preferred to remain a listener), but, obviously, for the most part politics.

These were the months just after the Munich Pact, and this, indeed, the Munich Pact and its consequences, was the subject that arose most often in our talk. What would Hitler do next, now that the Sudetenland had been incorporated into the Greater Reich? In which direction would he strike, now? For my part, I was not a pessimist, and for once, Malnate agreed with me. In my view, the agreement that France and England had been forced to sign at the end of last September's crisis would not last long. Yes,

Hitler and Mussolini had induced Chamberlain and Daladier to abandon the Czechoslavakia of Beneš to its fate. But then what? Replacing perhaps Chamberlain and Daladier with younger and more determined men (there was the advantage of the parliamentary system! I exclaimed), soon France and England would be able to hold their ground. Time—I insisted—could only be in their favor.

But if the talk, however, turned to the war in Spain, now at its last gasp, or if somehow we referred to the USSR, then Malnate's attitude towards Western democracies changed, and with it, his attitude towards me, present, considered their representative and supporter, and he immediately became less compliant. I can still see him, thrusting out his big dark head, his brow glistening with sweat, as his eyes stared into mine with their usual, unbearable attempt at blackmail, moral and sentimental, to which he recurred so easily, as the tone of his voice became low, warm, persuasive, patient. Would I mind telling him—he would ask—who had been really responsible for the Franco revolt? Hadn't it been, by chance, the French and English right wing, who had not only tolerated it, at first, but then, later, actually encouraged and applauded it? Just as Anglo-French behavior, formally correct, but actually ambiguous, had allowed Mussolini, in '35, to gobble up Ethiopia in one mouthful, so too in Spain the culpable uncertainty of Baldwin, Halifax, and also of Blum, had tipped the scales of fate in Franco's favor. No use blaming the USSR and the International Brigade—he insinuated, more and more gently—no use blaming Russia, which had become the convenient whipping boy, for every imbecile, if events there were now taking a dire turn. The truth was something else: only Russia had understood from the beginning who the Duce and the Führer really were, only Russia had clearly foreseen the inevitable accord between the two, and consequently had acted early. The French and English Right, on the contrary, subverting the democratic order, like all right wings of all countries in all times, had always looked on Fascist Italy and Nazi Germany with ill-concealed friendliness. For the reactionaries of France and England, the Duce and the Führer might seem slightly uncomfortable men, true, a bit rough and excessive, but preferable in every way to Stalin, nevertheless, because Stalin, as everyone knows, had always been the devil incarnate. After having attacked and annexed Austria and Czechoslovakia, Germany was already beginning to apply pressure on Poland. Now, if France and England had come to their present sorry position, namely, of standing by to watch, there could be no two ways about it: the responsibility for their present impotence had to be attributed precisely to those fine, decorative, worthy gentlemen in top hats and morning coats—perfect, at least in their dress, for satisfying the nineteenth-century nostalgias of so *many* literary decadents—who were still governing those countries.

Malnate's polemical tone became especially lively when Italian history of recent decades was brought up.

It was obvious—he said—that for me, also for Alberto, really, Fascism had been nothing but the sudden, inexplicable disease that treacherously attacks the healthy organism, or, to use a phrase dear to Benedetto Croce, "your common master" (Alberto, at this point, would shake his head in desolate denial, but Malnate would pay no attention), the invasion of the Hyksos. For the two of us, in other words, the liberal Italy of Giolitti, Nitti, Orlando, and even of Sonnino, Salandra, and Facta, had been all-lovely and all-holy: a kind of golden age, to which, if it were possible, it would be wise to go straight back. But we were wrong, we were very wrong! The disease had not attacked suddenly. On the contrary, it came from long ago, that is, from the first years of the Risorgimento, which had been achieved in the virtual absence of the masses, of the true populace. Giolitti? If Mussolini had been able to ride out the crisis after the Matteotti murder, in '24, when everything around him seemed to be falling apart, and even the king was wavering, we had *our* Giolitti to thank, and Benedetto Croce too, both prepared to swallow anything in order to prevent the advance of the people. It had been precisely they, the liberals of our dreams, who had given Mussolini time to catch his breath. Less than six months later, the Duce repaid their help by suppressing freedom of the press and dissolving political parties. Giovanni Giolitti had retired from political life, withdrawing to his country estate in Piedmont; Benedetto Croce had returned to his beloved literary and philosophical studies. But there had been others, far less culpable, or, rather, entirely innocent, who had paid a much heavier price. Amendola and Gobetti had been beaten to death; Filippo Turati had died in exile, far from that Milan of his, where, a few years before, he had buried poor Signora Anna; Antonio Gramsci had made the acquaintance of our nation's prisons (he had died in prison last year: didn't we know that?); the Italian peasants and workers, along with their natural leaders, had lost all real hope of social justice and human dignity, and for almost twenty years now had been vegetating and dying in silence.

It was not easy, for me, to rebut these ideas, and for various reasons: in the first place, because Malnate's political knowledge, as he had breathed Socialism and anti-Fascism at home, from infancy, surpassed mine; in the second place, because the role in which he wanted to confine me—the role of the decadent man of letters, the "hermetic," as he said, whose political formation came from the books of Benedetto Croce—seemed ill-fitting, not corresponding to my true personality, and so, even before any other argument was begun between us, something to be refused. In the end I preferred to remain silent, assuming a vaguely ironic smile. I submitted, and I smiled.

As for Alberto, he too was silent: partly because, as usual, he had no objection to raise; but chiefly to allow his friend to inveigh against me, and especially content with this, it was all too clear. Among three people, closed in a room arguing for days and days, almost inevitably two end by banding together against the third. In any case, to be in agreement with Giampi, to show his solidarity, Alberto seemed ready to accept everything from him, including the fact that he, Giampi, often lumped him with me. It was true: Mussolini and company were piling up against the Italian Jews very serious and infamous acts and abuses—Malnate said—for example, the notorious Manifesto of the Race, last July, drawn up by the so-called Fascist scholars: it was hard to know whether to consider it more shameful or more ridiculous. But granted this—he added—could we tell him how many anti-Fascist "Israelites" there had been, before '38, in Italy? Very few, he feared, a tiny minority, if even in Ferrara, as Alberto had told him several times, the number of them belonging to the party had always been very high. I myself, in '36, had taken part in the Fascist Youth Cultural Competition. Was I already reading, at that time, Croce's *History of Europe?* Or had I waited, for its revelation, until the following year of the *Anschluss* and the first storm-warnings of Italian racism?

I submitted, and smiled, sometimes rebelling, but, more often than not, won over, despite myself, by his frankness and sincerity, a bit too crude and pitiless, to be sure, a bit too *goyishe*—so I said to myself—but, at heart, truly merciful, because truly equalizing, fraternal. And when Malnate, forgetting about me for a while, turned against Alberto, good-humoredly accusing him and his family of being "after all" a bunch of filthy landowners, grim absentee-proprietors, and aristocrats, what's more, nostalgic for medieval feudalism, so it was not really so unjust, "after all," that now they should somehow pay the penalty for the privileges they had enjoyed for so many years (Alberto would laugh till tears came to his eyes, at these invectives, and at the same time he would nod his head, yes, he, for his part, was quite ready to pay), it was not without a private self-satisfaction that I listened to him fulminate against his friend. The little boy of the pre-1929 years, the one who, walking beside his Mamma along the paths of the cemetery, could hear her every time call the solitary monumental tomb of the Finzi-Continis "a real horror," rose suddenly, from my innermost depths, to applaud maliciously.

There were moments, however, when Malnate seemed almost to forget my presence. These were when, with Alberto, he recalled the Milan years, their common friendships, male and female, of those times, the restaurants where they used to eat together, the evenings at La Scala, the football games at the arena or at San Siro, the winter excursions to the mountains and to the Riviera. They had both belonged to a "group," membership in which—it seemed—had only two requisites: intelligence, contempt for every form of provincialism and bombast. Those were the finest years of their youth, the years of Gladys, a vaudeville dancer who performed periodically at the Lirico, and had been for a time his, Giampi's, girl friend, and then, having taken a fancy to Alberto, who for that matter would never have anything to do with her, had finally given up the pair of them. She wasn't at all bad, our Gladys—Malnate narrated—jolly, "good company," not a gold digger, and just enough of a whore.

"I never could understand why Alberto always rejected Gladys," he said one evening, suddenly winking at me. Then, looking back at Alberto:

"Come on. More than three years have gone by since then, we're almost two hundred miles from the scene of the crime: how about putting your cards on the table at last?"

But Alberto fended him off, blushing; and on the subject of Gladys, cards were never put on the table: not on that occasion, or on others.

He liked the job he had come to do in Ferrara—he repeated often—he liked Ferrara, too, as a city, and he couldn't understand why Alberto and I felt the way we did about it, considering it a kind of grave, or prison. But our error, as usual, was in believing ourselves members of the only per-secuted minority in Italy, not realizing that there were plenty of other mi-norities suffering as much or more than we. The workers in the plant where he was employed, for example: what did we think they were? Unfeeling brutes? He had met some, on the contrary, who not only had not joined the party, but, being Socialists or Communists, and beaten up for this reason, went on unswervingly attached to their ideas. He had been to some of their secret meetings, with the happy surprise of finding there not only workers and peasants who had come all the way from Mésola and Goro, but also three or four lawyers, among the best known in the city: this was proof that here too, in Ferrara, not all the bourgeoisie was on the side of Fascism, not all sectors of it were traitors. Had we ever heard the name of Clelia Trotti? No? Well, she was a former elementary-school teacher, a little old woman, who, from what they had told him, as a girl had been the guiding light of local Socialism, and she still was! Though well past seventy, she never missed a meeting. That's where he had encountered her and come to know her. From her humanitarian Socialism, in the Andrea Costa style, there wasn't much to be expected, obviously. And yet what ardor she had, what faith, what hope! She reminded him, even physically, especially in those blue eyes of a former blond, of Signora Anna, the comrade of Filippo Tu-rati, whom he had known well as a boy, in Milan, around '22. His father, a lawyer, had done almost a year of prison together with the Turati couple, in '98. A close friend of both, he had remained one of the few who, on Sun-day afternoons, still dared visit them in their humble apartment in the Gal-leria. And Giampi had often gone along with him.

No, no: Ferrara was far from being the jail that, to hear us, one might believe it. Naturally, seen from the Industrial Zone, closed as it appeared within the circle of its ancient walls, the city could easily give an impres-sion of isolation, especially on days when the weather was bad. Around Ferrara there was still the country: rich, alive, hard-working; and at the end of the countryside, to the east, only twenty-five miles away, the sea, with deserted beaches edged by splendid forests of ilex and pine: the sea, to be sure, is always a great resource. But apart from this, the city itself, if one penetrated it, as he had decided to do, observing it closely, without preju-dices, contained, like any other, such treasures of rectitude, intelligence, and goodness that only the blind and the deaf, or else the sterile, could have been unaware of them, or deny them.

# V

At the beginning, Alberto was constantly announcing his imminent departure for Milan. Then, gradually, he stopped talking about it, and the question of his thesis finally became, for me and perhaps also for Malnate, embarrassing, a subject to be cautiously avoided. He never referred to it; and, it was obvious that he also wanted us to forget it.

As I have mentioned before, his participation in our arguments was rare, and always slight. He was on Malnate's side: no doubt about that. But as a follower, never taking the least initiative. His eyes were on his friend every instant, happy if he was winning, concerned if, on the contrary, I seemed to be emerging the victor. Otherwise, he was silent, at most coming out from time to time with some exclamation ("Ah, that's a good one! . . ."; "Well, but only certain aspects  . . ."; "Wait a moment; let's look at this more carefully"), but confining himself for the most part to an occasional little laugh, or a clearing of the throat.

Even physically he tended to remain to one side, to disappear, to erase himself. Malnate and I generally sat facing each other, in the center of the room, one on the sofa, the other in one of the two armchairs: with the table between us, both of us in the light; and once seated, we didn't stand up, practically speaking, except to go into the little bath off the bedroom, or else to peer, through the panes of the broad window overlooking the park, at the state of the weather. Alberto, on the other hand, preferred to stay at the end of the room, sheltered behind the double barricade of the desk and the drafting table. Quite often we would see him, however, roam here and there about the room, on tiptoe, his elbows pressed against his sides. One after the other, he changed records on the gramophone, always making sure that the volume did not drown our voices; he supervised the ashtrays, taking care, when they were full, to empty them in the bath; he regulated the intensity of the indirect lighting; he asked softly if we wanted more tea; he corrected the position of certain objects. He had the busy and discreet look of a host concerned with only one thing: that his guests' important brains be allowed to function in the best possible atmospheric conditions.

And yet, I am certain, the chief reason for that vague sense of oppression which, on entering, I had immediately felt, was he, with his meticulous order, with his constant, obsessive attentions. When, for example, during the pauses in the conversation, he began illustrating, say, the virtues of the chair in which he was sitting, whose back—he said—had been "studied" deliberately to give the vertebrae the absolutely correct and proper "anatomical" position; or when, perhaps, having offered me his tobacco pouch, to fill my pipe, he would recall to me the various qualities of rough cut which, in his opinion, were indispensable to the optimum functioning of our respective Dunhill and G.B.D. (so much mild, so much strong, so much Maryland); or finally when, for reasons that were never very clear, known to him alone, he would announce, smiling, the temporary exclusion of one or two of the loudspeakers arranged for the diffusion of the gramophone's sound: in each of these circumstances, a nervous breaking point, an uncontrolled rebellion, was always latent in me, always just about to explode.

One evening, in fact, I was unable to restrain myself. Of course—I shouted, addressing Malnate—his dilettante attitude, a tourist's basically, allowed him to assume towards our city an indulgence, a forbearance that I envied him. But he who spoke so much about treasures of rectitude, intelligence, and goodness, how would he judge something that had happened to me, to me personally, only a few mornings before?

I had had the fine idea—I began to narrate—of settling down with my books and papers in the reference room of the Municipal Library on Via Scienze: a place where I had spent a great deal of time in the last few years, but where I had been known since my *ginnasio* days, mind you, because it was there, in fact, that I usually took refuge whenever a threat of being interrogated in mathematics counseled me to skip school. It was a second home for me, that room, and everybody there, especially since I had enrolled in literature at the university, had always overwhelmed me with kindness. Since then, the librarian, Dr. Ballola, had begun to consider me a colleague, and every time he saw me in the room, he would come and sit next to me and confide in me the progress of certain studies of his which for decades now had been devoted to the biographical material on Ariosto, preserved in his little private office, research thanks to which (he told me) he was counting on definitely surpassing Catalano's achievements, outstanding as they were, in this field. And what of the various employees? They behaved towards me with such friendliness and familiarity that they exempted me from the nuisance of filling out, every time, the little slip for each book I wanted to read, and they even allowed me, on days when there were few people in the room, to smoke an occasional cigarette.

Anyway, as I was saying, I had had the fine idea of spending that morning in the library. But I had barely had time to sit down at a desk in the reference room, and take my things from my leather briefcase, when one of the attendants, a certain Poledrelli, a man of about sixty, heavy, jovial, famous pasta-eater, and incapable of saying two words in a row that weren't dialect, had come over to order me to leave, and at once. Pulling in his belly, his chest thrown out, and managing even to express himself in proper Italian, that excellent Poledrelli had explained in a loud, official voice that the librarian had given explicit instructions in this matter: whereby—he had repeated—I would please get up and clear out. That morning the reference room had been particularly crowded with girls from the middle school. The scene had been observed, in a sepulchral silence, by no less than fifty pairs of eyes, and by the same number of pairs of ears. Well, for this reason too—I continued—it hadn't been at all pleasant for me to pull myself up, collect books and papers from the desk, replace everything in my case, and then, one step after another, reach the glass entrance door. All right: that wretched Poledrelli had only been carrying out orders. However, he, Malnate, should be very careful, if by chance he were to meet him (it wasn't impossible that Poledrelli also belonged to the circle of Signora Trotti!), he should be very careful not to be taken in by the false appearance of good nature on that broad, plebeian face. Inside that chest, thick as an armoire, there was housed a heart this tiny: rich in folk humors, all right, but not at all to be trusted!

And besides, besides—I insisted—wasn't it, to say the least, out of place for him, Malnate, to come and preach, not so much to Alberto, whose family had always kept aloof from the city's community life, but to me, who, on the contrary, had been born and had grown up in an environment all too prepared to open itself trustingly, to mingle in every possible way with the others? My father, a volunteer in the war, had taken out his party card in '19: I myself had belonged to the Young Fascist University Students until a short time before. In other words, we had always been very normal people, even banal in our normality: for which reason it seemed to me downright absurd that now, all of a sudden, exceptional behavior was demanded of us. Summoned to the provincial party headquarters to hear his expulsion from the party announced to him; expelled then from the Merchants Club as undesirable: it would have been really strange if my father, poor man, were to oppose to such treatment a countenance less anguished and bewildered than the one I had come to know. And my brother, Ernesto, who, in order to enter the university, had to emigrate to France and enroll at the Grenoble Polytechnic? And Fanny, my little sister, when barely thirteen, forced to continue her *ginnasio* studies in the Jewish school on Via Vignatagliata? Did he expect exceptional behavior of them, too, brusquely torn away from their childhood friends? No, no! One of the most odious forms of anti-Semitism was precisely this: to complain that the Jews were not *enough* like the others and then, vice versa, having ascertained their almost total assimilation into their surroundings, to complain of the opposite: that they were just like the others, not even a bit different from the average, the ordinary.

I had let my anger run away with me, and had overstepped the bounds of the debate, and Malnate, who had listened to me carefully, did not fail to point this out to me. Anti-Semite, him?—he grumbled. It was the first time, frankly, that he had heard such an accusation directed at him! Still aroused, I was about to reply, to go further. But at that moment, as he was passing behind my adversary's back with the jerky rapidity of a frightened bird, Alberto gave me an imploring look. "Please ! Enough!" his gaze said. That he, in secret from his bosom friend, should for once appeal to what was mòst intimate between the two of us, struck me as an extraordinary event. I didn't reply; I didn't say anything else. Immediately, the first notes of some Beethoven, played by the Busch Quartet, rose in the smoky atmosphere of the room, to seal my victory.

That evening, it must be added, was important not only for this. Towards eight it began to rain with such violence that Alberto, after a rapid telephone consultation in their private language, probably with his mother, suggested we stay to supper.

Malnate declared himself quite happy to accept. He almost always ate supper at Giovanni's—he told us—"as lonely as a stray dog": so nothing could please him more than spending a "family evening." I also accepted. I asked, however, if I could telephone home.

"Naturally!" Alberto exclaimed.

I sat down where he was usually seated, behind the desk, and I dialed the number. As I waited, I looked to one side, through the windowpanes streaked with rain. In the thick darkness the clumps of trees could barely be discerned. Beyond the black interval of the park, who knows where, a little light flickered.

My father's whining voice answered.

"Ah, it's you?" he said. "We were beginning to worry. Where are you calling from?"

"I won't be home for supper," I answered.

"With this rain!"

"Exactly."

"Are you still at the Finzi-Continis?"

"Yes."

"No matter what time you come home, look in on me, please. I can never get to sleep anyway, you know. . . ."

I hung up and raised my eyes. Alberto was looking at me.

"Done?" he asked.

"Done."

The three of us went out into the corridor, passed through various rooms, small and large, and descended a broad stairway at the foot of which, in white jacket and gloves, Perotti was waiting; and from there we went directly into the dining room.

The rest of the family was already present. There were Professor Ermanno, Signora Olga, Signora Regina, and one of the Venice uncles, the phthisiologist, who, seeing Alberto enter, stood up, went to him, kissed him on both cheeks, after which, as he absently depressed the lower lid of one eye with his finger, began to tell him why he was there: he had been called to Bologna for a consultation—he said—and then, on his way back, he had thought to stop off for supper, between trains. When we entered, Professor Ermanno, his wife, and his brother-in-law were sitting in front of the burning fire, with Jor stretched out full-length at their feet. Signora Regina, on the other hand, was seated at the table, directly under the central lamp.

Inevitably my recollection of my first supper at the Finzi-Continis (it was January, I believe) tends to be a bit confused, in me, with the memory of many other suppers I shared in the *magna domus* in the course of that same winter. Nevertheless I recall with curious precision what we ate that evening: a soup of rice and chicken livers in broth, minced turkey in galantine, jugged tongue with black olives and pickled celery stalks, a chocolate cake, fruit and nuts: walnuts, hazelnuts, pine nuts, raisins. I also remember that, almost at once, as soon as we were seated at the table, Alberto took it upon himself to report my story of the recent expulsion from the Municipal Library, and that once more I was impressed by the scant amazement this news aroused in the four old people. Their comments on the general situation, and on the Ballola-Poledrelli pair, mentioned from time to time throughout the meal, were in fact, on the part of those four, not even very bitter, but, as usual, elegantly sarcastic, almost merry. And merry, decidedly merry and content, was Professor Ermanno's tone of voice, later, when, having taken me by the arm, he suggested that from now on I should take advantage, freely, when and how I liked, of the almost twenty thousand volumes in the house, a considerable number of which—he told me—dealt with Italian literature of the middle and late nineteenth century.

But what struck me most, from that very first evening, was undoubtedly the dining room itself: its furniture of reddish wood, in art nouveau style, its vast fireplace with its curved, sinuous mouth, almost human, and the walls covered in leather, except for one, all glass, which framed the dark, silent tempest of the park like the porthole of the *Nautilus*: so intimate, so private, I would almost say so buried: so suited, especially, to the me of that time, now I understand it! to protect that kind of lazy ember that is so often the heart of the young.

Crossing its threshold, both Malnate and I were received with great cordiality, and not only by Professor Ermanno, kindly, jovial, and lively as always, but even by Signora Olga. She was the one who had arranged the seating. Malnate had been given the place at her right; I, at the other end of the table, that on the right of her husband; her brother Giulio was seated at her left: between herself—his sister—and their old mother. The last, meanwhile, beautiful, with her rosy cheeks, her silky white hair, thicker and more luminous than ever, looked around, benign and amused.

The place opposite mine, complete with plates, glasses, and cutlery, seemed to be waiting for a seventh person. As Perotti was going around with the tureen of soup, I asked Professor Ermanno for whom the place at his left was reserved. And he, in the same whisper, had answered that "presumably" that place was awaiting no one now (he checked the time with his big Omega wristwatch, shook his head, sighed), since that was the chair usually occupied by Micòl: "my Micòl," he said, to be precise.

# VI

Professor Ermanno had not been boasting. It was true: among the almost twenty thousand books of the house, many concerned with scientific or historical subjects, or with various erudite fields—in German, most of these last—there were several hundred devoted to the literature of the New Italy. Among the publications that had appeared in Carducci's circle at the end of the century, during the decades when Carducci taught in Bologna, you could say there was not one gap. There were not only the volumes of the master in verse and prose, but also the works of Panzacchi, Severino Ferrari, Lorenzo Stecchetti, Ugo Brilli, Guido Mazzoni, the young Pascoli, the young Panzini, the very young Valgimigli: first editions, as a rule, almost all inscribed to Baroness Josette Artom di Susegana. Collected in three isolated glass cabinets, which occupied an entire wall of a vast ground-floor room next to Professor Ermanno's private study; carefully catalogued: these books, taken all together, formed a collection that would have been the boast of any public library, not excepting Bologna's Archiginnasio. The collection included even the little volumes of prose lyrics, almost impossible to find, by Francesco Acri, the famous translator of Plato, known to me, at that time, only as translator: not so "sainted," after all, as Professor Meldolesi in the fifth *ginnasio* had assured us he was— Meldolesi had been Acri's pupil—if his dedications to the grandmother of Alberto and Micòl displayed, in the general chorus, perhaps the greatest gallantry, the greatest male awareness of the haughty beauty to which they referred.

Now I had an entire specialized library at my disposal, and I was curiously eager to be there every morning, in the great, warm, silent room, which received light from three high windows decorated with valences of white silk with vertical red stripes, and in whose center, covered by a mouse-colored cloth, the billiard table stood; and so in the two and a half months that followed, I succeeded in finishing my thesis on Panzacchi. If I had really tried, perhaps, I might have managed to complete it even sooner. But was this what I wanted? Or didn't I want, on the contrary, to retain as long as possible the right to turn up at the Finzi-Contini house *also* in the morning? The fact is that in about mid-March (meanwhile news of Micòl's degree had arrived: top marks), I was still there, lazily attached to that poor privilege of mine, the use, also in the morning, of the house from which she obstinately remained far away. Only a few days were left before the Christian Easter, which coincided that year more or less with Pesach, the Jewish Passover. Though spring was now almost upon us, it had snowed a week before with extraordinary abundance, and afterwards the cold had become intense again. It seemed as if winter refused to go away, in other words. And I, too, my heart inhabited by a dark, mysterious lake of fear, clung to the little desk which Professor Ermanno, the previous January, had had placed for me in the billiard room, beneath the central window, as if, in doing so, I were able to resist the irresistible advance of time. I would stand up, go to the window, look down into the park. Buried beneath a blanket of snow fifteen inches deep, the Barchetto del Duca, all white, appeared to me transformed into the landscape of a Nordic saga. At times I caught myself hoping precisely this: that snow and ice would never melt, that they would last forever.

For two and a half months my days had been, you could say, all the same. As punctual as an employee, I would leave home in the eight-thirty cold, almost always on my bicycle but sometimes on foot; after twenty minutes at most, I would be ringing the bell of the entrance at the end of Corso Ercole I d'Este, to cross the park then, pervaded, around the beginning of February, by the delicate scent of the yellow calicanthus flower; at nine I was already at work, in the billiard room, where I would stay till one, and where I would return at three in the afternoon; later, around six, I would drop in on Alberto, sure to find Malnate there too; and finally, as I said before, both of us were frequently invited to supper. It soon became so normal, for me, to stay out to supper, in fact, that I didn't even telephone home any more. On leaving, I may have said to Mamma: "I think I'll be staying there to supper this evening." There: no further clarification was necessary.

I would work for hours and hours, without anyone's putting in an appearance: except Perotti, around eleven, bringing a little cup of coffee on a silver tray. This, too, the coffee at eleven, became a daily rite almost at once, a recognized custom, on the subject of which neither he nor I felt it necessary to waste words. What Perotti did talk about with me, as he waited for me to finish sipping the coffee, was, if anything, the "running" of the house, gravely compromised, in his view, by the too-prolonged absence of the "signorina," who, to be sure, had to become a professoressa, although (and this "although," accompanied by a dubious grimace, could refer to many things: to the fact that the rich, lucky they, had no necessity to earn a living, or to the racial laws which, in any case, would make *our* diplomas mere pieces of paper, without the slightest practical use) . . . but, still, even a quick visit, because without her, the house was rapidly going to rack and ruin . . . she could have made a quick visit, perhaps every other week. With me, Perotti always found a reason to complain about the family. As a sign of mistrust and disapproval, he would purse his lips, wink, shake his head. When he mentioned Signora Olga, he would even touch his forehead with his rough forefinger. I didn't encourage him, naturally, firmly rejecting his repeated invitations to a servant's complicity, which not only revolted, but also offended me; and a little later, in the face of my silences, my cold smiles, Perotti could only go off, leaving me once more alone.

One day, in his place, his younger daughter came, Dirce. She also waited beside the desk until I had finished the coffee. I drank it, and I peered at her.

"What's your name?" I asked her, handing back the empty cup, as my heart meanwhile had begun racing.

"Dirce." She smiled, and her face was covered with blushes.

She was wearing her usual smock of heavy blue cotton, with its curious nursery smell. She ran off, avoiding any reply to my gaze, which was trying to meet hers. And a moment later I was already ashamed of what had happened (but what, after all, had happened?), as if of the most base and sordid betrayal.

Of the family, the only one who appeared every now and then was Professor Ermanno. He opened the door of his study, there at the end, with such caution, to proceed then, on tiptoe, across the room, that most times I became aware of him only when he was already there at my side, bent respectfully over the books and papers I had before me.

"How's it going?" he would ask, pleased. "We seem to be progressing under full sail!"

I started to get up.

"No, no, keep on with your work," he exclaimed. "I'll be going in a moment."

And as a rule, he never stayed more than five minutes, during which he always found a way to show me all the fondness, all the esteem that my tenacity at my work inspired in him. He looked at me with glowing, shining eyes: as if from me, from my future as a man of letters, as a scholar, he expected who knows what; as if he were counting on me for some secret ambition of his, that transcended not only himself, but me as well. . . . And I remember, on this score, how this attitude of his towards me, though it flattered me, also grieved me a little. Why didn't he expect as much of Alberto—I wondered—who was, after all, his son? For what reason did he accept, from Alberto, without protests or regrets—in fact, he never complained—the renunciation of taking a degree? And Micòl? In Venice, Micòl was doing the exact same thing I was doing: completing her thesis. And yet there was never a time that he mentioned Micòl, or if he referred to her, he sighed. He seemed to be saying: "She's a girl, and it's best for women to think of the home, to forget about literature!" But could I really believe him?

One morning he lingered longer than usual to converse. After some twists and turns, he brought up once more the Carducci letters and his own "little works" about Venice: all things—he said, nodding towards his study, behind my back—that he kept "in there." He was smiling mysteriously, meanwhile, a sly and inviting expression on his face. It was clear: he wanted to take me "in there," and at the same time, he wanted me to be the one to ask him to take me.

As soon as I realized what was wanted of me, I hastened to satisfy his wish. So we moved into the study, a room only a little less vast than the billiard room, but made smaller still—indeed, cramped—by an incredible congeries of disparate things.

To begin with, there were countless books here also. Those on literary subjects mixed with scientific works—mathematics, physics, economy, agriculture, medicine, astronomy—those of local history, of Ferrara or Venice, with those of "Judaic antiquity": the volumes filled, in disorder, at random, the usual glass cases, and òccupied a good part of the big walnut table beyond which, after Professor Ermanno sat down, only the top of his cap emerged; they were heaped up in precarious stacks on the chairs, had accumulated even on the floor, in piles scattered more or less everywhere. A big globe, a reading stand, a microscope, half a dozen barometers, a steel safe painted dark red, a snowy-white cot, like one in a doctor's office, various hourglasses of different sizes, a brass drum, a little upright piano, German, surmounted by two metronomes closed in their pyramidal cases, and many other objects, besides these, of uncertain function, which I cannot remember, gave the place the air of a Faustian study at which he, Professor Ermanno, was the first to smile and apologize, as if for a completely personal, private weakness: as if for a relic of youthful whims. I was forgetting, however, to say that, unlike almost all the other rooms of the house, generally overladen with paintings, here there was only one picture: an enormous life-size portrait, by Lenbach, looming like an altarpiece on the wall behind the table. The splendid blond lady portrayed in it, standing erect, her shoulders bare, a fan in her gloved hand, with the silken train of her white dress brought forward to emphasize the length of her legs and the fullness of her figure, was none other, obviously, than Baroness Josette Artom de Susegana. What a marble brow, what eyes, what a disdainful lip, what a bosom! She really seemed a queen. His mother's portrait was the only thing, among the countless things present in the study, at which Professor Ermanno did not smile: that morning, or ever.

It was on that same morning, moreover, that I was finally presented with the two little Venetian essays. In one of them—the Professor explained to me—he had collected and translated all the epitaphs in the Jewish cemetery on the Lido. The second, on the other hand, dealt with a Jewish poetess who had lived in Venice in the first half of the seventeenth century, as well known in her own day as, "unfortunately," she was now forgotten. Her name was Sara Enriquez (or Enriques) Avigdòr. In her house in the Ghetto Vecchio she had held for some decades an important literary salon, assiduously frequented not only by the learned Ferrarese-Venetian rabbi Leone da Modena, but also by many outstanding literary figures of the period, and not only Italians. She had written numerous "excellent" sonnets, which were still awaiting the person capable of reclaiming their beauty; she had kept up a brilliant correspondence, for more than four years, with the famous Ansaldo Cebà, a Genoese gentleman, author of an epic poem on Queen Esther; he had got it into his head to convert her to Catholicism, but then, finally, when he saw all his insistence was useless, he had been forced to give up the idea. A great woman, in short: an honor and a boast of Italian Jewry in the full tide of the Counter Reformation, and also "a kind of relative"—Professor Ermanno added, as he sat down to write a brief dedication—since it seemed established that his wife, in the maternal line, had descended from her.

He stood up, came around the table, took my arm, and led me to the window.

There was one thing, however—he went on, lowering his voice as if afraid someone might overhear—he felt obliged to inform me of. If, in the future, by any chance I happened to concern myself with this Sara Enriquez (or Enriques) Avigdòr—and the subject was one that deserved a far more careful and profound study than he, as a young man, had been capable of—at a certain point, inevitably, I would have to deal with some hostile . . . dissenting opinion . . . that is, with certain writings of fourth-rate scribblers, most of them contemporaries of the poetess (wretched libels, brimming over with envy and anti-Semitism), which tried to insinuate that not all the sonnets circulated with her signature, and not all the letters written by her to Cebà, were . . . hem . . . entirely her own work. Now he, in composing his monograph, had certainly not been able to ignore the existence of such gossip; and in fact, as I would see, he had dutifully recorded it; still . . .

He broke off, to look me in the face, suspicious of my reactions.

Still—he went on—even if I, "sometime in the future," were to think . . . hem . . . decide to attempt a new evaluation . . . a fresh approach . . . he advised me already not to pay too much attention to malicious stories, perhaps picturesque, yes, even amusing, but finally misleading. After all, what is the first-rate historian's job? To set, naturally, as his ideal, the arrival at the truth, without, however, losing his sense of propriety and justice along the way. Didn't I agree?

I nodded my head in a sign of assent, and he, relieved, gave me a little pat on the shoulder with the palm of his hand.

This done, he moved away from me, and crossed the study; then, hunched over, he bent to fiddle with the safe, opened it, and took out a little coffer covered in blue velvet.

He turned and, all smiles, came back towards the window, and even before opening the coffer, he said that he had guessed that I had guessed: in it were preserved the famous Carducci letters. They amounted to fifteen; and I would probably—he added—not consider all of them of great interest, since five of the fifteen dealt solely with a certain kind of sausage, "from our land," that the poet, having been presented with some, seemed to appreciate highly. Nevertheless, among the other letters, I would find one that would surely impress me. It was a letter of autumn '75, written, that is, when the crisis of the Historic Right was already becoming discernible on the horizon. In the autumn of '75, Carducci's political position was as follows: though a democrat, republican, and revolutionary, Carducci declared he could not side with the Left of Agostino Depretis. On the contrary, "the bristling vintner of Stradella," and the "hordes" of his friends, seemed to him vulgar, "petty" people. They would never be able to guide Italy to her destiny, to make of Italy a great nation, worthy of the ancient fathers . . .

We remained talking until midday-dinner time. With, then, the following result: from that morning on, the communicating door, instead of remaining always closed, was always open. The greater part of the time each of us spent in his own room, of course. But we saw each other far more frequently than before: Professor Ermanno, coming to me, and I, going to him. Through the door, when it was open, we even exchanged a few sentences: "What time is it?" "How's the work progressing?" and so on. A few years later, during the spring of '43, the words I was to exchange, in prison, with the unknown man in the next cell, shouting them towards the ceiling, towards the air vent, would be of that sort: uttered like that, chiefly through the need of hearing one's own voice, of feeling alive.

# VII

At our house that year, Passover was not celebrated with two successive suppers, but with only one.

My father made this decision. With Ernesto off studying in France—he said—there was really no point in our spending Passover as we had in past years. And, anyway, how could we? They, *my* Finzi-Continis, once again had been very clever: with the pretext of the garden, they had managed to keep all the maidservants they wanted, passing them off as farm workers assigned to raising vegetables. But what about us? Since we had had to discharge Elisa and Mariuccia, and take in their place that dreary old Cohen woman, we, practically speaking, no longer had anyone. In such conditions, not even our mother could work miracles.

"Isn't that so, my angel?"

His "angel" did not entertain sentiments much warmer than my father's towards the sixty-year-old Signorina Ricca Cohen, distinguished pensioner of the community. Enjoying herself, as always, when she heard one of us speak ill of the poor woman, my mother also accepted with sincere gratitude the idea of a more modest Passover. All right—she had approved—just one supper, the first evening, and with a maximum of ten guests: that was easy to prepare. She and Fanny would manage almost on their own, without "that one"—and she nodded meanwhile towards la Cohen, spontaneously self-exiled in the kitchen—throwing one of her usual fits of sulks. Yes, and another thing: so "that one" wouldn't be forced to make too many trips with plates and bowls, risking some disaster, unsteady on her legs as she was, we could make another change: instead of in the living room, so far from the kitchen, and this year, with the snow, colder than Siberia, instead of in the living room, we could prepare the table here, in the breakfast room. . . .

It was not a jolly supper. In the center of the table, the basket that, along with the ritual "morsels," contained the bowls of *haròset*, the clumps of bitter herbs, the unleavened bread, and the special hard-boiled egg for me, the first-born, stood there, in vain, under the cloth of blue and white silk, embroidered forty years ago by Grandmother Ester. Though set with great care, indeed, for this very reason, the table in the breakfast room had taken on an appearance quite similar to the one it presented on the evenings of Kippur, when it was prepared only for Them, for the family dead, whose bones lay there, in the cemetery, down at the end of Via Montebello, and yet They were quite present here, in spirit and in effigy. Here, in their places, we were seated, the living. But our number reduced, compared to the past, and no longer happy, laughing, vociferous, but sad and pensive like the dead. I looked at my father and mother, both aged considerably in the last few months; I looked at Fanny, who was now fifteen, but, as if an occult fear had arrested her development, she seemed no more than twelve; one by one, around me, I looked at uncles and cousins, most of whom, a few years later, would be swallowed up by German crematory ovens: they didn't imagine, no, surely not, that they would end in that way, but all the same, already, that evening, even if they seemed so insignificant to me, their poor faces surmounted by their little bourgeois hats or framed by their bourgeois permanents, even if I knew how dull-witted they were, how incapable of evaluating the real significance of the present or of reading into the future, they seemed to me already surrounded by the same aura of mysterious, statuary fatality that surrounds them now, in my memory; I looked at old Signorina Cohen, the few times she ventured to peep in from the kitchen door: Ricca Cohen, the respectable sixty-year-old spinster who had come from the home on Via Vittoria to act as servant in a house of well-to-do co-religionists, but who wanted nothing so much as to go back there, to the home, and, before times got worse, to die there; I looked, finally, at myself, reflected in the opaque water of the mirror opposite, I, too, already a bit gray, I, too, caught in the same mechanism, and yet rebellious, not yet resigned. I was not dead—I told myself—I was still quite alive! But then, if I was still living, why did I stay here with the others, to what end? Why didn't I evade, at once, that desperate and grotesque assembly of ghosts, or at least stop my ears so as to hear no more talk of "discrimination" and "patriotic merits" and "certificates of services," of "blood quotients," and so on, not to hear the petty lamenting, the monotonous, gray, futile threnody that family and kin were softly intoning around me? The supper would go on like that, among repetitions, discussions, for who knows how many hours yet, with my father recalling every now and then, with bitter delight, the various "insults" he had had to undergo during those last months, starting with the day when, at party headquarters, the provincial secretary, Consul Bolognesi, had announced, with guilty, grieving eyes, that he had been forced to "cancel" him from the list of party members, and ending when, with eyes no less sad, the president of the Merchants Club had sent for him to inform him that he was to consider himself "resigned." He had plenty to tell, all right! Until midnight, one, two in the morning! And then? Then there would be the grand finale, the scene of the farewells. I could already see it. We had all gone down, in a body, along the dark stairs, like an oppressed flock. Reaching the entrance, someone (perhaps I) had gone ahead, to open the big door on to the street, and now, for the last time, before separating, the good-nights were renewed by everyone, me included, the best wishes, the handshakes, the embraces, the kisses on the cheeks. But then, suddenly, from the door, which had remained half-open there, against the night's blackness, a gust of wind comes into the entrance. It is a storm wind, and it comes from the night. It bursts into the entrance, crosses it, passes, whistling, through the gates that separate the entrance passage from the garden, and meanwhile it has scattered, with its force, those who wanted still to linger, it has silenced abruptly, with its savage cry, those who were loitering to converse. Faint voices, then cries, promptly drowned. Swept away, all of them: like fragile leaves, like scraps of paper, like hairs from a head whitened by years, or by terror . . . Oh, Ernesto, after all, had been lucky to be unable to go to the university in Italy. He wrote, from Grenoble, that he was suffering hunger, that, with the little French he knew, he could understand almost nothing of the lectures at the polytechnic. But he was lucky to suffer hunger and to have trouble passing his exams: mathematics, especially! I had remained here, and for me, who had remained, and who once again, out of pride and sterility, had chosen solitude, nourishing it with vague, nebulous, impotent hopes, for me in reality there was no hope, no hope for *anything*.

But who could tell? What can we know, of ourselves, and of what lies ahead of us?

Towards eleven, in fact, while my father, with the obvious aim of dissipating the general gloom, had begun to sing the Passover jingle of the *Caprèt ch'avea comperà il signor Padre* (this song, "The goat the father had bought," was, as he said, his "best number"), I happened at a certain point, raising my eyes by chance to the mirror opposite, to notice the door of the telephone booth open slightly, slowly behind my back. Through the aperture, old Signorina Cohen's face cautiously peeped out. She was looking at me, yes, at me; and she seemed almost to be asking for help.

I got up, I went to her.

"What is it?"

She nodded towards the receiver, hanging by the line, and she disappeared in the other direction, through the door into the front hall.

Left alone, in the most absolute darkness, even before putting the receiver to my ear, I recognized Alberto's voice.

"I hear singing," he shouted, strangely festive. "How far have you got?"

"To the *Caprèt ch'avea comperà il signor Padre*," I answered.

"Ah, good. We've finished already. Why don't you drop by?"

"Now!" I exclaimed, amazed.

"Why not? The conversation here is beginning to languish, and you, with your well-known resources, could certainly liven it up." He laughed. "And besides . . ." he added, "we've prepared a surprise for you."

"A surprise? What might it be?"

"Come and you'll see."

"How mysterious!" My heart was beating furiously. "Cards on the table."

"Come on. Don't wait to be coaxed. I told you: you'll see when you get here."

I slipped into the hall, took my overcoat, muffler, and hat, I stuck my head into the kitchen, telling Signorina Cohen in a whisper to say, if they asked for me, that I had gone out for a moment; two minutes later I was on my way.

It was a splendid moonlit night, icy, very clear. In the streets there were no passersby, or almost none, and Corso Giovecca and Corso Ercole I d'Este, smooth and unencumbered, and of an almost saline whiteness, opened before me like two broad racetracks. I pedaled in the center of the street, in full light, my ears aching with the cold; but at supper I had drunk several glasses of wine, and I didn't feel the cold; in fact, I was sweating. My front tire barely rustled over the caked snow, and the dry flurry it raised filled me with a sense of risky joy, as if I were skiing. I went fast, with no fear of skidding. Meanwhile I was thinking of the surprise that according to Alberto's words, I was to expect at the Finzi-Continis'. What was it: had Micòl come back, perhaps? Strange, however. Why, then, hadn't she come, herself, to the telephone? And why, before supper, hadn't she been seen in temple? If she had been there, I would already have known it. My father, at table, making his usual review of those present at the service (he had done this also on my account: to reproach me indirectly for not having attended) would surely not have neglected to name her. He had named them all, Finzi-Continis and Herreras, but not her. Could she perhaps have arrived, on her own, at the last moment, on the 9:45 express?

In an even more intense brightness of snow and moon, I entered and rode through the Barchetto del Duca. Halfway, just before crossing the bridge over the Panfilio Canal, I saw a gigantic shadow loom up before me. It was Jor. I recognized him, my fright was changed into an almost equally paralyzing presentiment, within me. So it was true—I said to myself—Micòl had come home. Alerted by the bell from the street entrance, she had risen from the table, come downstairs, and now, having sent Jor ahead to meet me, she was waiting for me on the threshold of the little side door used exclusively by the family and intimate friends. A few more turns of my wheels, and then Micòl herself: a small dark form, engraved on a background of very white light, like a power station's, with her shoulders grazed by the protective breath of the radiator. Another few seconds and I would hear her voice, her "ciao."

"Ciao," Micòl said, standing in the doorway. "How good of you to come."

I had foreseen everything with great precision: everything except that I would kiss her. I had got down from my bicycle, I had answered: "Ciao. When did you get here?" She had still had time to answer: "This afternoon, I traveled with my uncles"; and then . . . then I had kissed her. It had happened suddenly. But how? I was still standing with my face hidden against her warm, perfumed neck (it was a strange perfume, a mixture of childish flesh and talcum), and I was already asking myself, How had it happened? I had embraced her, she had made a weak attempt to resist, and then had let me have my way. Was this how it had gone? Perhaps it had gone like this. But now?

I moved away slowly. Now she was there, her face ten inches from mine. I stared at her, without speaking or moving, incredulous, already incredulous. Leaning against the door jamb, her shoulders covered by a black woolen shawl, she too was staring at me in silence. She looked into my eyes, and her gaze entered me, straight, sure, hard: with the limpid inexorability of a sword.

I was the first to look away.

"Forgive me," I murmured.

"Forgive what? I was the one who did the wrong thing, perhaps, coming to meet you. It's my fault."

She shook her head. Then she smiled a brief, good, affectionate smile.

"What beautiful snow!" she said, pointing to the park with her chin. "Just think: it never snowed in Venice, not an inch. If I had known so much had fallen here . . ."

She ended with a gesture of her hand, her right hand. She had brought it out from beneath the shawl, and I immediately noticed a ring.

I grasped her wrist.

"What's that?" I asked, touching the ring with the tip of my forefinger.

"I'm *engaged*: didn't you know?"

Immediately afterwards, she burst into loud laughter.

"No, no, come . . ." she said. "Can't you see I'm joking? It's just a cheap little ring. Look."

She took it off with a great movement of her elbows, gave it to me, and it really was a cheap little ring: a gold band with a small turquoise. Her grandmother Regina had given it to her years ago—she explained—hiding it inside a chocolate Easter egg.

When I had given back the ring, she slipped it on again, then took my hand.

"Come in now," she whispered, "otherwise, upstairs"—and she laughed—"they might even be worried."

As we went, still holding hands (on the stairs she stopped, examined my lips in the light, concluding the examination with a nonchalant "Excellent!"), she never stopped talking a minute.

Yes—she said—the thesis business had come off better than she had dared hope. In the oral discussion, she had "held forth" for a good hour "haranguing left and right." In the end they had sent her out of the room, and from beyond the frosted glass door of the *aula magna* she had been able to overhear "clear as a bell" everything the committee of professors had said about her. The majority was in favor of a *cum laude*, but there was one, the German professor (a Nazi of the first water) who wouldn't hear of it. He had been quite explicit, "the worthy gentleman." According to him, the *cum laude* could not have been awarded without causing very serious scandal. What!—he cried—the young person was a Jew, and had not even been expelled, and now they were actually thinking of giving her honors! Good Lord! It was already a great concession, letting her take her degree. . . . The committee secretary, the English professor, had argued back very forcefully that school was school, that intelligence and serious study (too kind of him!) had nothing to do with blood strains, et cetera, et cetera. But it came time to reach conclusions; obvious, predictable triumph for the Nazi. And the only satisfaction left her—apart from the apologies, later, from the English professor, who had run after her down the steps of Ca' Foscari (poor thing: his chin was trembling, there were tears in his eyes)—the only satisfaction left her was to receive the verdict, giving them the most perfect Roman salute. The head of the department, as he named her doctor of letters, had raised his arm. What was she supposed to do? Confine herself to a pretty toss of her head? No, indeed!

She laughed gaily, and I also laughed, excited, telling her, for my part, with abundant comic details, about my eviction from the Municipal Library. But when I asked her why, after taking her degree, she had stayed on in Venice another month (in Venice—I added—where, to hear her, not only had she never felt at home, but also where she had no friends, male or female): at this point she turned grave, withdrew her hand from mine, giving me—her only reply—a rapid, sidelong glance.

A foretaste of the happy welcome we would receive in the dining room was given us by Perotti, waiting in the vestibule. As soon as he saw us come down the great staircase, followed by Jor, he flashed us an extraordinarily satisfied smile, almost a smile of complicity. On another occasion, his behavior would have irked me, I would have felt offended by it. But for some minutes I had been in a quite special mood. Stifling within me all reasons for uneasiness, I was proceeding, enriched with a strange lightness, as if borne on invisible wings. After all, Perotti was a good sort—I was thinking. He was also pleased that the "signorina" had come home. Could I blame him, poor old man? From now on he would surely stop grumbling.

We presented ourselves, side by side, in the doorway of the dining room, and our appearance was hailed, as I said, with great festivity. The faces of everyone at the table were rosy, flushed; all eyes, turning on us, expressed friendliness and benevolence. But the room, too, as it was suddenly revealed to me that evening, seemed more welcoming, warmer than usual, also rosy somehow with the polished blond wood of its furnishings, on which the high, flickering flame of the fireplace struck tender, flesh-colored glints. I had never seen the dining room illuminated like this. Besides the glow that burst from the mouth of the fireplace, on the table, covered now with a rich cloth of the whitest linen (plates and bowls had already been cleared, obviously), the big corolla of the central lamp poured down a positive cataract of light.

"Come in, come in!"

"Welcome!"

"We were beginning to think you wouldn't trouble to come!"

Alberto uttered these last words, but I could feel it: my coming filled him with genuine pleasure. All were looking at me: some, like Professor Ermanno, turning completely in their chairs; some leaning forward over the edge of the table, or pushing themselves away from it with stiff arms; some, finally, like Signora Olga, sitting there at the end of the table, with the burning fire behind her, extending her face and half-closing her eyelids. They observed me, they examined me, they scrutinized me from head to toe, and they all seemed quite pleased with me, with the way I looked at Micòl's side. Only Federico Herrera, the railway engineer, remained surprised, as if puzzled, and was late in joining in the general satisfaction. But it was the matter of an instant. Having sought information from his brother Giulio (I saw them confer briefly, their bald heads together behind the back of the old mother), he immediately multiplied his demonstrations of friendliness towards me. Not only did he make a grimace that bared his thick upper incisors, but he actually raised one arm: not so much in a gesture of greeting as in a sign of solidarity, of almost athletic incitement.

Professor Ermanno insisted I should sit at his right. It was my regular place—he explained to Micòl, who meanwhile had sat at his left, opposite me—the one I usually occupied when I stayed to supper. Giampiero Malnate—he then added—Alberto's friend, sat there (he pointed to the place), at Mamma's right. And Micòl listened with a curious air, at once nettled and sardonic: as if she disliked learning that the family's life, in her absence, had continued in directions she had not entirely foreseen, and also as if she were not sorry that things had gone, in fact, as they had.

I sat down and, at once, surprised at not having observed properly, I realized that the cloth was not at all cleared. In the center of the table there was a big, fine silver tray, and in the center of the tray, surrounded at a few inches' distance by a halo of little pieces of white cardboard, each of which bore a letter of the alphabet, written in red pencil, there stood a solitary champagne glass.

"What's that?" I asked Alberto.

"Why, that's the big surprise I told you about!" Alberto exclaimed. "It's absolutely amazing: all you have to do is have three or four people, in a circle, who each put a finger on the lip of the glass and, immediately, back and forth, one letter after another, it answers."

"Answers?"

"Certainly! It *writes*, very slowly, all the answers. And intelligent ones, too, you can't imagine how intelligent!"

It had been a long time since I had seen Alberto so euphoric, so excited.

"And where did it come from," I asked, "this latest thing?"

"It's only a game," Professor Ermanno interrupted, putting a hand on my arm and shaking his head. "Something Micòl brought down from Venice."

"Ah, then you're responsible!" I said, addressing Micòl. "And does it also read the future, *your* glass?"

"Of course!" she cried, with a sly wink. "I don't mind telling you, *that* is its great specialty."

Dirce came in, at that moment, holding aloft, balanced on one hand, a round platter of dark wood, brimming with Passover sweets. Dirce's cheeks, too, were rosy, gleaming with health and good humor. As guest, and the last to arrive, I was served first. The sweets, the so-called *zucarìn*, made of light pastry mixed with raisins, were more or less the same as the ones I had eaten reluctantly, a little earlier, at home. And yet these, at the Finzi-Continis', immediately seemed much better, much tastier: and I said so, too, addressing Signora Olga, who, intent on choosing a *zucarìn* from the dish Dirce was holding out to her, didn't seem to notice my compliment.

Then Perotti appeared, his heavy peasant hands clutching the edges of a second tray (this one of pewter), which held a flask of white wine and glasses for all. And afterwards, as we sat there, in disorder around the table, each taking little sips of Albana and munching *zucarìn*, Alberto was illustrating to me in particular the "divining powers of the chalice," which now stood there, mute like all the honest *verres* of this world, but which, until a short time before, as they had questioned it, had demonstrated an exceptional, admirable loquacity.

I asked what kind of questions had been addressed to it.

"Oh, a bit of everything."

They had asked it, for example—he continued—if he, Alberto, one of these days, would manage to take his engineering degree; and the glass, promptly, had replied with a very sharp "no." Then Micòl had wanted to know if she would be married, and when; and here the glass had been much less peremptory, indeed rather confused, giving a response worthy of a true classical oracle: subject, that is, to the most contradictory interpretations. They had questioned it even about the tennis court, the "poor sainted glass!": trying to discover if Papà would abandon his eternal fussing, postponing year after year the job of putting it in order. And on this subject, displaying great reserves of patience, the "Pythian" had become explicit once more, assuring them that the long-awaited improvements would be carried out very soon, within the present year.

But it was in the field of politics, especially, that the glass had worked wonders. Soon, in a few months, it had decreed, war would break out: a war that would be long, bloody, grievous for *all*, which would embroil the entire world, but which would end, after many years of dubious battles, with the complete victory of the forces of good. "Of good?" Micòl had asked at this point, always a specialist in *gaffes*. "And what, if you please, might the forces of good be?" At which the glass, leaving them all dumbfounded, had answered with a single word: "Stalin."

"Can you imagine," Alberto exclaimed, while all the others were laughing, "can you imagine how pleased Giampi would have been, if he had been here? I must write him about it."

"Isn't he in Ferrara?"

"No, he left day before yesterday. He's gone home for Easter."

Alberto continued, at some length, reporting what the glass had said, then the game was resumed. I too was urged to place my forefinger on the lip of the *coupe*, I too asked questions and awaited answers. But now, who knows why, nothing comprehensible would come forth from the oracle. Alberto insisted in vain, tenacious and stubborn as never before. Nothing doing.

I, in any case, didn't much care. Instead of paying attention to him and to the game of the glass, I was looking around, at the dining room, and outside, through the great porthole overlooking the park, and at Micòl, especially, seated opposite me on the other side of the table: Micòl, who, from time to time, feeling my gaze on her, smoothed her frowning brow, as when she played tennis, to devote to me a rapid smile, pensive, reassuring.

I stared at her lips, barely touched with lipstick. I myself had kissed them, I, yes, a little while ago. But hadn't it happened too late? Why hadn't I done it six months ago, when everything was still possible, or at least during the winter? How much time we had lost: I here, in Ferrara, and she in Venice! I could easily have taken the train, one Sunday, and gone to see her. There was a through train that left Ferrara at eight in the morning and arrived in Venice at ten-thirty. The moment I arrived, I would telephone her from the station, suggesting she take me to the Lido (and so, among other things—I would say to her—I could finally visit the famous

Jewish cemetery of San Niccolò). Later we would lunch together, in that same neighborhood, and afterwards, with a call to the uncle's house to keep the fraülein calm (oh, Micòl's face, as she telephoned, her grimaces, her clowning expressions!), afterwards we would stroll along the deserted beach. For this, too, there was plenty of time. For my departure, I had a choice of two trains: one at five and one at seven, both excellent, because my parents would still be unaware of anything. Ah, yes: to have done it then, when I *should* have, would all have been quite easy. It would have been a trifle. Whereas now it was late, on the contrary, terribly late.

What time was it? One thirty, perhaps two. In a little while I would have to leave, and it wasn't at all impossible that Micòl would accompany me again, downstairs, to the garden door.

Perhaps this is what she, too, was thinking about: it was this thought that made her restless. Room after room, corridor after corridor, we would walk side by side, now lacking the courage to look at each other or to exchange a word. We both feared the same thing, I could feel it: the farewell, the ever closer and ever less imaginable moment of farewell, of the good-bye kiss. And yet, if, for instance, Micòl refused to see me out, leaving the task to Alberto, or (as a little later it proved) even to Perotti, how could I face the rest of the night? And the next day?

But perhaps not—I was already dreaming again, stubborn and desperate—rising from the table was perhaps futile, unnecessary. That night, after all, would never end.

# Part

# Four

Immediately, the very next day, I began to realize that it would be very hard for me to re-establish with Micòl our relationship.

After long hesitation, around ten I tried telephoning her. I was told (by Dirce) that the "family" hadn't come down yet, and would I please call back around noon. To while away the time, I flung myself on my bed. I picked up a book at random: *Le rouge et le noir*; but try as I would, I couldn't concentrate. And what if, at noon—I let my imagination run—I didn't telephone? I soon changed my mind. Suddenly it seemed to me that I wanted only one thing of Micòl now: her friendship. Rather than disappear—I said to myself—it was much better for me to act as if the night before nothing had happened. Micòl, of all people, would understand. Impressed by my tact, fully reassured, she would soon trust me completely again, with the beloved intimacy of the past.

And so, at noon on the dot, I summoned my courage and, for the second time, dialed the Finzi-Continis' number.

I had to wait a long time, longer than usual.

"Hello?" I said finally, my voice choking with emotion. "Ah, it's you?"

It was the voice of Micòl herself.

She yawned.

"What is it?"

Disconcerted, devoid of conversation, for the moment I could think of nothing better to say than that I had already called once, two hours ago. Dirce—I added, stammering—had suggested I call back around noon.

Micòl listened. Then she began complaining of the day that lay ahead of her, with so many things to put in order after months and months of absence, suitcases to unpack, books and papers to arrange, et cetera, et cetera, and with the final prospect, not at all inviting for her, of a second *"àgape."* That was the trouble with every separation—she grumbled—afterwards, to get back into your groove, to resume your usual routine, you had to go to even more trouble than the already considerable trouble you had undergone in order to "clear out." Would she turn up later at temple—she asked, repeating my shy question—who knows? Maybe yes, but also maybe no. At the moment she simply couldn't promise anything.

She hung up without inviting me to come back to their house that evening, and without setting how and when we would see each other again.

That day I avoided calling her back, and going to temple: even if, as she told me, there was some probability of running into her there. Towards evening, all the same, passing along Via Mazzini, and seeing the Finzi-Continis' gray Dilambda parked around the corner, towards the cobblestones of Via Scienze, with Perotti in cap and chauffeur's uniform seated at the wheel, in attendance, I couldn't resist the temptation of stationing myself at the entrance of Via Vittoria, to wait. I waited a long time, in the biting cold. It was the hour of the most crowded evening strolling, the walk before supper. Along both sidewalks of Via Mazzini, covered with dirty, half-melted snow, people were hastening to and fro. In the end I was rewarded: because, at the conclusion of the service, though from a distance, I saw her suddenly appear at the door of the temple, and linger a long time on the threshold. She was wearing a short leopard coat, bound at the waist by a leather belt; and, her blond hair shining in the light of the shop windows, she looked here and there, as if seeking someone. Paying not the slightest attention to the many passersby who turned, amazed, to admire her, was she seeking me, perhaps? I was about to move from the shadow and step forward, when her relatives, who obviously had followed her down the stairs after a time, arrived, in a group, behind her. They were all there, even Grandmother Regina. Turning on my heel, I strode off rapidly down Via Vittoria.

The next day and the days after, I persisted with my telephone calls, though I succeeded in speaking with her only rarely. Almost always someone else came to answer: Alberto, or Professor Ermanno, or Dirce, or even Perotti, all of whom, with the sole exception of Dirce, curt and passive as a switchboard operator, embarrassing and chilling for this very reason, involved me in long, futile conversations. At a certain point I would cut Perotti short, true. But with Alberto and the Professor, on the other hand, it was much less easy. I let them speak. I kept hoping they would mention Micòl's name. Vain hope. As if both had decided to avoid it, and had even discussed the matter, it was to me, and to me alone, that father and brother left all initiative. With the result that very often I hung up the receiver without having found the strength to ask them to pass her to me.

Then I resumed my visits: both in the morning, on the pretext of my thesis, and in the afternoon, going to see Alberto. I never did anything to indicate to Micòl my presence in the house. I was sure she knew of it, and one day or another she would show up, spontaneously.

Though I had finished my thesis, I really did still have to make a clean copy of it. So I took my typewriter there from home, and its clicking, the first moment it broke the silence of the billard room, summoned Professor Ermanno immediately to the doorway of his study.

"What are you up to? Already making your final copy?" he cried gaily.

He came to me, and wanted to see the machine. It was an Italian portable, a Littoria, that my father had given me a few years before, when I had passed my university entrance examination. The Fascist trade name did not make the Professor smile, as I had feared. Quite the contrary. Observing that "also" in Italy they could now produce typewriters which, like mine, seemed to work perfectly, he actually appeared pleased. They, here in the house, had three—he said—one for Alberto, one for Micòl, and one for himself: all three American, Underwoods. The children's were portables: very sturdy, no doubt, but not, surely, as light as this one (meanwhile he tested its weight, lifting it by the handle). His, on the contrary, was the normal kind: office model, you might say. Cumbersome, no doubt, and antiquated, but solid, oh, yes, very solid! and also very practical and efficient. Did I know how many copies it could make, if necessary? Up to seven.

He took me into his study and showed it to me, lifting a lugubrious metal lid, painted black, which I had never noticed before. It was a genuine museum piece, obviously very seldom used, even when new. With my Littoria—I declared to the Professor, who listened to me with a quite unconvinced look—I wouldn't be able to make more than three copies, two of them on onionskin paper. I preferred to continue with that, however.

Chapter after chapter, I pounded the keys, but my mind was elsewhere. And it slipped off elsewhere also in the afternoon, when I was downstairs again, in Alberto's study. Malnate had returned from Milan a good week after Easter, filled with indignation at recent political events (the fall of Madrid—ah, but the war wasn't over yet!—the conquest of Albania: how shameful, what a farce!). With regard to the latter event, he reported sarcastically what he had learned from certain mutual friends of his and Alberto's in Milan. The Albanian enterprise had been desired chiefly by Ciano— he informed us—who was jealous of von Ribbentrop, and with that disgusting, cowardly invasion, had wanted to show the world how, when it came to Blitz-diplomacy, he was the German's equal. Did we realize? Apparently even Cardinal Schuster (of all people!) had expressed himself on the subject, deploring and admonishing; and though he had been speaking privately to a very few friends, all Milan had promptly heard about it. Giampi also told us about Milan: about a performance of Mozart's *Don Giovanni* at La Scala, which he had luckily managed to catch; and then about Gladys—yes, Gladys—whom he had run into in the Galleria. She was covered in mink, on the arm of a well-known industrialist; and Gladys, amiable as ever, had given him, as she passed, a little signal with her finger, as if to say: Phone me; or, I'll phone you. Too bad he had to come back at once to "the plant"! He would gladly have stuck a couple of horns on the well-known steel industrialist, imminent war profiteer. . . . He talked and talked: addressing me most of the time, as usual, but he seemed to me a bit less didactic and emphatic than in the past months: as if his trip to Milan, visiting family and friends, had given him a new indulgence towards others and their opinions.

With Micòl, as I said before, I had only rare contact, always by telephone, and we both avoided referring to personal things. Still, some days after I had waited for her outside the temple for over an hour, I couldn't resist the temptation of complaining to her of her coldness.

"You know," I said, "the second evening of Passover I saw you after all."

"You did? Were you in temple too?"

"No, I wasn't there. I was going along Via Mazzini, I noticed your car, but I decided to wait outside for you."

"What an idea."

"You were very elegant. You want me to tell you what you were wearing?"

"No, no, I'll take you word for it. Where were you?"

"On the sidewalk opposite, at the corner of Via Vittoria. At a certain point you looked in my direction. Had you spotted me? Tell the truth."

"No, I hadn't. Why should I lie to you? But you . . . I don't understand for what reason . . . Couldn't you advance and be recognized, really?"

"I was about to. Then, when I saw you weren't alone, I changed my mind."

"What a surprise! that I wasn't alone! But you're a funny character: you could have come and said hello to me anyway, I should think."

"Yes, of course, if you think logically. The trouble is that a person doesn't always manage to think logically. And besides: would you have been pleased?"

"Oh, God, what a fuss you make!" she sighed.

The second time I succeeded in speaking to her, no less than a dozen days later, she told me she was sick, with a "mighty" cold and with a slight fever. What a bore! Why did I never come to visit her? I had really forgotten her!

"You're . . . you're in bed?" I stammered, disconcerted, feeling myself the victim of an enormous injustice.

"Of course I am, and tucked in, too. Now I suppose you'll refuse to come for fear of 'flu.' "

"No, no, Micòl," I answered bitterly. "Don't make me out a worse coward than I am. I was just amazed that you could accuse me of having forgotten you, when on the contrary . . . I don't know if you remember," I went on, my voice breaking, "but before you left for Venice, it was very easy to phone you, whereas now, you have to admit, it's become a kind of feat. You know I've been to your house various times, these past few days? Did they tell you?"

"Yes."

"Well then! If you wanted to see me, you knew very well where to find me: mornings in the billiard room, afternoons down in your brother's study. The truth is you hadn't the slightest wish."

"What nonsense! I've never liked dropping in on Alberto, especially when he has friends visiting. As for coming to see you in the mornings:

aren't you supposed to be working? If there is one thing I *loathe*, it's disturbing people when they're at work. In any case, if it means all that much to you, tomorrow or the next day I'll drop by to say hello."

The next morning she didn't come, but in the afternoon, when I was with Alberto (it must have been about seven: Malnate had brusquely taken his leave a few minutes before), Perotti came in. The "signorina" asked if I would go up to see her a moment—he announced, impassive but, it seemed to me, in a bad humor. She apologized: she was still in bed, otherwise she would have come down herself. What did I prefer: to go up at once, or to stay to supper, and go up afterwards? The signorina, actually, would prefer to see me now, since she had a bit of a headache and wanted to go to sleep very early. But if I chose to stay on  . . .

"Oh, no, no," I said, looking at Alberto. "I'll come right away."

I stood up, preparing to follow Perotti.

"Don't be shy, for heaven's sake," Alberto was saying meanwhile, considerately accompanying me to the door. "I think that, this evening, there'll only be me and Papà at table. Grandmother is also in bed with flu, and Mama simply won't hear of leaving the sick room: not even for a moment. So, if you feel like having a bite with us, and going up to see Micòl afterwards  . . .  You know how glad Papà would be to see you."

I declined the invitation, alleging a nonexistent engagement for the evening, and I hurried after Perotti, already at the end of the corridor.

Without exchanging a word, we quickly reached the foot of the long spiral staircase that led upstairs, to the base of the skylight tower. Micòl's little apartment, I knew, was the highest in the house, only half a flight below the top landing.

I hadn't noticed the elevator, and I was starting up on foot.

"I know you're a young fellow," Perotti grinned, "but a hundred and thirty-three steps are a lot. Don't you want to come in the elevator? It works, you know."

He promptly opened the gate of the black outer cage, then the sliding door of the cabin, and he stood aside to let me pass.

To cross the threshold of the cabin, which was an antediluvian booth, all wine-colored gleaming wood, glistening crystal panels adorned with an *M*, an *F*, and a *C* elaborately intertwined, to be seized by the pungent, somewhat stifling odor, of mold, perhaps, and turpentine, which impregnated the air enclosed in that small space, was to feel suddenly an unmotivated sense of calm, of fatalistic tranquility, of actually ironic detachment. Where had I smelled an odor like this—I asked myself—when?

The cabin slowly began to rise up the stairwell. I sniffed the air, and meanwhile I looked at Perotti in front of me, his back sheathed in his striped canvas jacket. The old man had left the little seat covered with soft velvet at my complete disposal. Standing a few inches away, absorbed, tense, one hand gripping the brass handle of the sliding door, the other resting on the control panel, Perotti had shut himself up again in a silence pregnant with all possible meanings. But now I remembered and understood. Perotti was silent not because he disapproved, as I had imagined at a certain point, of Micòl's receiving me in her room, but rather because of the opportunity granted him to run the elevator—an opportunity perhaps rare—which filled him with a satisfaction the more intense for being private, secret. The elevator was no less dear to him than the carriage down in the coach house. On these things, on these venerable manifestations of a past by now also his, he released his torn love for the family he had served since a boy, his angry fidelity, like an old domestic animal's.

"It works beautifully," I cried. "What make is it?"

"It's American," he answered, half-turning his face, and twisting his mouth in the typical grimace of contempt behind which peasants often mask admiration. "It's over forty years old, but it could haul up a regiment."

"Probably a Westinghouse," I ventured, at random.

"Hmph, I wouldn't know . . ." he grumbled, "one of those names they have."

Here he started narrating to me how and when the elevator had been "put in." But the cabin, stopping abruptly, forced him to break off almost at once, with evident displeasure.

# II

In my mood of that moment, a temporary serenity without illusions, Micòl's welcome surprised me like an unexpected gift, undeserved. I had been afraid she would treat me badly, with the familiar cruel indifference of recent times. But I had only to enter her room (after letting me in, Perotti discreetly closed the door behind my back) to see her smiling at me, kindly, sweet, a friend. Even more than her explicit invitation to come closer, it was that luminous smile of hers, filled with tenderness and forgiveness, that persuaded me to move from the dark end of the room and approach.

So I went to the bed, the foot, staying there, my hands resting on the bedstead. Two pillows supported her back, Micòl had pulled the covers only up to her waist. She was wearing a high-necked dark-green pullover with long sleeves. Over her bosom glinting against the wool of the sweater, there was her little gold medal, the *shaddài*. . . . When I came in, she was reading: a French novel as I saw at once, recognizing from the distance the style of the binding, white and red; and more than her cold, her reading had probably made those hollows of weariness below her eyes. No, she was as beautiful as ever—I said to myself now, contemplating her—perhaps she had never been so beautiful and attractive.

Beside the bed, near the pillows, there was a walnut trolley, with two shelves, the upper one occupied by a lit gooseneck lamp, the telephone, a red earthenware teapot, two cups of gold-rimmed white porcelain, and a metal thermos. Micòl reached out to put the book on the lower shelf, then she turned, seeking the electric light switch, hanging on the other side of the head of the bed. Poor thing—she was muttering meanwhile—there was no excuse for her to keep me in such gloom! And the increase in light, the moment it came, was hailed by her with a deep "aah" of satisfaction.

She went on, speaking more Finzi-Continian than ever: about the "squalid" cold that had kept her in bed a good four days; about the aspirin tablets that, unknown to Papà, as well as to Uncle Giulio, bitter enemy of anything that made you sweat (and damaged the heart, according to them, but they were absolutely wrong!), she had tried, to hasten the conclusion of her illness; about the boredom of the endless hours of confinement, with no strength to do anything, not even read. Ah, read! Once, in the days of her famous influenzas with raging fevers, when she was thirteen, she was quite capable of devouring all of *War and Peace,* for example, in a few days, or the entire cycle of *The Three Musketeers,* whereas now, during the course of a wretched cold, head cold though it was, at most she had managed to "knock off" a few French novels, the kind with huge print and big margins. Did I know Cocteau's *Les Enfants terribles*?—she asked, picking up the book again from the trolley, and handing it to me. It wasn't bad; it was amusing and *chic.* But did I think it comparable to *The Three Musketeers,*

*Twenty Years After,* and *Le Vicomte de Bragelonne*? Those were real novels! Let's be frank: after all, even when it came to "chic," they were "far, far better."

Suddenly she broke off.

"Well? Why are you standing there like a stick?" she cried. "Good heavens, you're really worse than a child! Take that chair. That one"—she was pointing it out to me meanwhile—"and come and sit here, closer."

I hastened to obey, but that wasn't enough. Now I *had* to drink something.

"What can I offer you?" she said. "Would you like some tea?"

"No, thanks," I answered. "I don't like it before supper. It washes out the stomach and kills my appetite."

"Maybe some *Skiwasser*?"

"*Idem,* see above."

"It's steaming hot, you know! Unless I'm mistaken, you've only tasted the summer version, the basically *heretical* iced kind: *Himbeerwasser*."

"No, no thanks."

"Oh, my God," she whimpered. "Shall I ring and have them bring you an apéritif? We never drink them, but I believe there's a bottle of Bitter Campari somewhere in the house. Perotti, *honi soit,* surely knows where to find it. . . ."

I shook my head.

"You really don't want to drink anything!" she cried, disappointed. "What a character!"

"I would prefer not to."

When I said that she burst into loud laughter.

"Why are you laughing?" I asked, a bit offended.

She observed me as if perceiving my true features for the first time.

"You said 'I would prefer not to' just like Bartleby. With the same look on your face."

"Bartleby? And who might this gentleman be?"

"Now you'll tell me you haven't read the stories of Melville."

Of Melville—I said—I knew only *Moby Dick,* in the Cesare Pavese translation. Then she made me get up and go to the case opposite, between the two windows, take out the volume of *Piazza Tales,* and bring it to her. As I was hunting among the books, she was telling me the plot of the story. Bartleby was a scrivener—she said—a scrivener employed by a well-known lawyer in New York (an excellent professional man: active, capable, "liberal, one of those nineteenth-century Americans that Spencer Tracy plays so well"), to copy out legal documents, conveyances, and so on. Now he, Bartleby, as long as they set him to writing, sat there slaving away conscientiously. But if Spencer Tracy got the idea of giving him some little extra job, like examining a copy against the original text, or running down to the corner tobacconist's to buy a stamp, he would refuse: he would confine himself to an evasive smile, answering with polite firmness: *I would prefer not to.*

"And why not, after all?" I asked, coming back with the book in my hand.

"Because he didn't want to be anything but a scrivener. Just a scrivener, and nothing else."

"But still," I objected, "I imagine Spencer Tracy paid him a proper salary."

"Of course," Micòl answered. "But what of it? A salary pays the work, *not* the *person* who does it."

"I don't quite understand," I insisted. "Spencer Tracy took Bartleby into his office no doubt as a copyist, but also, I would think, to lend a hand in general, to keep things going. What was he asking of him, after all? Something *extra* that, perhaps, was something *less.* For a man who's obliged to remain seated all the time, running down to the corner tobacconist's can be a useful diversion, a necessary pause: in any case, a magnificent opportunity to stretch the legs a bit. No, I'm sorry. If you ask me, Spencer Tracy was absolutely right in insisting that your Bartleby should stop being such a bore and do what was asked of him."

We argued at some length about poor Bartleby and about Spencer Tracy. She reproached me, saying I didn't *understand,* that I was "banal," the same inveterate conformist. Conformist? She went on joking. The fact was, however, that before, with a commiserating look, she had compared me with Bartleby. Now, on the contrary, seeing that I was on the side of the "hateful bosses," she had begun to exalt Bartleby's "unalienable right, which is every human being's, to noncollaboration," that is, to freedom. She continued criticizing me, in other words, but for the opposite reasons.

At a certain point the phone rang. They were calling from the kitchen, to find out if, and when, they should bring up a supper tray. Micòl announced that for the moment she wasn't hungry, and she would call them back, later. Broth with noodles?—she replied, with a grimace, to a specific question from the receiver—certainly. But they weren't to prepare it yet, please: she had never been able to bear "soggy" pasta.

When she put down the receiver, she turned towards me. She was staring at me, her eyes both sweet and grave, and for a few seconds she said nothing.

"How's it going?" she asked finally, in a low voice.

I swallowed.

"So-so."

I smiled, and looked around.

"It's funny," I continued. "Every detail of this room corresponds exactly to the way I had imagined it. There's the Récamier, for example. It's as if I had already seen it. But, for that matter, I *have* seen it."

I told her about the dream I had had six months ago, the night before she left for Venice. I pointed to the rows of *làttimi,* glowing in the semidarkness on the shelves in their cases: the only objects, here—I said—that in the dream had appeared to me differently from reality. I explained the form in which I had seen them, and she listened to me, grave, intent, never interrupting.

When I finished, she grazed the sleeve of my jacket with a light caress. Then I knelt down beside the bed, embraced her, kissed her on the neck, on the eyes, on the lips. And she let me go on, but always staring at me, shaking her head slightly, always trying to prevent me from kissing her mouth.

"No . . . no . . ." she kept saying. "Stop it . . please. . . . Be good. . . . No, no . . . somebody might come. . . . No."

In vain. Slowly, first with one leg, then with the other, I climbed onto the bed. Now I was lying on her with my full weight. I kept blindly kissing her face, succeeding only rarely in gaining her lips, never managing to make her lower her eyelids. Finally I hid my face against her neck. And while my body, as if on its own, thrashed convulsively over hers, motionless as a statue beneath the blankets, suddenly, in an immediate and terrible sundering of my whole self, I had the distinct feeling that I was losing her, had lost her.

She was the first to speak.

"Get up, please," I heard her say, very close to my ear. "I can't breathe like this."

I was annihilated. Getting down from that bed seemed to me an enterprise beyond my strength. But I had no choice.

I pulled myself to my feet. I took a few steps about the room, swaying. Finally I sank down again in the little armchair beside the bed, and hid my face in my hands. My cheeks were burning.

"Why do you act like this?" Micòl said. "It's so useless."

"Useless, why?" I asked, sharply, raising my eyes. "May I ask why?"

She looked at me, the shadow of a smile hovering around her mouth.

"Don't you want to go in there a moment?" she said, nodding towards the door of the bath. "You're all red, absolutely flaming. Wash your face."

"Thanks, yes. Perhaps that would be a good idea."

I sprang up and headed for the bath. But then, at that very moment, the door to the stairs was shaken by a violent impact. Someone seemed to be trying to break in.

"What's that?" I whispered.

"It's Jor," Micòl answered calmly. "Open the door for him."

# III

In the oval mirror above the wash basin I looked at my reflected face.

I examined it carefully, as if it were not mine, as if it belonged to another person. Although I had plunged it several times into cold water, it was still all red, absolutely flaming—as Micòl had said—with darker patches between the nose and upper lip, over and around the cheekbones. I scrutinized with pedantic objectivity that large illuminated face, there, before me, attracted by the throb of the arteries under the skin of the brow and temples, by the thick network of little scarlet veins that, when I opened my eyes wide, seemed to be pressing the blue disk of the irises in a kind of siege, then the hairs of my beard, thicker on the chin and along the jaws, then a barely perceptible pimple. . . . I was thinking of nothing, really. Through the thin door, I could hear Micòl speaking into the telephone. To whom? To the kitchen staff, I supposed, telling them to bring up her supper. Good. The imminent farewell would be much less embarrassing. For both of us.

I went in as she was hanging up, and again, not without surprise, I saw she bore me no grudge.

She leaned from the bed to fill a cup with tea.

"Now, please, sit down," she said, "and drink something."

I obeyed in silence. I drank slowly, in long sips, without raising my eyes. Stretched out on the parquet behind me, Jor was sleeping. His heavy snores, like a drunken beggar's, filled the room.

I set down the cup.

And again it was Micòl who spoke first. Making no reference at all to what had happened a short while before, she began by saying how, for a long time, much longer, perhaps, than I imagined, she had been meaning to discuss with me frankly the situation that had gradually developed between us. Didn't I remember that day—she went on—last October, when, to escape the rain, we had ended up in the coach house, and had then gone to sit in the carriage? Well, as long ago as then, she had become aware of the nasty turn our relationship was taking. She had realized at once that between us something false had been born, something mistaken, very dangerous: and it was more her fault than mine if the landslide had gathered momentum, she was quite prepared to admit that. What should she have done? The answer was simple: take me aside then, and speak to me openly, "without letting any time go by." Instead, she hadn't: like a real coward, she had chosen the worst possible course, running away. Oh, yes, to cut and run is easy: but what does it lead to, almost always, especially in "unhealthy situations"? Ninety-nine times out of a hundred, the embers continue burning under the ash: with the fine result that later, when the two see each other again, it has become very difficult, almost impossible for them to talk calmly, like good friends.

I understood too—I spoke up at this point—and, in the final analysis, I was very grateful to her for being sincere.

There was one thing, however, that I would like her to explain to me. She had run away, on the spur of the moment, without even saying goodbye, after which, as soon as she had arrived in Venice, she had had only one concern: to make sure I kept seeing her brother Alberto.

"Why?" I asked. "If, as you say, you really wanted me to forget you (excuse the expression; don't burst out laughing in my face!), couldn't you have left me alone, absolutely alone? It would have been difficult, true, but it wasn't impossible, either, that for lack of nourishment, let's say, the embers might have finally gone out completely, on their own.''

She looked at me, not hiding a moment's surprise: amazed perhaps that I could find the strength to counterattack, even if, all things considered, with scant conviction.

I wasn't wrong—she agreed then, pensive, shaking her head—I wasn't at all wrong. Still, she begged me to believe her. In behaving as she had, she hadn't, for a moment, the least intention of stirring anything up. My friendship was important to her, that was all, perhaps in a somewhat too possessive way; and besides, really, even more than of me, she had been thinking of Alberto, who, except for Giampiero Malnate, had remained here without anybody to exchange a few words with. Poor Alberto—she sighed. Hadn't I also noticed, seeing something of him these past months, what *need* he had of companionship? For someone like him, now accustomed to spending the winter in Milan, with theaters, films, and all the rest at his disposal, the prospect of remaining here, in Ferrara, shut up in the house for months and months, and moreover with practically nothing to do, was not jolly, I had to admit. Poor Alberto!—she repeated. She, in comparison, was much stronger, much more *autonomous:* capable, if necessary, of putting up with the most ferocious solitude. And, as she thought she had already told me: Venice, when it comes to dreariness, in winter was perhaps even worse than Ferrara, and her uncles' house was no less sad and ''cut off'' than this one.

''This house isn't at all sad,'' I said suddenly, moved.

''You like it?'' she asked brightly. ''Ah, then I'll confess something to you: but you mustn't scold me, eh, don't start accusing me of hypocrisy, or maybe of ambiguity! . . . I was very anxious for you to see it.''

''Why?''

''I don't know why. I really couldn't tell you why. For the same reason, I suppose, that, when I was a little girl, in temple, I would have been so happy to drag you, too, under Papà's *talèd* . . . Ah, if only I could have! I can still see you there, under your *talèd*, your Papà's, there on the bench in front of ours. I felt so sorry for you! It's absurd, I know: and yet, when I looked at you, I felt sorry, as if you had been an orphan, with no father or mother.''

Having said this, she was silent for a few moments, her eyes staring at the ceiling. Then, propping her elbow against the pillow, she resumed talking to me: but serious, now, earnest.

She said she was sorry to hurt me, she was very sorry, but anyway I would have to convince myself: it would be absolutely wrong for us to ruin, as we risked doing, the beautiful childhood memories we had in common. Make love? The two of us! Did it really seem possible to me?

I asked why it seemed so impossible to her.

For all sorts of reasons—she answered—but chiefly because the thought of making love with me upset her, embarrassed her: just as if she were to imagine making love with a brother, say, with Alberto. It was true: as a child, she had had a little "crush" on me; and who knows, perhaps this was the very thing that now, in her, created such a block towards me. I . . . I was *beside* her, did I understand?, not *facing*, whereas love—at least, the way she imagined it—was something for people reciprocally determined to get the upper hand: a cruel, fierce sport, far more cruel and fierce than tennis! to be played with no holds barred, and without ever calling on goodness of soul or sincerity of purpose, to mitigate it.

> *Maudit soit à jamais le rêveur inutile*
> *qui voulut le premier, dans sa stupidité,*
> *s'éprenant d'un problème insoluble et stérile*
> *aux choses de l'amour mêler l'honnêteté*

Baudelaire, who knew a thing or two, had warned. And us? Stupidly sincere, both of us: exactly alike in everything, identical as two drops of water ("and like doesn't fight like, believe me!"): could we have got the upper hand, one or the other? Us? Or really want to *tear each other limb from limb*? No, it wasn't possible. In her opinion, seeing the way the good Lord had made us, the thing wouldn't have been possible or desirable.

But even assuming, purely as a hypothesis, that we had been different from what we were, that there had been, in other words, between us, even a slight possibility of a relationship of the *bloodthirsty* sort, how were we to act? *Become engaged,* for instance, with the consequent exchange of rings, visits of parents, et cetera? What an edifying tale! If he were still alive, and were informed of it, Israel Zangwill himself would have drawn a tasty codicil from it to add to his *Dreamers of the Ghetto.* And what smug satisfaction, what *pious* satisfaction, for everybody, when we appeared together at the Italian synagogue next Kippur: a bit wan of face, thanks to our fasting, but beautiful, all the same, a well-matched couple! Some, on seeing us, would surely bless the racial laws, declaring, in the face of such a splendid union, that there was one thing still to say: every cloud has a silver lining. And who knows? Perhaps even the party secretary would have been touched, in Viale Cavour! Even if, in secret, he hadn't remained a great philo-Semite, that excellent man Consul Bolognesi! Ugh!

I was silent, oppressed. She seized the opportunity to pick up the receiver and tell them, in the kitchen, that they could bring her supper: but in a half-hour, not before, because—she repeated—that evening she "wasn't the least hungry." Only the next day, when I was thinking it all over, did I remember that, when I was in the bath, I had heard her speak on the phone. So I had been mistaken—I was to tell myself the next day—she could have been speaking with anyone, in the house (and also outside) but *not* with the kitchen.

Now I was immersed in quite different thoughts. When Micòl put down the receiver, I raised my head.

"You said the two of us are alike," I said. "In what sense?"

We were, we were—she exclaimed—and in the sense that I, too, like her, lacked that instinctive taste for things that characterized *normal* people. She could tell very clearly: for me, as for her, the past counted more than the present, possession counted less than memory of it. Compared with memory, all possession, in itself, can only seem disappointing, banal, inadequate. . . . How she understood me! my eagerness for the present to become *immediately* past, so that I could love it and cherish it at ease, was also hers, just the same. It was *our* vice, this: proceeding always with our heads turned back. Wasn't she right?

She was right—I couldn't help admitting to myself—she was exactly right. When was it that I had embraced her? An hour ago, at most. And already, as always, everything had become unreal once more, fabulous: an event to disbelieve, or to fear.

"Who knows?" I answered. "Maybe it's still simpler: maybe I don't attract you physically. It's only that."

"Don't talk nonsense," she protested. "What's that got to do with it?"

"It has plenty to do with it!"

"*You're fishing for compliments,*" she said, in English, "and you know very well you are. But I don't want to give you any satisfaction: you don't deserve it. And besides, even if I tried to tell you all the good things I've

always thought of your famous glaucous eyes (and not only of your eyes),
what result would I achieve? You'd be the first to think ill of me. A terrible
hypocrite: that's what you'd think. Yes, after the stick, the carrot, the con-
solation prize . . ."

"Unless . . ."

"Unless what?"

I hesitated, but finally I took the plunge.

"Unless," I resumed, "there's somebody else involved."

She shook her head, staring at me.

"There's absolutely nobody else involved," she answered. "Who could
there be?"

I believed her. But I was desperate, and I wanted to hurt her.

"You're asking me?" I said, pursing my lips. "Anything can happen.
How do I know that, during this winter, in Venice, you didn't meet somebody?"

She burst out laughing: a gay, fresh, crystalline laugh.

"What ideas you have!" she cried. "Why, I did nothing but slave the
whole time on my thesis!"

"You surely don't mean to insist that in these five years at the university
you haven't been in love with anyone! Come on: there must have been
some character, at school, who was after you!"

I was sure she would deny it. But I was wrong.

"Yes, I've had admirers," she confessed.

It was as if a hand had clutched my stomach and was twisting it.

"Many?" I managed to ask.

Lying supine as she was, her eyes staring at the ceiling, she barely raised
one arm.

"Mmm . . . I wouldn't know," she said. "Let me think."

"So you had quite a few, then?"

She gave me a sidelong glance, with a sly, definitely sneaky expression,
which I didn't know and which terrified me.

"Well . . . let's say three or four. No, five, to be exact . . . But all
little flirtations, mind you, very innocent . . . and also fairly tiresome."

"What kind of flirtations?"

"Oh, you know . . . long walks on the Lido . . . two or three trips
to Torcello . . . a kiss now and then . . . lots of holding hands . . .
and *lots* of movies. Orgies of movies."

"Always with classmates?"

"More or less."

"Catholics, I imagine."

"Naturally. But not out of principle, however. You know how it is: you have to take what you find."

"Never with . . ."

"No. With *judìm* I'd say not, definitely. Not that there weren't some at school. But they were so serious and ugly!"

She turned again to look at me.

"In any case, none this winter," she added, smiling: "I can even swear that to you. All I did was study and smoke: so much that Fraülein Blumenfeld herself used to urge me to go out."

From under the pillow she took out a pack of Lucky Strikes, unopened.

"You want one? I've started smoking the strong kind, as you see."

I pointed in silence to my pipe, thrust in the pocket of my jacket.

"You too!" she laughed, hugely amused. "Why, that Giampi of yours has a whole raft of followers!"

"And you were complaining you had no friends, in Venice!" I lamented. "The lies! You're just like all other girls, you really are."

She shook her head, I don't know whether out of compassion for me or for herself.

"Flirtations, even trifling ones, are also things you don't carry on with friends," she said, in a sad tone; "and so, when I was speaking to you about friends, you have to admit I was lying only up to a point. Still you're right. I'm just like all the other girls: liar, traitor, *unfaithful*. . . . Not very different from an ordinary Adriana Trentini, after all."

She had said "unfaithful," underlining the syllables, as usual, but with, in addition, a kind of bitter pride. Continuing, she added that if there was one mistake I made, it had always been to overestimate her a bit too much. Not that she was trying to excuse herself, oh, no. Still, it was a fact: she had always read so much "idealism" in my eyes that she had felt herself somehow obliged to appear better than she really was.

There was not much else to say. A little later, when Gina came in with the supper (it was now past nine), I stood up.

"Sorry, but I'm going now," I said, holding out my hand.

"You know your way, don't you? Or would you rather have Gina show you out?"

"No, there's no need. I can manage very well on my own."

"Be sure to take the elevator."

"Of course."

In the doorway, I turned. She was already raising the spoon to her lips.

"Ciao," I said.

She smiled at me. "Ciao. I'll call you tomorrow."

# IV

But the worst began only about three weeks later, when I came back from a trip to France I made in the second half of April.

I had gone to France, to Grenoble, for a very specific reason. The few hundred lire that could be sent monthly by legal means to my brother, Ernesto, sufficed only, as he himself repeated constantly in his letters, for him to pay for the room where he slept, in Place Vaucanson. So it was urgent to supply him with more money. And my father, one night when I came home later than usual (he had stayed up—he said—expressly to talk with me) had insisted I go, to take Ernesto the money in person. Why didn't I take advantage of the opportunity? Breathe some air that was different from "the air here," to see a bit of the world, amuse myself: all this would undoubtedly do me good, both physically and spiritually.

So I went. I stopped over for two hours at Turin, four at Chambéry, and finally I reached Grenoble. There, in the pension where Ernesto went for his meals, he immediately introduced me to various Italians his age, all in his same condition and all polytechnic students: a Levi from Turin, a Segre from Saluzzo, a Sorani from Trieste, a Cantoni from Mantua, a Castelnuovo from Florence, a Pincherle girl from Rome. Still, instead of making friends with them, during my dozen days there, I had spent most of my time at the Bibliothèque Municipale, leafing through the Stendhal manuscripts. It was cold in Grenoble, and rainy. The mountains, just above the city, rarely allowed a glimpse of their peaks, hidden by fog and clouds, while, in the evenings, experimental total blackouts discouraged going out. Ferrara seemed to me very far away: as if I were never to go back there again. And Micòl? Since leaving, I heard her voice constantly in my ear, her voice when she had said to me: "Why do you act like this? It's so useless.'' One day, nevertheless, something happened. I chanced to read in one of Stendhal's notebooks these English words: *all lost, nothing lost,* and suddenly, as if by miracle, I felt myself free, healed. I took a picture postcard, wrote Stendhal's words on it, then sent it to her, to Micòl, like that, without a greeting, without even a signature, let her think of it what she liked. All lost, nothing lost. How true that was!—I said to myself— And I could breathe.

I had deceived myself, of course. Coming back to Italy at the beginning of May, I found spring in full flower, the meadows between Alessandria and Piacenza with vast yellow patches, the roads of the Emilian country-side full of girls out on their bicycles, arms and legs already bared, the great trees of the Ferrara walls laden with leaves. I arrived on a Sunday, around noon. As soon as I was home, I had a bath, dined with the family, answered a number of questions with smug patience. But the sudden frenzy that had seized me, the very moment when, from the train, I had seen the towers and spires of Ferrara loom on the horizon, did not brook further de-lay. At two thirty, not daring to telephone, I was already speeding on my bicycle along the Mura degli Angeli, my eyes fixed on the motionless, flourishing vegetation of the Barchetto del Duca, coming nearer and nearer on the left. Everything was again as it had been before, as if I had spent the last two weeks sleeping.

They were playing, down below, on the tennis court, Micòl against a young man in long white trousers, whom I easily recognized as Malnate; and soon I was spotted and recognized, for the pair stopped their volleying and began to wave their arms in broad gestures, brandishing their rackets. They weren't alone, however; Alberto was also there. I saw him, emerging from the foliage, run into the center of the court, look towards me, then raise his hands to his mouth. He whistled twice, three times. What was I doing up there, on the walls?—he seemed to say to me—why didn't I come into the garden, odd character that I was? I was already heading towards the mouth of Corso Ercole I, already riding along outside the garden wall, I was in sight of the entrance, when Alberto from time to time made his ''oliphant'' resound still. Mind you, no stealing away! his whistles were now saying, still very powerful, but having become, in the meanwhile, somehow good-humored, only faintly admonishing.

''Hi!'' I shouted, as always, coming out into the open from the tunnel of climbing roses.

Micòl and Malnate had resumed playing and, without stopping, they answered together, with another "Hi." Alberto stood up and came towards me. "Would you mind telling us where you've been hiding all these days?" he asked me. "I called your house several times, but you were never in."

'He's been in France," Micòl answered for me, from the court.

"In France!" Alberto exclaimed, his eyes filled with an amazement that seemed sincere to me. "Doing what?"

"I went to visit my brother, in Grenoble."

"Ah, yes, that's right, your brother's studying in Grenoble. And how is he? How's he getting along?"

Meanwhile we had sat down, in two deck chairs, side by side facing the gate to the court: in an excellent position to follow the course of the game. Unlike the previous autumn, Micòl was not in shorts. She was wearing a skirt of pleated white flannel, very old-fashioned, a blouse, also white, with the sleeves rolled up, and strange long stockings, white cotton, like a nurse's. All sweating, flushed, she doggedly sent balls into the farthest corners of the court, overdoing it; but Malnate, though heavier and breathless, was giving her determined, successful opposition.

One ball came rolling towards us, stopping nearby. Micòl approached to collect it, and for a moment her gaze met mine.

This annoyed her, obviously, and she wheeled around towards Malnate.

'Shall we try a set?" she shouted.

'All right," he grumbled. "How many games' handicap will you give me?"

"Not one," Micòl replied, frowning. "At most, I'll let you have first serve. Go on, serve!"

She threw the ball over the net, then went to take up her position, ready to return her opponent's serve.

For a few minutes Alberto and I watched them play. I was filled with malaise and unhappiness. The *tu* Micòl had used, to address Malnate, her ostentatious ignoring of me, suddenly allowed me to measure the length of time I had been away. As for Alberto, he, as usual, had eyes only for Giampi. But for once, I noticed, instead of admiring and praising him, he never stopped criticizing him for a moment.

There was a character—he confided to me in a whisper: and it was such a surprising thing that, for all my anguish, I couldn't help paying attention to him—there was a character who even if he took tennis lessons every blessed day from a Nüsslein or a Martin Plaa, would *never* become an even mediocre player. What was he lacking? What prevented his making progress? Let's see. Legs? No, surely not legs, otherwise he wouldn't be the fairly good rock-climber he certainly was. Breath? No, that neither, and for the same reason. Muscular strength? He had all too much of that: just try shaking his hand. Well then? The fact is that tennis—Alberto decreed, with extraordinary sententiousness—is not only a sport: it's an art, and like all arts it requires a special talent, that certain "natural class," in other words, without which "a dog is a dog for the rest of his life."

"What's going on?" Malnate shouted at a certain point. "What are you two criticizing, you over there?"

"Play, keep playing," Alberto retorted, "and try at least not to be defeated by a woman!"

I couldn't believe my ears. Was it possible? What had become of Alberto's meekness, all his submission to his friend? I looked at him closely. His face suddenly appeared to me wan, emaciated, as if wrinkled by a precocious old age. Was he ill?

I was tempted to ask him, but my courage failed me. I asked instead if this was the first day they had resumed playing tennis, and why Bruno Lattes, Adriana Trentini, and the rest of the "gang" weren't there, like last year?

"Why, then, you don't know anything at all!" he cried, baring his gums in a big laugh.

About a week before—he went on to tell me—given the fine weather, he and Micòl had decided to make a round of phone calls, perhaps ten, "for the noble purpose," in fact, of renewing the "tennistic splendors" of the previous year. They had called Adriana Trentini, Bruno Lattes, young Sani, young Collevatti, and various "other magnificent specimens of both sexes in the rising generation," to whom, the past autumn, "consideration had not been given." All had accepted the invitation with "praiseworthy" alacrity: such as to guarantee, on the opening day, Saturday, May first (too bad I hadn't been able to be there) a success that was "to say the least, sensational." Not only had they played tennis, gossiped, flirted, et cetera, but they had even danced, there, in the *Hütte,* to the sound of the Philips "installed for the occasion."

An even greater success—Alberto went on—had crowned the second session, Sunday afternoon, May second. But then, Monday morning, May third, the "trouble" began to emerge. Preceded by a sibylline card, there, in fact, towards eleven, the lawyer Tabet turned up on his bicycle—yes, that big Fascist, the lawyer Geremia Tabet in person—who, after shutting himself up in the study with Papà, had communicated to him the party secretary's explicit order to cease *"ipso facto"* the scandal of those daily, provocatory receptions which had for some time been taking place in his house, and which moreover had no healthy athletic scope. It was absolutely inconceivable—Consul Bolognesi informed him, by way of their "common" friend Tabet—absolutely inconceivable, and for obvious reasons, that the garden of the Finzi-Contini house should be gradually transformed into a kind of club, competing with the Eleonora d'Este Tennis Club: that worthy institution of municipal sports. So that was that: to avoid official sanctions (for the uncooperative there was the ready threat of exile to Urbisaglia!), from now on, nothing: no member of the Eleonora d'Este would be able to be seduced from his "natural environment."

"And your father," I asked, "what did he say?"

"What do you think he said?" Alberto laughed. "He could only behave like Don Abbondio. Bow his head, and murmur: 'I am always disposed towards obedience.' I believe he expressed himself more or less like that."

"If you ask me, it's Barbicinti's fault," Micòl shouted from the court; obviously the distance had not prevented her from following our conversation. "Nobody can convince me he didn't go to Viale Cavour to complain. I can just visualize the scene. But we have to excuse him, after all, poor man: when you're jealous, you're capable of anything. . . ."

Although uttered perhaps in all innocence, these words of Micòl's struck me painfully. I was about to get up and go away.

And, who knows, maybe I would really have succeeded in going away, if, at that very moment, as I was turning towards Alberto, almost to summon his aid and witness, I had not stopped once again to consider the pallor of his face, the worn thin shoulders, lost in a pullover now become too big (he winked, as if to urge me not to take it to heart, and meanwhile was already talking of other things: the tennis court, that is, and the work to improve it "from the bottom up," work that, in spite of everything, would begin within the week), and if at the same moment I had not seen appear, in the distance, at the edge of the clearing, the black, mourning, paired forms of Professor Ermanno and Signora Olga, returning from their afternoon walk in the park, and heading in our direction.

# V

The long period of time that followed, till the fatal last days of August '39—till the eve of the Nazi invasion of Poland and the *drôle de guerre*—I remember as a kind of slow, progressive descent into the bottomless funnel of the maelstrom. There were four of us left—me, Micòl, Alberto, and Malnate—sole masters of the tennis court which soon had been covered with a good six inches of red earth from Imola (there was no counting on Bruno Lattes, presumably lost in the wake of Adriana Trentini). Alternating partnerships, we spent whole afternoons in long doubles matches, with Alberto, even if he was tired and short of breath, always ready, for some reason, to begin again, giving himself and us no respite.

Why did I stubbornly go back every day, to a place where I knew I would find only humiliation and bitterness? I couldn't say. Perhaps I was hoping for a miracle, in an abrupt change in the situation, or perhaps, yes, I was actually seeking out humiliations and bitterness. . . . We played tennis; or, stretched out, during the rare intervals Alberto allowed, in four deck chairs, lined up in the shade in front of the *Hütte*, we talked, Malnate and I especially, about the usual questions of art and politics. But if I then suggested to Micòl, who had remained polite, after all, with me, and sometimes even affectionate, that we take a turn in the park, it was very rarely that she said yes. If she did consent, she never followed me gladly, but always with an expression between disgust and condescension on her face, which soon made me regret having dragged her away from Alberto and Malnate.

And yet I wouldn't give up, I wouldn't resign myself. Torn between the impulse to break it off, to vanish forever, and the other, opposite impulse, not to renounce being there, not to surrender at any cost, practically speaking I never failed to turn up. At times, true, a glance from Micòl, colder than usual, was enough, an impatient gesture of hers, a grimace of sarcasm or of boredom; I believed then, with complete sincerity, that I had decided, that I had broken it off. But how long could I succeed in staying away? Three days, four at most. On the fifth, there I would be again, displaying the merry, nonchalant face of one who has come back from a trip (I always spoke of trips, on returning: trips to Milan, Florence, Rome: and thank goodness, all three of them made a sufficient show of believing me!), but with a sore heart, and with eyes that immediately began seeking in Micòl's an impossible reply. That was the hour of the "conjugal scenes"—as Micòl called them—during which, if the opportunity arose, I tried also to kiss her, and she tolerated me with great patience, was never rude.

One June evening, however, about the middle of the month, things went differently.

We had sat down side by side on the front steps of the *Hütte,* and though it was eight o'clock, it was still light. I glimpsed Perotti, in the distance, busy taking down and rolling up the net of the tennis court, whose terrain, since the new red dirt had arrived from Romagna, never seemed sufficiently tended to him: and this too was strange, on his part. Malnate was having a shower inside the *Hütte* (we could hear him, behind us, snorting noisily under the jet of hot water); Alberto had taken his leave a little earlier, with a melancholy "bye-bye." The two of us had remained alone, in other words, Micòl and I, and I immediately seized the occasion to begin again my boring, absurd, eternal siege. As always, I insisted in my attempt to persuade her she was wrong to believe a sentimental relationship between us would be out of place; as always, I accused her (in bad faith) of having lied to me, when, not even a month before, she had assured me there was nobody else between her and me. According to me, there was somebody, on the contrary; or at least there had been, in Venice, during the winter.

"For the umpteenth time, I tell you you're wrong," Micòl was saying, in a low voice, "but I know it's hopeless, I know you'll begin again tomorrow with the same business. What can I say? That I'm carrying on a secret intrigue, that I lead a double life? If that's what you really want, I can satisfy you."

"No, Micòl," I answered, in an equally low, but more agitated voice. "I may be anything, but not a masochist. If you only knew, on the contrary, how normal, how terribly banal my aspirations are! Go ahead and laugh, if you like. If there is one thing I want, it would be this: to hear you *swear* what you told me is true, and to believe you."

"As far as I'm concerned, I'll swear right away. But would you believe me?"

"No."

"So much the worse for you then!"

"Of course: so much the worse for me. In any case, if I *could* really believe you . . ."

"What would you do? Let's hear it."

"Oh, more normal, banal things, that's the trouble! This, for example."

I grasped her hands, and began covering them with kisses and tears.

For a little while she let me go on. I hid my face against her knees, and the smell of her smooth, tender skin, faintly salty, dazed me. I kissed her there, on the legs.

"That's enough," she said.

She slipped her hands from mine, and stood up.

"Ciao, I'm cold," she went on: "I have to go in. Supper must be ready by now, and I still have to wash and dress. Come on, get up: don't act like a child."

"Good-bye!" she shouted then, turning towards the *Hütte.* "I'm going."

"Good-bye," Malnate answered from inside. "Thanks."

"See you soon. Are you coming tomorrow?"

"I don't know about tomorrow. We'll see."

She and I set off towards the *mogna domus,* tall and dark in the air filled with mosquitoes and bats, the air of the summer sunset. We were divided by my bicycle, whose handle bars I was clutching convulsively. We were silent. A wagon piled high with hay, drawn by a pair of yoked oxen, was coming from the opposite direction. Hoisted on the top of the hay, there was one of Perotti's sons, who, passing us, wished us good evening and took off his cap. Even if I was accusing Micòl in bad faith, without believing it, I would still have wanted to shout at her, tell her to stop play-acting, insult her, maybe slap her. And then? What would I have got from it?

But this, however, is where I was mistaken.

"There's no use your denying," I said. "For that matter, I know who *the person* is."

The moment I had finished uttering these words, I was already repentant. She looked at me gravely, sorrowfully.

"There," she said, "and now, according to your plan, I should probably challenge you to spit out the name that's choking you, if there really is one. Anyway, that's enough. I don't want to hear any more. Only, at this point, I'd be grateful to you if, from now on, you were a little less constant . . . yes, . . . if, I mean, you came to our house less often. I'll tell you frankly: if I weren't afraid of causing talk in the family: why? how is it that? et cetera, I'd ask you not to come back at all: never again.''

"Forgive me,'' I managed to murmur.

"No, I can't forgive you,'' she replied, shaking her head. "If I did, you'd start all over again in a few days.''

She added that, for some time, my way of behaving had not been seemly, for her or for me. She had told me and repeated to me a thousand times that it was useless, that I should not try to shift our relationship to a different plane from friendship and affection. But no: the moment I could, on the contrary, I was at her "with kisses and what not,'' as if I too didn't know that, in situations like ours, there is nothing more unpleasant and less "indicated.'' Good Lord! Was it impossible for me to control myself? If there had been, in the past, a physical bond between us, something a bit deeper than a few kisses, then yes, perhaps, she might also have been able to understand that I . . . that she had, so to speak, got under my skin. But considering what our relationship had always been, my mania for hugging her, for rubbing against her, was the sign, perhaps, of only one thing: my basic aridity, my constitutional inability really to love. And after all: what was the meaning of the sudden absences, the abrupt returns, the inquisitorial or tragic stares, the sulky silences, the rudeness, the far-fetched insinuations: the whole repertory of thoughtless and embarrassing actions I was constantly displaying, without the least shame? If I had saved the conjugal scenes for her alone, in privacy, it wouldn't have been so bad: but with her brother and Giampi Malnate as spectators, no, not that.

"Now it seems to me you're exaggerating,'' I said. "When did I ever make a scene in front of Alberto and Malnate?''

"Always, constantly!'' she replied.

When I came back after a week's absence—she went on—declaring that I'd been somewhere or other, Rome, and then laughing, with that nervous laughter, like a lunatic, for no reason: did I perhaps deceive myself that Alberto and Malnate weren't aware I was telling lies, and that my bursts of hilarity, "right out of *The Jest*'' were dedicated to her? And in arguments, when I jumped up yelling and inveighing like one possessed, constantly creating personal issues (one of these days Giampi would finally get mad, and he wouldn't be all wrong, poor thing!): did I think people didn't realize that she, and no other, was the cause, however "innocent," of my "ravings"?

"I understand," I said, bowing my head. "I understand that you really don't want to see me any more."

"It's not my fault. You're the one who, little by little, has become unbearable."

"You said," I stammered, after a pause, "you said, though, that I can come back every now and then, or rather, that I *must*. Isn't that so?"

"Yes."

"Well . . . then you decide. How am I to behave, so as not to do anything wrong? How often should I put in an appearance?"

"Oh, I don't know," she answered, shrugging. "I'd say that, for now, you should let at least three weeks go by. Then, start coming back, if you want. But please: *even afterwards,* don't turn up more than twice a week."

"Tuesday and Friday: all right? Like piano lessons."

"Fool," she grumbled, smiling in spite of herself. "You really are a fool."

# VI

Though the effort was very great, especially at the beginning, I made it a point of honor to observe Micòl's prohibitions scrupulously. Suffice it to say that, having taken my degree on June 29, and having immediately received from Professor Ermanno a warm note of congratulations, also including an invitation to supper, I thought it best to say no, I was sorry but I couldn't go. I wrote that I had a sore throat, and Papà forbade me to go out in the evening. If I refused, however, I was led to do it simply because, of the twenty-one days' exile imposed on me by Micòl, only sixteen had gone by.

The effort was very great. And though I hoped, obviously, that sooner or later it would be somehow rewarded, that hope remained vague, content as I was for the moment to obey Micòl, and to be bound, through my obedience, to her and to the paradisiacal places from which I had been banished. As for Micòl, moreover, if I had had something for which to reproach her in the past, now there was nothing: I was the only guilty one, the only one who had something to be forgiven. How many mistakes I had made!—I said to myself—I remembered, one by one, all the times that, often by violence, I had succeeded in kissing her on the mouth, but only to agree that she alone was right, she who, though rejecting me, had put up with me for so long, and also to be ashamed of my satyr lust, masked in sentimentality and idealism. When the three weeks had gone by, I ventured to reappear, restricting myself thereafter, with discipline, to two weekly visits. But Micòl did not, for this, descend from the pedestal of purity and moral superiority, where I had placed her, since I had gone into exile. She continued to remain there, up above. I, for my part, considered myself lucky to be admitted to admire, every so often, the distant image, as beautiful within as without. "*Like the truth / like it, sad and beautiful*": these first two verses of a poem I never finished, though written later, just after the war, allude to the Micòl of August '39, to the way I saw her then.

Driven from Paradise, I had not then rebelled, waiting in silence to be received there once more. All the same, I suffered: certain days, atrociously. And it was for the sole purpose of somehow lightening the burden of an often intolerable separation and a solitude that, about a week after my last, disastrous talk with Micòl, I thought of seeking out Malnate, keeping up contact at least with him.

I knew where to find him. He, too, like Professor Meldolesi in the past, lived in the quarter of little villas outside Porta San Benedetto, between the City Pound and the Industrial Zone. The quarter, in those days, was far more solitary and respectable than now, overwhelmed as it has been in these last fifteen years by the most unrestrained building speculation. The little villas, almost all of two stories, and each with its own garden, not spacious but attractive, belonged to magistrates, teachers, officials, city employees, and on passing by there, especially in the late afternoons of summer, it was usual to see, through the bars of bristling gates, gentlemen in pajamas, busy watering, pruning, and hoeing industriously. Malnate's landlord, a certain Dr. Lalumìa, if I remember the name correctly, was in fact a court judge: a Sicilian of about fifty, very thin, with a great mop of gray hair, who, as soon as he noticed me, standing on the pedals of my bicycle, clutching the stakes of the gate with both hands, to look into the garden, immediately set on the ground the rubber hose with which he was watering the flower beds.

"Yes?" he asked, moving towards the gate.

"Is this where Dr. Malnate lives?"

"Yes, he lives here. Why?"

"Is he at home?"

"I've no idea. Do you have an appointment?"

"I'm a friend of his. I was going by, and I thought I'd stop off a moment to say hello to him."

During this exchange, the judge finished covering the ten yards that separated us. Now I could see only the upper part of his bony, intense face, his black eyes, sharp as pins, peering over the sheet-metal edge that bound the stakes of the gate at a man's height. He was examining me with obvious distrust. Still the examination must have ended in my favor, because the lock clicked almost at once, and I could enter.

"Go around there," the judge said finally, raising his skeletal arm, "follow the sidewalk around the villa. The little door on the ground floor is Signor Malnate's apartment. Ring the bell. He may be in; if he isn't, my wife will open the door. She must be downstairs at this time, preparing his bed for the night."

Having said this, he turned his back on me, picking up again his rubber hose, and paying me no further attention.

Instead of Malnate, at the threshold of the little door described to me by Judge Lalumìa, there appeared a mature, buxom blond woman in a bathrobe.

"Good evening," I said, "I was looking for Signor Malnate."

"He hasn't come home yet," Signora Lalumìa answered, very politely. "But he shouldn't be long. Almost every evening, as soon as he leaves the factory, he goes to play tennis at the home of the Finzi-Continis, you know, the ones who live in Corso Ercole I. . . . But, as I said, he should be here any moment. Before supper," she smiled, lowering her eyelids, rapt, "before supper he always stops by the house to see if there's any mail."

I said I would come back later, and started to collect my bicycle, which I had propped against the wall, beside the door. But the signora insisted I should remain. She had me come in, take a seat in an easy chair, and meanwhile, standing over me, she informed me she was from Ferrara, "pure-bred Ferrarese," that she knew my family very well, and my mother in particular ("your mamma"), with whom, "something like forty years ago"—at this, she smiled again and gently lowered her eyelids—she had gone to the Regina Elena Elementary School, the one near the church of San Giuseppe, in Via Carlo Mayr. How was she, my mamma?—she asked—I mustn't forget to say hello to her, from Edvige, Edvige Santini, she would surely remember. She mentioned the imminent dangers of war, she hinted, with a sigh, at the racial laws, after which excusing herself (the "girl" being off for a few days, she had to do everything herself, including the cooking), she left me alone.

When the signora had gone out, I looked around. I was in a spacious room, but with a low ceiling, a room that obviously served as bedroom, study, and sitting room. It was after eight: the sunset's rays, penetrating from the broad horizontal window, illuminated the motes of dust in the air. I observed the furniture: the day bed, half-bed and half-sofa, at the head a thick white pillow, the foot covered by a cheap, worn counterpane, with red flowers; the little black table, Moorish in style, placed between the sofa and the one easy chair, of imitation leather, where I was sitting; the lamps with pseudoparchment shades more or less everywhere; the white telephone, clearly meant to be smart, which stood out against the funereal black of a lawyer's desk, in bad shape, full of drawers; the banal oil paintings, hung on the walls: and though I told myself that Giampi had his nerve, turning up his nose at Alberto's "modern" furniture (how could his moralism, which made him so severely censorious of others, allow him such indulgence towards himself and his own things?), suddenly, feeling my heart gripped by the thought of Micòl—it was as if she herself had gripped it, with her hand—I renewed my solemn vow to be good, with Malnate, not to argue any more, not to quarrel. When she was informed, Micòl would take this into account, too.

In the distance, the siren of one of the sugar refineries at Pontelagoscuro sounded. A moment later, heavy footsteps crunched on the gravel of the garden.

The judge's voice rose, very near, beyond the wall.

"Ah, Signor Malnate," he said, with a marked nasal intonation, "there's a friend waiting for you in your place."

"A friend?" Malnate asked. "Who is it?"

"Go along, go along . . ." the man urged him. "I said a friend."

Tall, heavy, seeming taller and heavier than ever, perhaps because of the low ceiling, Malnate entered.

"Well, well!" he exclaimed, his eyes widening with amazement, as he adjusted his glasses on his nose.

He shook my hand vigorously, slapped me several times on the shoulder, and it was very strange, for me, who, since we had met, had always had him against me, now to find him so kindly, thoughtful, talkative. Why was it?—I asked myself, confused. Had a decision developed, also on his side, to change tone radically, towards me? Who knows? Certainly, now, in his house, there was nothing left in him of the harsh debater with whom, before the intent eyes of Alberto first, then later, also of Micòl, I had fought so often. It had been enough for me to see him, and I had understood: between us, away from the Finzi-Contini house (and to think that, lately, we had quarreled to the point of insulting each other and, almost, coming to blows!), all reasons for conflict were destined to fall away, to dissolve like mist in the sun.

Meanwhile Malnate was talking: incredibly garrulous and cordial. He asked me if, crossing the garden, I had run into the landlord, and if he had been polite. I answered that I had run into him, and, laughing, I described the scene.

"Thank goodness."

He continued, telling me about the judge and about his wife, not giving me time to inform him that I had also met the latter: excellent people—he said—though, in general, something of a nuisance in their mutual determination to protect him against the snares and dangers of the "vast world." Though definitely anti-Fascist (he was an ardent monarchist), the judge didn't want trouble, and therefore he was constantly on the alert, fearing that Malnate, whom the landlord said he could recognize, by the scent, as a very likely future customer of the Special Political Tribunal, would secretly bring into his house some dangerous types: an ex-prisoner, or someone under surveillance, or a subversive. As for Signora Edvige, she too was always on the alert, spending whole days perched behind the slats of the blinds on the second floor, or turning up at his door at the most unlikely moments, even at night, when she heard him come in. But her fears were of quite a different sort. Good Ferrarese that she was—for she was Ferrarese, the signora, her maiden name was Santini—she knew very well, she assured him, what the women in the city were like, married or single. In her opinion, a young man on his own, a university graduate, a stranger in town, with a little apartment having a private entrance, in Ferrara could be considered ruined: one way or another, in no time the women would reduce his spinal column to a genuine *oss boeucc,* a hollow bone. And he? He, naturally, had always done his best to reassure her, his landlady. But it was obvious: only when she had succeeded in transforming him into a sad boarder, always in his undershirt, pajama pants, and slippers, his nose always sniffing pots in the kitchen, only then would "Madama" Lalumìa find peace.

"Well, after all, why not?" I protested. "I believe I've heard you grumbling often about restaurants and eating places."

"It's true," he admitted with unusual docility: a docility which never ceased to amaze me. "Anyway, it's hopeless. Freedom is, no doubt, a fine thing, but if you don't find some boundaries at a certain point" (with this, he gave me a wink), "where will it all end?"

It was beginning to grow dark. Malnate stood up from the day bed, where he had stretched out full-length, and went to turn on the light, then into the bath. His beard felt a bit itchy—he said, from the bath—Would I give him time to shave? Afterwards, we would go out together.

We went on conversing like that, he from the bath, I from the room.

He reported that that afternoon he had also been at the Finzi-Continis', that he had just left. They had played for more than two hours: first he and Micòl, then he and Alberto, finally all three together. Did I like two-against-one games?

"Not very much," I answered.

"I understand," he agreed. "For you, who're a good player, I realize games like that haven't much sense. But they're fun."

"Who was the winner?"

"Two against one?"

"Yes."

"Micòl, naturally!" he chuckled. "It takes quite a man to keep her down, that girl. On the court, too, she's a cannonball. . . ."

He asked me, then, why I hadn't shown up for several days. Had I been away?

And remembering what Micòl had told me, namely, that nobody believed me when, after every period of absence, I told them I had been on a trip, I answered that I had grown annoyed, that often, lately, I had the impression of being unwelcome, especially to Micòl, and so I had decided to "keep my distance."

"Why, what are you talking about?" he said. "If you ask me, Micòl doesn't have a thing against you. Are you sure you're not mistaken?"

"Very sure."

"Hm." He sighed.

He added nothing further, and I also kept quiet. A little later he reappeared in the doorway of the bath, shaven and smiling. He noticed I was examining the ugly paintings hung on the walls.

"Well then," he said, "what do you think of my den? You haven't expressed your opinion yet."

He grinned in his old way, ready and waiting for my answer, but at the same time, I could read in his eyes the decision to keep the peace.

"I envy you," I answered. "If only I could have something of the sort for myself! I've always dreamed of it."

He gave me a pleased, grateful look. He said then that he, too, of course, realized well the Lalumìas' limitations, as far as taste in interior decoration went. However, their taste, typical of the petty bourgeoisie ("which, finally"—he remarked parenthetically—"is the mainspring, the spinal column of the nation"), still had something vivid, vital, healthy about it: and this probably stemmed directly from its very banality and vulgarity.

"After all, objects are only objects," he exclaimed. "Why make ourselves their slaves?"

I should look at Alberto, on this score—he continued—my God! If he kept on surrounding himself with exquisite things, perfect, flawless, one of these days he himself would end up becoming . . .

He started towards the door, leaving his sentence unfinished.

"How is he?" I asked.

I had also stood up, and had overtaken him at the door.

"Who? Alberto?" he said, with a start.

I nodded.

"Ah, yes," I went on. "Lately he's seemed a bit tired to me, a bit run down. Don't you agree? I have the impression he isn't well."

He shrugged, then turned off the light. He preceded me outside, in the darkness, and didn't utter another word from there to the gate, except to reply, halfway, to the "Good evening" of Signora Lalumìa, who was leaning out of a window, and then to suggest, at the gate in fact, that I come and have supper with him, at Giovanni's.

# VII

I wasn't deceived. No, I had no illusions. Malnate knew very well—I realized perfectly even then—all the reasons, without exception, that were keeping me away from the Finzi-Contini house. The fact is that in our talk the subject never arose again. On the subject of the Finzi-Continis we both showed exceptional reserve and delicacy, and I was particularly grateful that he pretended to believe what I had said to him about the matter the first evening: grateful that he was playing along with me, in short, that he was supporting me.

We saw each other very often, almost every evening. At the beginning of July, the heat, suddenly stifling, emptied the city. As a rule I went to his place, between seven and eight. When I didn't find him at home, I would wait for him patiently, entertained perhaps by Signora Edvige's chatter. But most times, he was there, alone, stretched out on the day bed in a polo shirt, his hands clasped behind his head, his eyes staring at the ceiling, or else seated, writing a letter to his mother, to whom, I discovered, he was bound by deep, even slightly excessive affection. In any case, as soon as he saw me, he would quickly shut himself up in the bath to shave, after which we would go out together, it being understood that we would also have supper together.

We went almost inevitably to Giovanni's, sitting outside, opposite the towers of the Castle, high over our heads like Dolomite cliff-faces, and, like them, grazed at the peaks by the last light of the day; or else to I Voltini, a little restaurant beyond Porta Reno, from whose tables, lined up beneath a fragile arbor facing on to the open country to the south, it was possible to see all the way to the immense fields of the airport. On the hottest evenings, however, instead of heading for the city, we would go off down the lovely Pontelagoscuro road, cross the iron bridge over the Po, and riding side by side along the embankment, with the river on our right and the Veneto countryside on our left, after another fifteen minutes we would reach the big isolated farmhouse halfway between Pontelagoscuro and Polesella, the Dogana Vecchia, famous for its fried eels. We always ate very slowly. We stayed at the table until late, drinking Lambrusco or mild Bosco wine and smoking our pipes. When we ate in town, however, we would put down our napkins at a certain point, each would pay his bill, and then, pushing our bicycles, we would begin strolling along Corso Giovecca, up and down from the Castle to the Prospect, or else along Viale Cavour, from the Castle to the station. It was he, then, usually around midnight, who would offer to see me to my door. He would take a look at his watch, announce that it was time to head home and sleep (it was true—he explained—that the factory siren, for them, the "technical staff," blew only at eight, but it was also true that he always had to drag himself out of bed at six forty-five "at the very latest"); and though I insisted, at times, on accompanying him, there was no way I could make him allow me. The last image of him left to me was always the same: standing in the middle of the street, astride his bicycle, he waited there until I had carefully locked the downstairs door of the house in his face.

Two or three evenings, after eating, we ended up on the bastions of Porta Reno, where, that summer, in the open space overlooking the gasometer on one side, and Piazza Travaglio on the other, an amusement park had been set up. It was a tawdry affair: half a dozen shooting galleries, collected around the mushroom of tan canvas that housed a little circus. The place attracted me. I was attracted and moved by the melancholy society of poor prostitutes, young louts, soldiers, wretched homosexuals from the city's outskirts, who usually frequented the place. I would quote Apollinaire, I would quote Ungaretti. And though Malnate, with the look of someone pulled along against his will, accused me of the "worst sort of literary decadence," at heart he also, after we had eaten at I Voltini, liked to climb up to the dusty clearing, linger there to eat a slice of watermelon beside the acetylene lamp of a melon stand, or spend half an hour at a shooting gallery. He was an excellent marksman, Giampi. Tall and corpulent, distinguished in the well-ironed, cream-colored bushjacket I had seen him wear since the beginning of summer, very calm as he took aim through his thick tortoise-shell-rimmed glasses, he had obviously taken the fancy of the painted and lewd Tuscan girl—a sort of queen of the place—at whose stand, the moment we appeared from the stone stair that went up from

Piazza Travaglio to the bastion, we were imperiously invited to stop. As Malnate shot, she, the girl, did not spare him obscene comments, of a sexual nature, to which he, calling her *tu*, replied with great wit, with the easy nonchalance typical of someone who had spent many hours of his early youth in brothels.

One August evening, especially sultry, we happened instead on an outdoor movie, where, I remember, they were showing a German picture with Cristina Söderbaum. We went in after the film had begun, and immediately, paying no attention to Malnate, who kept telling me to be careful, to stop "vociferating," since, really, it wasn't worth the trouble, I had begun whispering ironic remarks. He was a thousand times right, Malnate. In fact, suddenly rising to his feet against the milky background of the screen, a character in the row ahead ordered me, threateningly, to shut up. I replied with an insult, the man shouted, "Get out, you lousy Jew!" and at the same time, flung himself on me, grabbing me by the neck. And I was lucky that Malnate, without a word, was quick to shove my assailant back into his seat and pull me away.

"You really are an idiot," he reproached me, after we had, in great haste, recovered our bicycles, left in the parking lot. "And now, let's clear out: praying to your God that the pig in there was just guessing."

And so, one after the other, we spent our evenings, always with the air of congratulating each other, reciprocally, that now, unlike the days in Alberto's company, we could converse without squabbling, and so we never considered the possibility that he, Alberto, summoned by a simple phone call, could also leave the house and join us.

We neglected political subjects now. Both relying on the certainty that France and England, whose diplomatic missions had reached Moscow some time ago, would finally come to an understanding with the USSR (the agreement, which we considered inevitable, would at once save the independence of Poland and the peace, and would provoke, in consequence, not only the end of the Pact of Steel, but at least the downfall of Mussolini), now it was of literature and art that we talked almost always. Keeping his tone moderate, never going too far in the debate (besides—he declared—he understood art only up to a point, it wasn't his field), Malnate remained firm in rejecting, in a body, everything I loved most: Eliot along with Montale, García Lorca and Esenin alike. He would listen to me recite, with emotion, Montale's *Do not ask of us the word,* or passages of Lorca's *Lament for Ignacio,* and I would hope in vain, each time, that I had roused some warmth in him, converted him to my taste. Shaking his head, he would say no, Montale's line about "what we are *not,* what we do *not* want" left him cold, indifferent, true poetry could not be based on negation (please, I wasn't to bring Leopardi into it! Leopardi was another matter, and besides he had written *La ginestra,* I shouldn't forget that!), but instead, on the affirmative, on the *yes* that the poet, in the final analysis, *cannot* fail to shout against hostile Nature and Death. The paintings of Morandi didn't convince him either—he said—very fine, no doubt, delicate, but, in his view, too "individual," too "subjective" and "without an anchor." The fear of reality, the fear of making a mistake: that was what Morandi's still lifes basically expressed, those famous pictures of bottles and little flowers; and fear, also in art, has always been a poor adviser. . . . To which, though deploring his views in silence, I could never find arguments in rebuttal. The thought that the next afternoon, he, the lucky one, would certainly see Alberto and Micòl, and perhaps talk about me with them, was enough to make me suppress any whim of rebellion, to force me back into my shell.

All the same, I was champing at the bit.

"Well, look at yourself, after all," I protested one evening. "Towards contemporary literature, the only living literature, you hold the same radically negative attitude that you won't tolerate, on the other hand, in it, *our* literature, if it expresses any negation towards life. Does this seem fair to you? Your ideal poets are still Victor Hugo and Carducci. Admit it."

"Why not?" he answered. "If you ask me, Carducci's republican poems, the ones before his political conversion—before his neoclassical, monarchist senility, it would be more correct to say—are all to be rediscovered. Have you reread them lately? Try, and you'll see."

I answered that I had not reread them, and that I had no wish to. For me, they were and remained empty, "hot air," those poems, also swollen with patriotic bombast. Downright incomprehensible. And, if anything, amusing for this very reason: because incomprehensible, and therefore, in the final analysis, "surreal."

One evening, nevertheless, not so much because I wanted to look good in his eyes, but, who knows, impelled perhaps by a vague need that I had felt urgently inside me, for some time, to confess, to pour out everything, I succumbed to the temptation of reciting a poem of mine to him. I had written it on the train, returning from Bologna after the defense of my thesis, and though for some weeks I had continued deluding myself that it faithfully reflected my profound desolation of those days, the horror I had felt towards myself then, now as I recited it to Malnate, I could see gradually, clearly, with discomfort more than dismay, all its falsity, all its literary airs. We were walking along Corso Giovecca, down towards the Prospect, beyond which the darkness of the countryside seemed dense, a kind of black wall. I declaimed slowly, making an effort to underline the rhythm, charging my voice with pathos in the attempt to make my poor spoiled goods pass for the real thing, but more and more convinced, as I was approaching the end, of the inevitable failure of my exhibition. I was wrong, however. As soon as I had finished, Malnate stared at me with extraordinary gravity, then, taking my breath away, he assured me he liked the poem very much, very much indeed. He asked me to recite it to him a second time (and I obliged at once), after which he declared to me that, in his humble opinion, my "lyric" alone was worth more than all the "painful convulsions of Montale and Ungaretti put together." You could feel a real grief in it, a "moral commitment," absolutely new, genuine. Was Malnate sincere? At least on that occasion I would say yes. The sure thing is that, having soon learned my verses by heart, he quoted them constantly, insisting that in them it was possible to see a "new path" for a poetry that, like contemporary Italy's, was arrested in the dry shoals of the calligraphic, hermetic school. As for me, I am not ashamed to confess that I let him have his say, without contradicting him. Against his hyperbolic praise, I confined myself to venturing some weak protests, my heart filled with a gratitude and a hope much more moving than they were despicable, now that I think back.

In any case, as far as Malnate's tastes in poetry are concerned, here I feel obliged to add that neither Carducci nor Victor Hugo was his favorite poet. Carducci and Victor Hugo he respected, as an anti-Fascist, a Marxist. But his real passion, like a true Milanese, was Porta: a poet who, till then, I had always found inferior to Belli, but this was wrong—Malnate insisted—how could I compare the funereal, counterreformation monotony of Belli with the various and warm humanity of Porta?

He knew hundreds of verses by heart.

> *Bravo el mè Baldissar! bravo el mè nan!*
> *l'eva poeù vora de vegnì a trovamm.* . . .
> *T'el seet mattascion porch che maneman*
> *l'è on mes che no te vegnet a ciollamm?*
> *Ah Cristo! Cristo! com'hin frecc sti man!*

> [Good for you, my Baldassare! Good for you,
>       my little man!
> It was high time you came to see me. . . .
> Do you know, you crazy pig, that it's almost
> A month since you've come to screw me?
> Ah! Christ! Christ! how cold these hands are!]

He would start declaiming aloud, with his heavy, slightly hoarse Milanese voice, every night as, strolling, we approached Via Sacra, Via Colomba, and went slowly up along Via delle Volte, peeping through the doors, left ajar, at the lighted interiors of the brothels. He knew *La Ninetta del Verzee* from beginning to end; it was he who revealed it to me.

Threatening me with his finger, winking his eye in a sly and allusive expression (alluding to some remote episode of his Milanese adolescence, I supposed), he would often whisper:

> *Nò Ghittin: no sont capazz*
> *de traditt: nò, stà pur franca.*
> *Mettem minga insemma a mazz*
> *coj gingitt e cont i s'cianca.*

> [No, Margheritina, I'm not capable
> of being unfaithful to you: no, rest assured.
> Don't lump me together
> with rogues and rascals.]

et cetera. Or else, in a bitter, heart-rent tone, he would begin:

> *Paracar, che scappee de Lombardia* .
> [You sentries, who are running away
>       from Lombardy . . .]

underlining each verse of the sonnet with sly references dedicated, not to the French of Napoleon, naturally, but to the Fascists.

He would quote with equal enthusiasm and intensity also the poems of Ragazzoni and Delio Tessa; Tessa, in particular, who still—and I didn't fail, once, to point this out to him—did not seem to me possible to call a "classic" poet, steeped as he was in decadent sensitivity. But the fact is that anything connected somehow with Milan and with its dialect always inspired in him an extraordinary indulgence. Of Milan he accepted everything, he smiled good-humoredly at everything. In Milan, even literary decadence, even Fascism had something positive about it.

He declaimed:

> *Pensa ed opra, varda e scolta,*
> *tant se viv e tant se impara;*
> *mi, quand nassi on'altra volta,*
> *nassi on gatt de portinara!*
>
> *Per esempi, in Rugabella,*
> *nassi el gatt del sur Pinin . . .*
> *. . . scartoseij de coradella,*
> *polpa e fidegh, barettin*
>
> *del patron per dormigh sora . . .*
>
> [Think and work, look and listen,
> the more you live, the more you learn;
> I, if I'm born another time,
> would be born a concierge's cat!
>
> For example, in Rugabella,
> were I born the cat of Signor Giuseppino . . .
> . . . packages of lung and heart,
> meat and liver, and the cap
>
> of the master, to sleep upon . . .]

and he would laugh to himself; he laughed, full of tenderness and nostalgia.

I didn't understand everything in Milanese, obviously, and when I didn't understand, I would ask.

"Tell me, Giampi," I asked one evening, "What's Rugabella? It's true, I've been to Milan, but I certainly can't say I know the city. Would you believe it? It's probably the hardest city for me to get my bearings in: even worse than Venice."

"What!" he retorted, with strange impetuosity. "Why there's no city so clear, so rational! I don't understand how you dare mention it in the same breath with that depressing, damp latrine, Venice!

But then, immediately becoming calm, he explained to me that Rugabella was a street: the old street, not very far from the Duomo, where he was born, where his parents still lived, and where in a few months, perhaps even before the end of the year (provided that the General Management Office, in Milan, didn't tear up his application for transfer!), he also hoped to be able to go back and live. Because, mind you—he clarified— Ferrara was a fine city, lively, interesting in many ways, including its politics. He considered important, indeed fundamental, the experience of the two years he had spent here. But home is home, and Mamma is Mamma, and the sky of Lombardy, "so beautiful, when it is beautiful," couldn't be compared, for him at least, to any other sky in the world.

# VIII

As I have said before, when the twenty-first day of exile was over, I began to go back to the Finzi-Continis' every Tuesday and Friday. Still not knowing how to spend my Sundays (even if I had wanted to resume relations with old *liceo* companions, with Nino Bottecchiari or with Otello Forti, just to name a couple, or with my more recent university acquaintances, made these last few years in Bologna, it would have been impossible: all of them had left for their summer holidays), I allowed myself to go there also sometimes on Sunday. And Micòl had let it pass, she had never held me to the letter of our agreement.

Now we were very considerate of each other, too much so. Aware of the precarious balance we had attained, we were careful not to break it, to remain in a neutral zone, of reciprocal respect, excluding not only excessive coldness but also excessive confidence. When Alberto felt like playing, and this happened more and more rarely, I gladly lent myself to be a fourth, but avoiding, if possible, being Micòl's partner. Most of the time, however, I didn't even change. I preferred to referee the long, dogged singles between her and Malnate, or else, sitting under the big umbrella at the side of the court, I kept Alberto company.

Visibly worse, his health worried me, distressed me. I thought about it all the time. Little by little, Alberto's condition had become, for me, another secret ache, the source of a rage perhaps even more acute and painful than the thought of Micòl, constant as that was. I looked at his face which, growing thinner, seemed to have lengthened, I examined his neck carefully: it, on the contrary, had thickened, and the passage of his respiration seemed to me more toilsome every day, and my heart grieved, oppressed by a mysterious remorse. There were moments when, to see him bloom again, I would have given anything.

"Why don't you go away for a while?" I asked him one day.

He turned to look at me.

"You find me run down?"

"No, not exactly run down . . I'd say you've lost weight. Does the heat bother you?"

"Very much." He huffed.

He raised his arms, accompanying a long inhalation.

"For some time now, my friend, I've been drawing every breath by the skin of my teeth. Go away . . . but go away *where?*"

"I think the mountains would do you good. What does your uncle say? Has he examined you?"

"Of course. Uncle Giulio swears there's nothing wrong with me; and it must be the truth, don't you think? Otherwise, he would have ordered some sort of treatment for me! . . . According to my uncle, actually, I can play tennis as much as I like. What more can you ask? It's the heat, of course, that has got me down like this. In fact, I don't eat anything, hardly a morsel."

"Well, since it's the heat, why don't you go to the mountains for a couple of weeks?"

"The mountains, in August? Good Lord, no. And besides . . ."— here he smiled—"and besides, *Juden sind* everywhere *unerwünscht.* Have you forgotten that?"

"Nonsense. Not at San Martino di Castrozza, for example. Anyone can go freely to San Martino, and, for that matter, also to the Lido in Venice, to Gli Alberoni. . . . The *Corriere della sera* said so, last week."

"How dismal. To spend the mid-August holiday in a hotel, elbow to elbow with athletic throngs of merry Levis and Cohanìm; no, sorry, I don't feel up to that. I prefer to stay where I am, sitting it out till September."

The following evening, taking advantage of the new atmosphere of intimacy created between us after I had ventured to submit my verses to his judgment, I made up my mind to speak with Malnate about Alberto's health. There was no doubt—I said—in my opinion, that something was wrong with Alberto. Hadn't he also noticed how difficult it was for Alberto to breathe? And didn't it seem to him strange, to say the least, that nobody in the family, neither his uncle nor his father, had so far taken the slightest initiative to treat him? The doctor uncle, the one from Venice, didn't believe in medicines, all right. But all the others, his sister included? Calm, smiling, seraphic: nobody was lifting a finger.

Malnate heard me out in silence.

"I hope you're not being overanxious," he said finally, with a faint tinge of embarrassment in his voice. "Does he really seem so bad to you?"

"Why, good heavens!" I blurted. "He must have lost twenty-five pounds in two months!"

"Oh, come now! Twenty-five pounds is a lot!"

"Well, if it's not twenty-five, it must be twenty, eighteen, At least."

He was silent, pensive. He admitted then that, for some time now, he too had noticed Alberto wasn't well. But then—he added—were we really sure, the two of us, that we weren't getting upset over nothing? If the closest members of his family weren't making a move, if even Professor Ermanno's face betrayed not the slightest uneasiness, then . . . Professor Ermanno, there you were: if Alberto were really ill, presumably his father would never have thought to order those two truckloads of red earth from Imola for the tennis court! And, while we were talking about the tennis court: did I know that in a few days they were going to start also enlarging the famous out-of-bounds zone?

And thus, starting with Alberto and his presumed illness, we had imperceptibly introduced into our nightly conversations also the subject—taboo till then—of the Finzi-Continis. We were well aware, both of us, that we were treading on a minefield, and for this very reason, we always proceeded with great caution, very careful not to go too far. Every time we spoke of them as a family, however, as an "institution" (I don't know which of us was the first to use this word: I remember that we liked it, that it made us laugh), Malnate didn't spare his criticisms, even the most harsh. What impossible people!—he would say. What a curious, absurd tangle of insoluble contradictions they represented "socially"! At times, thinking of the thousands of acres of land they owned, thinking of the thousands of farm laborers who hoed that land, meek, disciplined slaves of the Corporative Regime, sometimes he almost preferred to them the grim "normal" landowners, those who in '20 and '21 and '22, determined to set up and supply the lousy squads of bullies and castor-oil-givers in black shirts, hadn't hesitated a moment to open their purses. They, *at least,* were Fascists. When the occasion arose, there would surely be no doubts as to how to deal with them. But the Finzi-Continis?

And he would shake his head, with the look of one who, if he liked, could also understand, but who didn't want to, didn't feel up to it: split hairs, complications, infinitesimal distinctions, however interesting or amusing, at a certain point—enough—they also have to come to an end.

One night in mid-August, late, we had stopped to drink some wine in a tavern in Via Gorgadello, beside the Duomo, a few steps from what until a year and a half before had been the office of Dr. Fadigati, the well-known ear-nose-and-throat specialist. Between glasses, I told Malnate the story of the doctor, of whom, in the five months preceding his suicide "for love," I had become such a good friend, the last one he had left in the city (I said "for love": and Malnate, at this point, couldn't restrain a little sarcastic laugh, as if at a students' joke). From Fadigati in particular to speaking about homosexuality in general had been a short step. Malnate, on this subject, had very simple ideas: like a true *goy*—I thought to myself. For him, homosexuals were only "poor bastards," "obsessed" creatures, not worth considering from a medical point of view or from the point of view of social assistance. I, on the contrary, sustained that love justifies and sanctifies everything, even homosexuality; and more: that love, when it is pure, completely without material interest, is always abnormal, antisocial, et cetera, just like art—I had added—which, when it is pure, hence useless, annoys all priests of all religions, including the Socialist religion. Casting aside all our fine proposals of moderation, for once we grew heated, arguing almost as in the early days, until the moment when, suddenly realizing we had had a bit to drink, we burst out together in a big laugh. Afterwards we left the tavern, crossed the half-deserted paved area of the Listone, went up San Romano, to find ourselves finally walking, aimlessly, along Via delle Volte.

Without sidewalks, with many gaps among the cobblestones, the street seemed even darker than usual. As always, while we advanced, almost groping, and with the sole aid, to guide us, of the light that came from the slightly opened doors of the bordellos, Malnate had struck up some stanzas of Porta: not of *Ninetta,* I remember, but of the *Marchionn di gamb avert.*

He declaimed in a low voice, in the bitter and grieving tone he always assumed, reciting the *Lament:*

> *Finalment l'alba tance voeult spionada*
> *l'è comparsa anca lee di filidur*
>
> [Finally the dawn, so often sighed for,
> has also appeared, at the blinds]

But here, suddenly, he broke off.

"What would you say?" he asked me, pointing his chin towards the door of a brothel, "if we went inside for a look?"

There was nothing exceptional about the suggestion; still, coming from him, with whom I had always discussed only serious things, it amazed and embarrassed me.

"It's not one of the best," I answered. "It must be a ten-lire place, or less. . . . But let's go in, anyway."

It was late, almost one in the morning, and the reception given us was anything but warm. The woman at the door, seated on a straw chair just inside the little entrance, began at once making a fuss because she didn't want us to bring in our bicycles; next, the madam, a little woman of undefinable age, thin, livid, with eyeglasses, dressed in black like a sort of nun, started complaining about the bicycles and the hour. A maid, then, who had already begun cleaning up the various little sitting rooms, with broom, dust rag, and dustpan under her arm, as we crossed the brief hall, gave us a look charged with contempt. And even the girls, all collected in a single room, calmly conversing, around a little group of regular visitors, didn't make a show of welcome. Nobody came up to us. And at least ten minutes passed, while Malnate and I, seated facing each other, in the little separate room to which the madam had shunted us, exchanged hardly a word (through the walls the girls' laughter reached us, the coughing, the sleepy voices of their customer-friends), before a little refined-looking blond, her hair pulled into a knot on her neck, dressed as soberly as a high-school girl of good family, made up her mind to appear in the doorway.

She didn't seem all that annoyed.

"Good evening," she greeted us.

She examined us calmly, her pale eyes full of irony. Then she said, addressing me: "Well, Blue Eyes, what are we going to do?"

"What's your name?" I managed to stammer.

"Gisella."

"Where are you from?"

"Bologna!" she exclaimed, widening her eyes, as if to promise who knows what.

But it wasn't true. Calm, in perfect control, Malnate realized this at once.

"Bologna, hell," he said. "If you ask me, you're from Lombardy, and not even from Milan. You must come from around Como somewhere, eh?"

"How did you guess?" the girl asked, dumbfounded.

Meanwhile, behind her back, the madam's weasel face had appeared.

"Well," she grumbled, "we don't seem to be doing much in here."

"No, no," Gisella protested, smiling and pointing to me. "Blue Eyes there has serious intentions. Shall we go?"

Before standing up and following her, I turned towards Malnate. But he also looked at me with an encouraging, affectionate expression. "What about you?"

He emitted a brief laugh, making a vague gesture with his hand, as if to say: I have nothing to do with it, count me out.

"Don't worry about me," he added. "Go on up. I'll wait for you."

Everything went very quickly. When we came downstairs again, Malnate was conversing with the madam. He had taken out his pipe: he talked, and smoked. He inquired about the "economic treatment" of prostitutes, the "mechanism" of their two-week shifts, the "medical control," et cetera; and the woman answered him with equal seriousness and commitment.

*"Bon,"* Malnate said at last, noticing my presence; and he stood up.

He passed in front of me, crossed the hall, heading for our bicycles, which we had propped against the wall beside the exit, as the madam, very polite now, ran ahead to open the door for us.

"Good night," Malnate said to her.

He dropped a coin into the extended palm of the doorkeeper, and went out ahead of me.

" 'Bye, darling," Gisella shouted, yawning, before she disappeared into the little room where the other girls were gathered. "Come back, eh!"

" 'Bye," I answered, as I also left.

"Good night, gentlemen," the madam whispered respectfully, at my back; and I heard her close the door and bolt it.

Gripping the handlebars of our bicycles, we walked up Via Scienze to the corner of Via Mazzini. Arriving there, we turned right, along Via Saraceno. Now Malnate was doing the talking. He reported to me what he had learned from the proprietress of the brothel. In Milan, until a few years before—he said—he had been a fairly regular customer of the famous brothel in San Pietro dell'Orto (where—he added—he had tried on several occasions, without any success, also to take Alberto), but it was only now that he had bothered to collect some information on the laws that regulated the "system." Good God— he deplored—what a life, the life whores led! And how base and backwards "the ethical state" was, organizing such a commerce in human flesh!

Then, noticing that I answered him curtly, reluctantly, he asked: "What's wrong? Don't you feel well?"

"No, no."

*"Omne animal post coitum triste,"* he sighed. "But don't think about it. Get a good night's sleep, and you'll see, tomorrow everything will be magnificent again."

"I know, I know."

We turned left, onto Via Borgo di Sotto.

"Signora Trotti, the schoolmistress, must live around here," he said, nodding towards the humble little houses on the right, towards Via Fondo Banchetto.

I didn't answer. He coughed.

"Well . . . how's it going, with Micòl?"

Suddenly I was assailed by a great need to confide, to open my heart to him.

"It's going badly. . . . I've fallen hard."

"Eh, we realized that," he laughed, good-humoredly. "A long time ago. But how are things now? Is she still treating you badly?"

"No. As you must have seen, lately we've achieved a certain *modus vivendi.*"

"Yes, I've seen you don't bicker the way you did before. I'm glad you're becoming friends again. It was absurd."

My mouth twisted in a grimace, as tears clouded my eyes. Malnate must have noticed my condition.

"Come on," he exhorted me, embarrassed, "you *mustn't* let yourself go like this."

I gulped, with an effort.

"I don't think we'll be friends again," I murmured. "It's useless."

"Nonsense," he said. "If you only knew, really, how fond she is of you. When you're not there, and she speaks of you—she speaks of you very often—woe to anybody who dares criticize you. She turns into a viper. Alberto is fond of you too, and he respects you. In fact, a few days ago (maybe I was a bit indiscreet, excuse me . . .) I recited your poem to them. My God! You can't imagine how much they liked it: both of them, mind you, both of them. . . ."

"Their fondness is no good to me, nor their respect," I said.

Meanwhile we had come out into the little square in front of Santa Maria in Vado. Not a living soul was in sight, there, or along Via Scandiana as far as the Montagnone hill. We headed in silence towards the drinking fountain set beside the churchyard. Malnate bent over to drink; and after him, I, too, drank and rinsed my face.

"Look," Malnate continued, walking on, "in my opinion, you're wrong to talk like that. Fondness and respect, especially in times like these, are the only values you can really count on. What is less materialistic than friendship? And besides, it doesn't seem to me—at least, as far as I know—it doesn't seem to me that, between you two, anything happened that . . . It's quite possible that, with time . . . For example: why don't you come and play tennis more often, the way you did a few months ago? The absence tactic isn't necessarily the best! I have the impression, my friend, that you don't know women very well."

"But she herself told me to come less often!" I burst out. "You want me to disobey her? After all, it's her house!"

He was silent a few seconds, pensive.

"It seems impossible to me," he said finally. "I might even understand perhaps, if, between the two of you, before, there had been something . . . how can I say it . . . something serious, irreparable. But, after all, what happened?"

He examined me, hesitantly.

"Forgive me if the question isn't very . . . diplomatic," he went on, and he smiled: "Did you ever go so far as to kiss her, at least?"

"Ah, lots of times," I sighed, in despair. "Unfortunately for me."

I told him, then, in the greatest detail, the story of our relationship, going back to the beginning, and without omitting the episode of last May, in her bedroom, an episode that I considered—I said—decisive, in the negative sense, and beyond repair. I also described how I had kissed her, or at least how, on several occasions and not only that time in the bedroom, I had tried to kiss her, along with her various reactions, when she was more disgusted and when less.

He let me unburden myself; and I was so absorbed, so lost in these bitter recollections, that I paid no heed to his silence, which had meanwhile become hermetic.

We had been standing outside the door of my house: for almost half an hour by now. Suddenly I saw him start.

"Damn," he muttered, checking the time. "It's two-fifteen. I really have to go. Otherwise, who'll get me up tomorrow morning?"

He sprang onto his bicycle.

"So long, eh," he said, leaving. "And cheer up!"

His face was strange, I noticed, as if it had turned gray. Had my confidences about love bored him, irritated him?

I stood and watched him as he rapidly rode off. It was the first night that he had left me there, like that, without waiting till I had gone into the house.

# IX

Late as it was, my father still hadn't turned out his light.

Ever since, beginning with the summer of '37, the racial campaign had been launched in all the newspapers, he had been affected by a serious form of insomnia, which was at its worst in summer, with the heat. He would spend whole nights without closing his eyes, reading a bit, or roaming about the house, or, in the breakfast room, listening to the Italian-language broadcasts from foreign radio stations, or chatting briefly with Mamma in her room. If I came in after one in the morning, it was difficult for me to pass along the corridor, where, one after the other, the bedrooms opened (the first was Papà's, the second Mamma's, then came those of Ernesto and Fanny, and finally, at the end, mine), without his noticing. It was all very well for me to advance on tiptoe, or even to remove my shoes: my father's ear, very sensitive, perceived the faintest creaks and rustles.

"Is that you?"

As was to be foreseen, that night, too, I did not escape his control. As a rule, his "Is that you?" achieved the effect only of making me walk faster: I would go straight on without answering him, pretending not to have heard. But that night, no. Though imagining, with some annoyance, the sort of questions I would have to answer, always the same, for years— "Why so late?" "Do you know what time it is?" "Where have you been?" et cetera—I preferred to stop. Opening the door slightly, I stuck my head inside.

"What are you doing there?" my father said at once, from the bed, peering at me over his eyeglasses. "Come in, come in for a moment."

He was not lying down, but sitting up, in his nightshirt, his back and his nape against the bedstead of carved blond wood, and covered only up to the base of his stomach with just a sheet. I was struck by the way everything, in him and his surroundings, was white: his silver hair, his wan face, his snowy nightshirt, the pillow beneath his back, the sheet, the book set down, open, on his stomach; how that whiteness (a hospital whiteness, I thought) harmonized with the surprising, extraordinary serenity, the unfamiliar expression of goodness charged with wisdom that illuminated his pale eyes.

"How late it is!" he remarked, smiling, as he glanced at his waterproof Rolex wristwatch, which he never removed, not even in bed. "You know what time it is? Twenty-seven past two."

For the first time, perhaps, since, at eighteen, I had been given the latchkey to the house, this ritual sentence did not irritate me.

"I've been out," I said calmly.

"With that Milanese friend of yours?"

"Yes."

"What does he do? Is he still a student?"

"Student? He's twenty-seven years old! He has a job. He works as a chemist in the Industrial Zone, in a synthetic rubber factory of the Montecatini."

"Imagine! And I thought he was still at the university! Why don't you ever invite him to supper?"

"Oh . . . I thought it wasn't a good idea to make more work for Mamma than she already has."

"No, no, not at all! What difference does it make? One more bowl of soup, it's nothing. Bring him, bring him along. And . . . where did you have supper. At Giovanni's?"

I nodded.

"Tell me what you had to eat."

Politely, not without some surprise at my own indulgence, I made myself list for him the various dishes: the ones I had chosen, and those chosen by Malnate. Meanwhile I sat down.

"Good," my father agreed finally, pleased.

"And after that," he went on, after a pause, "what in the world have you been up to, the pair of you? I bet"—here he raised a hand, as if to forestall any denial on my part—"I bet you're been with women."

There had never been any confidences between us on this subject. A fierce modesty, a violent and irrational need of freedom and independence, had always impelled me to freeze at the start all his shy attempts to bring up such subjects. But not that night. I looked at him: so white, so fragile, so old. And meanwhile, within me, it was as if something (a kind of knot, an age-old secret tangle . . . ) were slowly dissolving.

"Of course," I said. "You guessed it."

"You went to a brothel, I presume."

"Yes."

"Very good," he approved. "At that age, at yours especially, brothels are the most sensible solution from every point of view: including health. But tell me: how do you manage for money? Is the allowance Mamma gives you enough? If you run short, just ask me: I'll help you out, as far as possible."

"Thanks."

"Where did you go? To Maria Ludargnani's? She was already active in my day "

"No. A place on Via delle Volte."

"The only thing I urge you," he continued, suddenly assuming the language of the medical profession which he had practiced only as a young man, until, at my grandfather's death, he had devoted himself exclusively to managing our land at Masi Torello, and the two buildings he owned on Via Vignatagliata, "the only thing I urge you is *never* to neglect the necessary prophylactic measures. It's a nuisance, I know, one would gladly skip them. But it's so easy to catch a nasty blennorrhagia, *vulgo*, the clap, or worse. And most of all: if in the morning, when you wake up, you happen to notice something wrong, come *at once* to the bathroom and show me, eh? If necessary, I'll tell you what must be done."

"I understand. Don't worry."

I sensed he was seeking the best way to ask me something else. Now that I had taken my degree—I guessed he was about to ask me—did I have any ideas about the future, any plans? Instead he digressed into politics. Before I came in—he said—between one and two, he had managed to pick up various foreign stations: Monteceneri, Paris, London, Beromünster. Now, on the basis of the latest news, he had become convinced the international situation was rapidly worsening. Ah yes, unfortunately: it was really a "bad business." In Moscow, the Anglo-French diplomatic missions now seemed about to leave (without having achieved a thing, of course!). Would they really leave Moscow like that? It was to be feared: afterwards there would be nothing left for any of us but prayer.

"What do you think?" he exclaimed. "Stalin isn't the type to have scruples. If it suited his game, I'm sure he wouldn't hesitate a moment to come to an agreement with Hitler!"

"An agreement between Germany and the Soviet Union?" I smiled weakly. "No, I don't think so; it doesn't seem possible to me."

"We'll see," he answered, and smiled in his turn. "God help us!"

At this point, from the next room, a groan was heard. My mother had waked up.

"What did you say, Ghigo?" she asked. "Hitler's dead?"

"No such luck," my father sighed. "Go to sleep, go to sleep, angel, don't be upset."

"What time is it?"

"Almost three."

"Send that boy to bed!"

Mamma murmured a few more incomprehensible words, then was silent.

My father stared at me for a long time, into my eyes. Then, in a low voice, almost whispering:

"Forgive me, if I take the liberty of speaking to you about these things," he said, "but you must understand . . . both your mother and I have been quite aware, this past year, that you're in love with . . . with Micòl Finzi-Contini. That's true, isn't it?"

"Yes."

"And how are things, now, between you? Still going badly?"

"They couldn't be worse," I murmured, suddenly realizing with extreme clarity that I was speaking the precise truth, that in fact things between us could not be worse, and that, despite Malnate's opinion to the contrary, I would never be able to regain ground, to scale the slope at the bottom of which I had been struggling, for months.

My father heaved a sigh.

"I know, these are great sorrows. .    But, after all, it's much better this way."

I stood with my head bowed, saying nothing.

"Yes," he went on, raising his voice slightly. "What would you have liked? To be engaged?"

Micòl too, that evening in her room, had asked me the same question. She had said: "How are we to act? *Become engaged*, for instance?" I hadn't breathed a word. I had had nothing to answer. Like now—I reflected—like now, with my father.

"Why not?" I said, all the same, and I looked at him.

He shook his head.

"You think I don't understand you?" he said. "I like the girl too. I always have, ever since she was a child . . . when she used to come down, in temple, to receive the *berahà* from her father. Pretty, even beautiful (too beautiful, perhaps), intelligent, full of spirit . . . But an en-gage-ment!" he articulated, widening his eyes. "An engagement, my dear boy, means then getting married; and in times like these, and without a steady profession furthermore . . . now I ask you if . . . I imagine that, to support the family, you wouldn't count on my help (which I wouldn't be able to give you, for that matter, at least to the necessary extent), or, still less, on hers. The girl will surely have a fine dowry," he added, "no doubt about that! But I don't think you . . ."

"Never mind the dowry," I said. "If we had been in love, what difference would the dowry have made?"

"You're right," my father agreed. "You are absolutely right. I myself, when I became engaged to Mamma, back in '11, paid no attention to these things. But times were different them. You could look ahead, to the future, with a certain serenity. And though the future didn't prove so jolly and easy as the two of us imagined (we were married in '15, as you know, after the war had begun, after I had volunteered), it was society that was different then, a society that guaranteed . . . Besides, I had studied medicine, while you . . ."

"While I?"

"That's right. Instead of medicine, you preferred literature, and you know that, when the moment to decide came, I didn't put any obstacles in your way. That was your passion, and both of us, you and I, did our duty: you, in choosing the path you felt you had to choose, and I, in not preventing you. But now . . . Even if you had hoped for a university career, as a professor . . ."

I shook my head.

"Worse," he went on, "worse still! It's true that nothing, even now, can prevent you from continuing to study on your own . . . continuing your cultivation, in order to attempt, one day, if it's possible, the far more difficult and risky career of the writer, of the critic like Edoardo Scarfoglio, Vincenzo Morello, Ugo Ojetti . . . or else, why not? the novelist, the . . ." and he smiled, "the poet. . . . But for this very reason: how could you, at your age, barely twenty-three, and with everything before you, still to come . . . how could you think of taking a wife, of starting a family?"

He spoke of my literary future—I said to myself—as a beautiful and seductive dream, not translatable into something concrete, real. He spoke of it as if he and I were already dead, and now, from a point outside space and time, we were conversing together about life, about everything that, in the course of our respective lives, could have been and had not been. Would Hitler and Stalin come to an agreement? I also asked myself, Why not? Quite probably, Hitler and Stalin would come to an agreement.

"But apart from this," my father went on, "and apart from a number of

other considerations, will you allow me to say something to you frankly . . . to give you some friendly advice?''

"Go ahead.''

"I realize that when a young man, especially at your age, loses his head
over a girl, he doesn't stop and calculate. . . . I also realize that your
character is somewhat special . . . and don't think that two years ago,
when that wretched Dr. Fadigati . . ."

Since Fadigati had died, in our house, his name had never been mentioned. What did Fadigati have to with anything, now?

I looked him in the face.

"Yes, let me say it!" he said. "Your temperament (I have the impression you take after your grandmother Fanny), your temperament . . .
You're too sensitive, that's it, and so you are never satisfied . . . you are
always looking for . . ."

He didn't finish. He indicated, with his hand, ideal worlds, inhabited by
pure fancies.

"In any case, forgive me," he resumed, "but even as a family, the
Finzi-Continis were not right . . . they weren't people for us. . . .
Marrying a girl of that sort, you would, I'm sure, have found yourself in
trouble sooner or later. . . . Yes, yes," he insisted, perhaps fearing some
word or gesture of protest from me, "you also know what my opinion has
always been, on that score. They are different . . . they don't even seem
*judìm*. . . . Ah, I know: Micòl, perhaps, attracted you for that very reason . . . because she was superior to us . . . socially. But listen to me:
it's better that things have ended this way. You know the old proverb:
'wife and oxen from your own town.' And despite appearances, that girl
was not from your town. Not in the least.''

I had hung my head again, and I was staring at my hands, open on my
knees.

"You'll get over it," he went on, "you'll get over it, and much quicker
than you think. Naturally I'm sorry: I can imagine what you're feeling at
this moment. But you know? I also envy you a little. In life, if one wants
seriously to understand how the world works, he *must* die at least once.
And, since this is the rule, better to die young, when you still have so much
time ahead of you to pull yourself together and resuscitate. . . . To understand, when you're old, is bad, much worse. What's to be done then?
There's no time left to start over again from the beginning, and our genera-

tion has made so many mistakes! In any case, thank God, you're so young! In a few months, you'll see, it won't seem possible to you that you went through all this. You will, perhaps, even be pleased. You'll feel richer, I don't know . . . more mature. . . ."

"Let's hope so," I murmured.

"I'm happy to get this off my chest, to rid myself of this burden that was weighing on me. . . . And now, one last suggestion. May I?"

I nodded.

"Don't go there any more, to their house. Start studying again, concern yourself with something, give lessons perhaps, since, as I hear, there is a great demand. . . . And don't go there any more. It would be more manly, for one thing."

He was right. For one thing, it would be more manly.

"I'll try," I said, raising my eyes. "I'll do my best."

"That's the spirit!"

He looked at the time.

"And now, go off to sleep," he added, "you need it. And I'll try to close my eyes for a moment, too."

I stood up, bent over him to kiss him; but the kiss we exchanged turned into a long, silent, tender embrace.

# X

That was how I gave up Micòl.

The next evening, strictly maintaining the promise I had made to my father, I stayed away from Malnate's; the following day, a Friday, I didn't turn up at the Finzi-Contini house. And so, a week, the first, went by without my seeing anyone: neither Malnate nor the others. Luckily nobody sought me during all this time, and this fact surely helped me. Otherwise I probably wouldn't have held out, I would have let myself be caught again.

About ten days after our last meeting, towards the twenty-fifth of the month, Malnate phoned me. It had never happened until then, and since I hadn't answered the phone, I was tempted to have them say I was out. But I immediately repented. I already felt myself sufficiently strong: if not to see him again, at least to speak to him.

"Are you all right?" he began. "You've really dropped me."

"I was away."

"Where? Florence? Rome?" he asked, not without a hint of irony.

"A bit farther this time," I answered, already sorry for the pathetic phrase.

"*Bon.* I don't mean to question you. Well: how about seeing each other?"

I said I wasn't free that evening, but the next evening I would surely come by his place, at the usual hour. If, however, he saw I was delayed—I added—he wasn't to wait for me. In that case we would meet directly at Giovanni's. Wouldn't he be having supper at Giovanni's?

"Probably," he confirmed, curtly. And then:

"Have you heard the news?"

"I've heard."

"What a mess! Do come, please, and we can talk about it all."

"Good-bye then," I said softly.

And he hung up.

The following evening, as soon as I had finished supper, I rode on my bicycle to about a hundred yards from the restaurant. I wanted to see if Malnate was there, nothing more: and, in fact, having ascertained that he was there, all right (he was sitting as usual at an outdoor table, wearing his eternal cream-colored bush jacket), instead of joining him, I turned back, taking up a position at the head of one of the Castle's three drawbridges, the one directly opposite Giovanni's. I reckoned that in this way I could observe him better, with no danger of being noticed. And so it was. My chest against the stone edge of the parapet, I observed him at length, while he ate. I watched him and the other customers over there, arrayed in a line, the wall at their backs; I saw the swift bustle of white-jacketed waiters among the tables; and it seemed to me, suspended as I was in the darkness, over the glassy water of the moat, as if I were in the theatre, clandestine spectator of a pleasant, mindless performance. Malnate was by now on the fruit. He listlessly picked at a heavy bunch of grapes, one grape after the other, and every so often, certainly expecting me to show up, he would turn his head sharply to the right and left. As he did, the lenses of his thick glasses ("those telescopes," Micòl called them) would glint: throbbing, nervous. . . . Having finished the grapes, he summoned the waiter with a gesture, conferring with him for a moment. I assumed he had asked for the bill, and I was already preparing to go away, when I saw the waiter coming back with a cup of coffee. He drank it in one gulp. Then, from one of the two breast pockets of his bush jacket, he took out some very small object, a notebook, and began writing on it with a pencil. What the devil was he writing—I smiled—a poem? He too? And here I left him, busily writing, hunched over that notebook of his, from which, at rare intervals, he raised his head, as if seeking above, in the starry sky, inspiration and ideas.

A few more evenings I went on roaming idly through the streets of the city, observing everything, attracted impartially by everything: by the heavy newspaper headlines, in huge letters, underlined in red ink, that covered the kiosks downtown; by the stills of films and the photographs of stage shows, displayed outside the theatre entrances, by the clumps of drunks, standing in the middle of the narrow streets of the old city; by the licenses of the automobiles lined up in Piazza del Duomo; by the different types that came out of the brothels, or appeared, straggling, from the dark bushes of the Montagnone, to come and order ices, beer, or soft drinks at the metal counter of a stand that had recently been set up on the ramparts of San Tomaso, at the end of Via Scandiana. One evening, around eleven, I found myself in the neighborhood of Piazza Travaglio, peering at the gloomy interior of the famous Caffè Scianghai, frequented almost exclusively by streetwalkers and by workers from the nearby Borgo San Luca; then, immediately afterwards, I was on the top of the bastion above, watching two young characters lazily competing at the shooting gallery, under the hard eyes of the Tuscan girl, Malnate's admirer.

I stood there, to one side, saying nothing, not even getting off my bicycle: and the Tuscan girl, at a certain point, hailed me directly.

"Hey you," she said, "over there. Why don't you come up and fire a few shots, too? Come on, don't be afraid. Show these weaklings what you can do."

"No, thanks," I answered.

"No, thanks," she repeated. "Jesus, these young people! What've you done with that friend of yours? There was a real man, all right! Did you bury him?"

I didn't answer, and she burst out laughing.

"Poor kid!" she commiserated with me. "Go on home, run along, or your dad will give you a licking. It's way past your bedtime!"

The following evening, towards midnight, without even knowing, myself, what I was really seeking, I was at the opposite end of the city, riding along the packed-earth track, smooth and only slightly winding, that followed the inner edge of the Mura degli Angeli. There was a magnificent full moon: so clear and luminous, in the perfectly serene sky, that my headlight was superfluous. I rode slowly. More and more lovers were revealed to me, lying in the grass, at the foot of the trees. I counted the couples one by one, automatically. Some, entwined, were writhing one on the other, half-naked; some were stretched out, already separated, hand in hand; others, embracing but motionless, seemed to be asleep. I finally counted more than thirty couples. And though, at times, I passed so close to them that I grazed them with my wheel, none showed any sign of being aware of my silent presence. I felt, and was, a kind of strange, passing phantom: full of life and of death at once; of passion, and of detached pity.

When I had come to the point above the Barchetto del Duca, I stopped. I got off my bicycle, propped it against a tree trunk, and for a few minutes, turned towards the still, silvery expanse of the park. I stood there, looking. I was thinking of nothing specific, I would say: but of many things, one after the other, not dwelling on any one in particular. I looked, I listened to the subtle and immense crying of the crickets and the frogs, and I was myself amazed by the vaguely embarrassed smile that smoothed my lips. "Here we are," I murmured. I didn't know what to do, what I had come to do. I was filled with the vague sense of uselessness of all commemorations.

I began to walk along the edge of the grassy slope, my eyes fixed on the *magna domus*. All was dark, down there, and though the windows of Micòl's room faced south, and therefore I couldn't see them, still I was sure, who knows why, that even from them not the dimmest light shone. When I had finally arrived at the exact spot from which I dominated the part of the wall "sacred," as Micòl said, "*au vert paradis des amours enfantins*," I was suddenly seized by an idea. What if I were to enter the park, secretly scaling the wall? As a boy, one far-off June afternoon, I hadn't dared do it, I had been afraid. But now? What could I possibly be afraid of, now?

I took a rapid look around, and a moment later I was at the foot of the wall, suddenly rediscovering in the sultry shadow the same smell of nettles and dung of ten years before. But the wall, no, it was different. Perhaps because it was ten years older (I, too, had aged ten years, in the meanwhile, and grown in height and strength), it didn't seem to me as high or as impervious as I remembered it. After a first unsuccessful attempt, I lighted a match. There were all the necessary footholds, and even the big rusty spike was there still, sticking up from the wall. On the second attempt, I reached it, and grasping it, I easily pulled myself to the top.

Once I was seated up there, my legs hanging over the other side, the first thing I noticed was a ladder, against the wall below. I wasn't surprised by it; if anything, the discovery amused. "Well," I said to myself: "the ladder, too." Before beginning my descent, however, I turned back for a moment towards the Mura degli Angeli. My bicycle was still in its place: propped against the trunk of a linden, where I had left it. It was an old bicycle, a heap of scrap metal unlikely to appeal to anyone.

Quickly, with the help of the ladder, I reached the ground, and, at once abandoning the path parallel to the wall, I cut across the field dotted with fruit trees, planning to reach the main driveway at a point about equidistant from the Perottis' farmhouse and the wooden bridge over the Panfilio. I trod on the grass soundlessly, my mind still blank: gripped, true, every now and then, by a faint misgiving, but each time, with a shrug, promptly suppressing all anxiety and concern. How beautiful it was, the Barchetto del Duca, at night—I said to myself—how softly the moon illuminated it! I was looking for nothing, among those milky shadows, in that sea of milk and silver. No one, even if I had been caught wandering there, could have accused me of anything. On the contrary. If you thought about it, I even had some rights, by now. . . .

I stepped into the drive, I crossed the bridge over the Panfilio, then, turning left, I was soon in the tennis court clearing. Yes, Professor Ermanno had kept his word. The metal fence, pulled down, was lying in a confused, glistening heap beside the court, opposite the part where, as a rule, the wicker chairs and the deck chairs for the spectators were lined up. And more: the job of extending the playing area had already begun, for, along the entire perimeter of the court, for a breadth of almost three yards along the sides and five beyond the ends, the lawn was being dug up. Alberto was ill, gravely ill. In some way, also in *that* way, the seriousness of his illness had to be hidden from him! "Perfect," I approved. And I went further.

I stepped into the open, with the intention of making a wide turn around the clearing, and I was not surprised, when I was already quite far from the court, to see advancing, trotting from the direction of the *Hütte*, the big, familiar form of Jor. I stood still and waited for him; and when he was about ten yards away, the dog also stopped. "Jor," I called in a stifled voice. "Jor!" Jor recognized me. His tail gave a brief, peaceful, festive wag, then he slowly retraced his steps.

He turned every so often, as if to make sure I was following him. But I was not following him; on the contrary; or, rather, though I was gradually drawing nearer the *Hütte*, I did not move away from the far edge of the clearing. I was walking at about twenty yards from the crescent of great, dark trees of that part of the park, my face always turned to the left. The moon, now, was at my back. The clearing, the tennis court, the blind corner of the *magna domus*, and then, there at the end, looming over the frilled crowns of apple trees, figs, plums, pears, the bulwark of the Mura degli Angeli: all appeared clear, distinct, as if in relief, in a light better than daylight.

Proceeding in this way, I noticed that at a certain point I was only a few steps from the *Hütte*: not facing it, that is, not on the side of it that overlooked the tennis court, but behind, among the trunks of the young firs and larches against which it rose. Here I stopped. I stared at the dark, rough form of the *Hütte* against the light. Suddenly uncertain, I no longer knew where to go, which direction to take.

"What shall I do?" I said meanwhile, in a low voice, puzzled, "What shall I do?"

I kept staring at the *Hütte*; and now I thought—without my heart's even beating faster at this idea: receiving it indifferently, as stagnant water allows the light to pierce it—now I thought, yes, after all, it was here, to meet Micòl, that Giampi Malnate came every night after leaving me at my door. (Why not? Wasn't this perhaps the reason he always shaved so carefully, before going out to supper with me?) Well, in this case, the dressing room–hut of the tennis court would have been a magnificent refuge, for the two of them.

Yes, yes—I went on calmly reasoning, in a kind of rapid, inner whisper—of course. How could I have been so blind? He roamed around with me only to kill time until it was late enough, and then, after having tucked me in, so to speak, off he rode, full tilt, to her, who, naturally, was waiting for him in the garden. . . . Why, of course. Now I understood the real reason of his gesture, there in the brothel. Naturally: he was making love every night, or almost, that was it! To be sure, the moment soon comes when you long for Mamma, the sky of Lombardy, et cetera. . . . And the ladder, there, against the inside wall? Only Micòl could have put it there, at *that* spot.

I was lucid, serene, calm. As in a puzzle, every piece fit perfectly, all calculations worked out.

Micòl, of course. With Giampi Malnate. With the intimate friend of her sick brother. In secret from him and from all the others in the house, parents, relatives, servants; and always at night. In the *Hütte*, normally, but who knows? some nights perhaps also up there, in her bedroom, in the room of the *làttimi*. Really in secret? Or did the others, as always, pretend not to see, and let things go, or even, subtly, encourage them, because, after all, it's only human and right that a girl, at twenty-three, if she doesn't want to be married, or can't marry, should still have what nature ordains? They also pretended not to see Alberto's illness, in the house. It was their system.

I pricked up my ears. Absolute silence.

And Jor, meanwhile? Where had Jor gone off to?

I took a few steps, on tiptoe, towards the *Hütte*.

"Jor!" I called, loudly.

But then, as if in reply, a faint sound, heartsick, almost human, suddenly arrived from very far away, through the night air. I recognized it at once: it was the old, beloved voice of the clock in the square, striking the hours and the quarter-hours. What was it saying? It was saying that, once again, it had grown very late, that it was foolish and wicked, on my part, to continue torturing my father in this way, who, surely, also that night, concerned because I hadn't come home, was unable to fall asleep: and that finally it was time for me to resign myself. Truly. Forever.

"What a fine novel," I sneered, shaking my head, as if at an incorrigible child.

And, turning my back on the *Hütte*, I went off among the trees, in the opposite direction.

# Epilogue

My story with Micòl Finzi-Contini ends here. So it is just as well for this story to end, too, now, for anything I might add would no longer concern her, but, if anyone, only myself.

Already, at the beginning, I have told of her fate and her family's.

Alberto died of a malignant lymphogranuloma, before the others, in '42, after a very long death-agony, in which all Ferrara took an interest, from afar, despite the deep rift made in the citizenry by the racial laws. He was suffocating. To help him breathe, oxygen was needed, oxygen in ever greater quantities. And since, because of the war, there was a scarcity of oxygen tanks in the city, towards the end the family virtually cornered the supply throughout the region, sending people to buy them, at any price, in Bologna, Ravenna, Rimini, Parma, Piacenza. . . .

The others, in September of '43, were taken by the Fascist *repubblichini*. After a brief stay in the prison of Via Piangipane, they were sent off, the following November, to the concentration camp of Fòssoli, near Carpi, and from there, later, to Germany. As far as I am concerned, I must still say that during the four years between the summer of '39 and the autumn of '43, I had not seen any of them again. Not even Micòl. At Alberto's funeral, the old Dilambda, converted from gasoline to methane, proceeded slowly at the end of the cortège, and then, as soon as the hearse had crossed the entrance to the cemetery at the end of Via Montebello, immediately turned back. Behind its windows, I thought, for a moment, I could discern the ash-blond of her hair. No more. Even in a city as small as Ferrara, you can manage, if you like, to disappear for years and years, one from another, living side by side like the dead.

As for Malnate, summoned to Milan as early as November '39 (he had tried in vain to reach me by phone, in September; he had even written me a letter), I didn't see him again either after the August of that year. Poor

Giampi. He believed—ın that, yes!—in the honest Lombard and Communist future that beckoned him, smiling, then, from beyond the darkness of
the imminent war: a distant future—he admitted—but certain, infallible.
But who knows the heart, really? When I think of him shipped off to the
Russian front with the Italian Expeditionary Force, in '41, never to return,
I always recall, vividly, how Micòl reacted every time that, between tennis
games, he would start once more "catechizing" us. He would talk in his
calm, low, buzzing voice; but Micòl, unlike me, never paid much attention
to him. She never stopped laughing, taunting him, making fun of him.

"Whose side are you on? The Fascists'?" I remember him asking her,
one day, shaking his heavy, sweating head. He couldn't understand.

What had there been, then, between the two of them? Nothing? Who
can say?

It is certain that, as if prescient of the approaching end, her own and all
her family's, Micòl repeated constantly also to Malnate that his democratic
and social future meant nothing to her, for the future, in itself, was something she detested, preferring to it by far *"le vierge, le vivace et le bel au-
jourd'hui,"* and, even more, the past, the dear, sweet, *sainted* past.

And as these, I know, were only words, the usual deceitful and desperate words that only a true kiss would have prevented her from uttering: let
them, and only them, seal here what little the heart has been able to remember.